SLAVERY IN
COLONIAL GEORGIA,
1730–1775

Slavery in

Colonial Georgia

1730–1775

BETTY WOOD

The University of Georgia Press

Athens

Copyright © 1984 by the University of Georgia Press
Athens, Georgia 30602

Designed by Richard Hendel

Set in 10 on 12 Linotron 202 Sabon

The paper in this book meets the guidelines for permanence
and durability of the Committee on Production Guidelines for
Book Longevity of the Council on Library Resources.

Printed in the United States of America

Library of Congress Cataloging in Publication Data
Wood, Betty.
    Slavery in colonial Georgia, 1730–1775.
    Includes index.
        1. Slavery—Georgia—History—18th century.
    2. Georgia—History—Colonial period, ca. 1600–1775.
    3. Plantation life—Georgia—History—18th century.
    4. Afro-Americans—Georgia—History—18th century.
    I. Title.
E445.G3W66 1984   975.8'00496073   83-4808
ISBN 0-8203-0687-8

For my parents

CONTENTS

ACKNOWLEDGMENTS

During the time it has taken to write this book I have received tremendous assistance from a great many people on both sides of the Atlantic. Enormous scholarly and personal debts have accumulated which can never be adequately repaid.

First and foremost my deepest thanks go to Jim Potter, who supervised my postgraduate work at the London School of Economics, and to Richard Beeman and Richard Dunn, who did likewise at the University of Pennsylvania. But for their sympathy and patience this book would not have been begun, let alone completed.

Since 1971 I have been in the very privileged position of holding a Fellowship at Girton College. Girton has provided a most congenial and stimulating environment in which to work, and I am immensely grateful to Professor M. C. Bradbrook, the Mistress of Girton at the time of my election to a Fellowship, and to the present Mistress, Professor B. E. Ryman. Although all the Fellows of Girton over the past ten years have contributed in some way to the writing of this book, I would like to say a special word of thanks to Alison Duke, Margaret Smith, Elisabeth Stopp, and Dorothy Thompson. These wise and generous friends have helped me in more ways than perhaps they realize, as have two former Fellows of the College, Philip Davis and Mary-Ann Radzinowicz.

I am deeply indebted to my colleagues and former colleagues in the Faculty of History at Cambridge University, but especially to Jack Pole and John Thompson, two friends who have taken immense interest in my work and who in every way have encouraged me to finish this book. I am very grateful to them both. Robert Fogel and Eugene Genovese, who visited Cambridge as Pitt Professors, have been exceptionally generous with their time. I greatly appreciate all the help that I have received from them. To a third Pitt Professor, Eric McKittrick, goes my warmest thanks for making it possible for me to visit Columbia University in the summer of 1976.

Three friends whose interests are somewhat removed from eighteenth-century Georgia but whose friendship has been important in other ways are Brendan Bradshaw, Dermot Fenlon, and Jack Ravensdale. Many other Cambridge friends, and friends no longer in Cambridge, have helped me in various ways, but one to whom I am particularly indebted is Isobel Grace. Her house on the Norfolk coast provided the ideal retreat in which to think and to write.

I met Phinizy and Margie Spalding on the first of what proved to be many research trips to Georgia, and I cannot thank them enough for their many acts of friendship. They are more responsible than perhaps they know for the completion of this book. Other friends in Georgia have also been immensely helpful and supportive, but none more so than the late Professor E. Merton Coulter. Professor Hardy Jackson and his family are friends who were made only recently, but their kindness and enthusiasm came at an important time.

My friends elsewhere in the United States, but especially those in Greencastle, are to be thanked for their constant support and encouragement. Particular thanks go to Ralph and Sally Gray and to Jim and Sheila Cooper for their help and, not least, for their boundless hospitality.

Last, but by no means least, I am deeply grateful to Charles East, of the University of Georgia Press, for his patience and understanding during the time it took to prepare my manuscript for publication.

My greatest thanks are reserved for my parents. The dedication of my book to them is a grossly inadequate acknowledgment of the most enduring debt of all.

Betty Wood
Girton College,
Cambridge

CHAPTER ONE

A NEW COLONY

The founding of Georgia in 1733 was the culmination of a longstanding British and colonial interest in establishing a permanent settlement in the disputed lands to the south and southwest of the Carolinas.[1] The strategic and economic significance of the southern borderlands to both Spain and Britain had been evident since the mid-seventeenth century. The settlement of Georgia differed in one vital respect from all previous proposals to plant a British colony in the region to the south of the Savannah River. Indeed, the first fifteen years of Georgia history constituted a unique episode in the annals of colonial North America because this was the only British colony in which a sustained attempt was made to prohibit black slavery.[2]

By 1733 the black population of the mainland colonies numbered just over ninety thousand, and everywhere in British America the African endured the legal status of slave. The processes involved in the enslavement of the African have generated a wide-ranging and often heated debate among scholars. The seventeenth-century American experience was distinguished by two important characteristics. First, in all the mainland colonies, with the notable exception of South Carolina, which was to prove an influential model for all the participants in the Georgia experiment, the emergence of slavery reflected the outcome of what Winthrop D. Jordan has called "unthinking decisions" rather than the result of a premeditated plan to enslave blacks. Second, the fate of the African once in British America rested squarely in the hands of the colonists, and they neither felt the need nor were required by either the British authorities or dissidents in their midst to explain or justify their treatment of blacks.³ The exceptional case of Georgia must be set and examined in the context of a rapidly growing black population elsewhere in the mainland; a black population whose economic significance, at least in the plantation colonies, went unchallenged; and, finally, a black population whose status and conduct were defined and regulated by the colonists rather than from London. As is well known, the decision to exclude slavery from Georgia was taken not by the settlers but by the founders of the colony, the Trustees, and simply imposed on the new settlement. Those settlers who disagreed with the prohibition were the only American colonists who, before the mid-eighteenth century, were called upon by their critics on both sides of the Atlantic to make out a case for slavery. All the arguments, all the forces and pressures that prompted the enslavement of the African and that can only be speculated about for most of the other mainland colonies, are laid before us in abundant detail. Between 1735 and 1750 a deliberate and well-thought-out policy of exclusion was confronted by an equally deliberate decision on the part of some, but by no means all, of the Georgia settlers that black slavery was "the one thing needful" for the economic success of the colony. There were no "unthinking decisions" in the debate that preceded the introduction of slavery into Georgia.

The Georgia Charter of 1732 named twenty-one Trustees who would assume overall responsibility for the proposed new colony and, during the next twenty years, seventy-one men were to serve in this capacity.⁴ The private, political, and philanthropic interests of these ministers, merchants, and parliamentarians clearly reveal the charitable and imperial concerns that converged to bring the Georgia project into being.⁵ The immediate impetus to the venture came from the Parliamentary Gaols Committee, which met in 1728 and 1729, and, in particular, from two members of that committee: its chairman, James Oglethorpe, and Sir John Percival, afterward first Earl of Egmont. Although by mid-1732 the Trustees named in the charter assumed a collective responsibility for Georgia, Oglethorpe and Egmont were to play the decisive part in shaping the initial scheme of settlement and, during the next ten years, assumed the main burden of defending the "Georgia Plan" against a rising tide of opposition on both sides of the Atlantic. On 13 February 1730 Egmont recorded in his diary that he and Oglethorpe had met that day and agreed in principle to combine the resources of two legacies which they administered with a view to settling "a hundred" former prisoners in the West Indies.[6] Within months the proposed location of the settlement had changed from vague references to the West Indies to more concrete plans for a colony in the southern borderlands. By mid-1730 the scheme had changed in another respect: Egmont, Oglethorpe, and their associates now determined "not to confine this charity to prisoners, but to extend it as far as their funds would allow to all poor families as might be desirous of it."[7] This decision indicated a desire to expand their "charity and humanity" and reflected their belief that the planting of as many "miserable wretches" as possible in America would not only relieve Britain of a pressing social and economic burden but also add significantly to the national wealth. These aspirations, especially when combined with a very clear idea of the standard and quality of life that ought to characterize Georgia, generated compelling reasons for the exclusion of black slavery.

Some forty-four years after he had led the first embarkation of settlers to Georgia, Oglethorpe explained to Granville Sharp, a leading British opponent of black slavery and the African slave trade, that the Trustees had "determined not to suffer slavery" in their colony because they believed the institution to be "against the Gospel, as well as the fundamental law of England" and, for these weighty reasons, they had steadfastly "refused . . . to make a law permitting such a horrid crime." But they had been thwarted by "slave merchants and their adherents" who managed to persuade the House of Commons to rescind "the charter by which no law could be passed without our consent." Part of this retrospective account is indisputable: Parliament did play a key role in the slavery debate that raged after 1735. But that the Trustees were prototype abolitionists is a more dubious proposition.[8]

By 1776, and no doubt influenced by the Georgia experience, Oglethorpe might well have believed that slavery was "unjust" and sympathized with those who were demanding the universal abolition of the institution. But there is little evidence to suggest that he or any other Trustee subscribed to such an overtly abolitionist sentiment during the 1730s and 1740s. Oglethorpe, who had held high office in the Royal African Company, and his colleagues on the Georgia Board acquiesced in the continued existence of slavery and the African slave trade as significant facts of contemporary economic life.[9] Although Oglethorpe was instrumental in securing the release from slavery of the African Job Jalla, his concern on that occasion was with the injustice that had been perpetrated on an individual African (and, significantly, a highly placed African) and not with the injustice inherent in slavery and the African slave trade.[10]

The Trustees did not shape their scheme of settlement around a prior commitment to prohibit slavery. The institution was not specifically proscribed by the Georgia Charter but by legislation drafted in 1734 and accorded royal approval in 1735.[11] The posture adopted by the Trustees before 1734 was, to say the least, ambiguous. In 1733, for example, they allowed black slaves to be used in Savannah, and a year later the Salzburgers who settled at Ebenezer were permitted to employ blacks. That the Trustees actually made a point of requesting black workers from South Carolina to assist with the building of Savannah (which they must have known would mean slave labor) casts considerable doubt upon Oglethorpe's subsequent account of their motivation. Moreover, there is no evidence to suggest that during the 1730s and 1740s any of the Trustees believed that slaveholding was inconsistent with Christian teaching. Essentially their thinking on this point followed that elaborated by the bishop of London in 1727: the freedom implicit in Christian teaching was freedom from the bondage of sin. Conversion to Christianity made no difference to the individual's secular status and did not constitute a compelling argument in favor of manumission. The duty of the Christian master did not extend beyond attending to the spiritual welfare of his slaves.[12]

The Trustees were not abolitionists in that they seldom expressed any concern for the African and never called for the universal extinction, either immediately or gradually, of black slavery. In their capacity as colonizers, however, they were confronted by a set of circumstances, albeit mainly of their own making, which persuaded them to adopt an antislavery stance. As a matter of long-term policy their decision to outlaw slavery reflected the three principal objectives they had in mind when founding Georgia: their colony would serve as a safety valve for Britain's dispossessed and discontented and a haven for persecuted European Protestants, as the long contemplated military buffer between Florida and the Carolinas, and as the producer of such highly prized commodities as silk and wine. The Trustees banned slavery not because they were opposed to the institution as a matter of principle but because they believed the introduction of black slaves would be both undesirable and unnecessary in carrying out their expectations for the colony.

Of paramount importance to the Trustees, indeed the very essence of their plan, was the nature of the society that would develop in their colony. The Trustees' vision of Georgia was based on the irresistible prospect of both secular and spiritual redemption for the settlers. The unfortunates to be sent as charity settlers would be removed from a life of unmitigated misery and distress in Britain, from a society that offered "such temptations to vice . . . as they are scarce able to resist," and placed in "a Christian, moral and industrious way of life, and [instructed] how by labour to gain a comfortable subsistence." Once in America they would be afforded every opportunity for self-improvement and for moral regeneration.

The "bad courses, such as begging, cheating or robbing" which these unfortunates might indulge in in England were prompted, the Trustees believed, by "idleness and necessity."[13] Both conditions would be excluded from Georgia and the settlers encouraged to earn their redemption through work. But the redemption, and thereby the nature of society, envisaged by the Trustees could not be left to chance or the settlers to their own devices. From the outset the Trustees emphasized that the attainment of the virtues and the virtuous society which they contemplated would necessitate the close and continuing supervision of the "miserable wretches" and "drones" to be sent "on the charity" to Georgia. The Trustees would not only lay down the broad outlines of Georgia's development but also concern themselves with the minutiae of life in the colony. Their avowed intention was to create "a simple and stable society made up of contented citizens."[14]

The Trustees thought the plantation societies of British America revealed only too clearly the nature of the threat posed by slavery to their social vision. In their estimation of the deleterious effects of slavery on white manners and morals, in their unswerving belief that slavery both symbolized and generated most of the social and moral evils they were determined to avoid, they anticipated most of the arguments postulated by the antislavery movement that gathered force on both sides of the Atlantic during the middle years of the eighteenth century.

The Trustees did not dispute the economic value of the plantation economies of the West Indies and the southern mainland colonies to Britain but rather the social and moral cost of economic systems that, because of their heavy dependence upon slave labor, encouraged "idleness" and "luxury" in white society. For the Trustees, the vices associated with an unfettered agricultural capitalism that depended upon slave labor were potentially as damaging to white morals as those that derived from grinding poverty. They determined to avoid both extremes: there would be no great inequalities of wealth in Georgia. Prospective settlers were promised a "comfortable subsistence," but the Trustees emphasized that the attainment of this goal would depend upon their willingness to work. Slavery would be prohibited not because of a concern for the rights of the African but for the morals of the European. The Trustees believed that the introduction of slavery would inevitably "result not only in the corruption of the colonists . . . but also in the repudiation of the basic principle of the colony that independent men could gain a decent living by their own labour."[15] The institution could have no place in a society that placed such a heavy requirement of industry and virtue on its white inhabitants.

The Trustees' critique of slavery would have been familiar to John Woolman and those who followed in his footsteps during the era of the American Revolution.[16] But the Georgia Board never applied, at least not explicitly, its antislavery argument to the other American colonies. Nowhere in their published records or private papers is there any suggestion that the Trustees wished or secretly hoped to undermine the slave systems of British America. The Trustees' crusade against slavery, in actuality their concern with the manners and morals of white American society, never crossed the Savannah River. They were keenly aware of the southern colonists' commitment to slavery, both as an economic regime and as a means of securing racial control, and probably appreciated the futility, at least for the foreseeable future, of mounting a sweeping campaign against the institution. Moreover, they realized that they could ill afford to alienate influential South Carolinian and British interests who were firmly committed to slavery and the African slave trade and whose support was essential to the success of their colonizing venture. Any doubts that might have been entertained about the Trustees' intentions concerning slavery elsewhere in the mainland were effectively removed by their promise to return to bondage any black fugitive apprehended in Georgia.[17]

If the Trustees' social vision provided a set of compelling arguments in favor of excluding slavery, then so did the proposed strategic and economic roles of Georgia. The Trustees' social design, their paramount objective, could be promoted by recourse to pragmatic arguments that suggested that the successful functioning of Georgia, and thereby its value to both Britain and the other southern colonies, depended upon the prohibition of slavery. For this part of their scheme the Trustees drew heavily from earlier proposals to establish a British settlement in the borderlands.

Although differing in detail as well as in practicability, the plans of such men as Sir Robert Montgomery, John Barnwell, and Francis Nicholson emphasized that the widely dispersed settlement patterns associated with the plantation economies of the Carolinas and Virginia must be avoided in the borderlands. A favorite notion was that the essential strategic requirements that would lessen the chances of successful Spanish invasion could be met by establishing a chain of fortified townships along the southern frontier. The Trustees incorporated this idea into their design but took additional steps to ensure a compact settlement pattern. The maximum size of individual land grants was set at five hundred acres, with these holdings confined to those who transported themselves and ten servants to Georgia. Charity settlers conveyed at the Trustees' expense would be allocated fifty acres of land. To retain a low land-to-man ratio and to ensure that each grant would always be occupied by a potential soldier, the Trustees imposed rigid restrictions on the tenure of landholdings.[18] Their land policy served an obvious military function but, equally important, it was entirely compatible with their social design. Settlers would be unable to acquire massive estates either to work or for speculative purposes. This land policy, with all its implications for the economic life of Georgia, became the subject of bitter complaint and constituted an essential ingredient of the slavery debate. By the mid-1730s some settlers were demanding permission to establish a plantation economy similar to that of South Carolina. To achieve that objective would necessitate a thoroughgoing revision of the Trustees' land policy and thus also reopen the question of black slavery.

If the Trustees were convinced that their social design and the security of Georgia depended upon a compact settlement pattern, they also needed little persuading that the introduction of slavery would jeopardize the colony's role as a military buffer.[19] The experience of the other plantation colonies taught that the presence of blacks would depress the price of free labor so that whites would be discouraged from settling, and white settlers were vital because only they could be "relyed on for the Defence and Security" of Georgia.[20] One of the Trustees' (and by extension Britain's) most urgent priorities had to be attracting a white population, and they could not risk any deterrent to migration to this exposed outpost.

But the employment of slaves would have an even more serious consequence than that of deterring white migrants. The Trustees believed, and correctly so, that slaves would be encouraged to flee to Florida, where they would be armed and turned against their former owners as part of the Spanish war effort.[21] They pointed to the "Insurrections Tumults and Rebellions" of the black populations of British America and argued that the same would "Ruin" Georgia. As their secretary, Benjamin Martyn, remarked, "Every man is naturally fond of liberty, and he will struggle for it when he knows his own strength."[22] It was patently obvious to the Trustees that the Spanish presence in Florida would add greatly to the "strength" of any blacks brought to Georgia. As we shall see, one of the Trustees' most important pragmatic arguments against the introduction of slavery was to be seriously undermined in 1742 when Oglethorpe repelled the Spanish at the Battle of Bloody Marsh. Ironically, the military victory which virtually guaranteed the survival of Georgia and the security of South Carolina proved an important nail in the coffin of the Trustees' social design.

If the proposed military role of Georgia combined with the Trustees' perception of the African as a potential rebel to generate persuasive arguments in favor of a compact, slave-free settlement pattern, so did the Trustees' economic aspirations for the colony. These aspirations reflected the blending of three themes: the standard of living deemed appropriate for the settlers; the desire to produce commodities that would lessen Britain's dependence upon its European rivals and, in the process, enhance the case for the public support of Georgia; and the economic possibilities presented by the physical environment of the region to the south of the Savannah River.

The Trustees had no firsthand experience of the borderlands, and they based their economic blueprint upon secondhand information of varying, but in the main dubious, accuracy. They accepted wholesale the extravagant accounts of such earlier authorities as Montgomery.[23] Martyn and Oglethorpe, who wrote two of the Trustees' most influential promotional tracts, followed Montgomery and Jean-Pierre Purry in depicting the region's physical environment in the most glowing terms.[24] According to Oglethorpe, the borderlands enjoyed a surprisingly benign climate which was conducive to good health. Newcomers might be "apt to have a seasoning; an ague or sort of fever," but otherwise such ill health as might occur would be the result of "intemperance (which indeed is too common)" rather than the climate. Land clearance would be simplicity itself because there was practically "no underwood, and the trees do not stand generally thick on the ground." Once the land had been cleared the settlers would need only "scratch the earth and . . . cover the seed" in order to be rewarded with unbelievably large yields.[25] The implication was clear: if Georgia proved less successful than anticipated the blame must attach to the settlers and not to the environment or the Trustees' design.

This highly romanticized image, which might be termed the "Georgia myth," was of the utmost importance because it persuaded the Trustees that a range of highly prized commodities, including "wine, oil, cotton, drugs, [and] dying stuff," could be produced in the borderlands. But by the end of 1732 another item, silk, had been added to the list. From a mercantilist standpoint silk made as much sense as these other commodities. Should Georgia ever produce raw silk on a significant scale, and the Trustees claimed that eventually the silk industry would employ "forty or fifty thousand persons," the benefits to Britain would be enormous. Sir Thomas Lombe, Britain's premier silk expert, assured the Trustees that the quality of the silk produced in the borderlands compared most favorably with that of the Piedmont, and they in turn assured prospective settlers that they could "be certain of selling their raw silk to the utmost extent of the British demand for that commodity."[26] Silk culture strengthened the Trustees' argument for excluding slavery because they believed that it would require light but skilled labor rather than the physical strength of gangs of unskilled Africans. The first colonists' lack of experience in silk production was deemed to be of little consequence; the Trustees assumed that the necessary skills could be imparted by Piedmontese experts who would accompany the first embarkation of settlers to America.

In their promotional literature the Trustees hammered home the economic, military, and social significance of Georgia for Britain but said relatively little about their potentially controversial intentions regarding slavery.[27] The first priority was to secure public and private backing for their venture and, strongly assisted by the fact that ten of the original Trustees sat in Parliament, the Georgia Board was to prove eminently successful in this endeavor. Between 1732 and 1752 the House of Commons appropriated over £150,000 for the Georgia project, approximately 90 percent of all the money expended on the colony during the Trusteeship.[28] Parliamentary aid, however, came in the form of annual appropriations and not as a block grant making the Trustees, and especially their social design, dependent upon the continuing goodwill of Parliament, their own lobbying effectiveness, and, ultimately, the success of their project.

Given their aspirations for Georgia, the information at their disposal, and their need to secure government backing, it is readily apparent why the Trustees embarked on an economic course that soon earned them the disapprobation of many settlers, the scorn of the South Carolinians, and, by the late 1730s, the opposition of many members of Parliament. Their mistake was not having created a false image of the environment of the borderlands, and thereby of the economic possibilities, but rather having clung to that image long after it had been demolished by the practical experience of the settlers. The optimistic impressions of the Georgia Board and the experience of the early settlers were diametrically opposed. The Trustees imagined an idyllic environment in which peaches, vines, white mulberries, and other desirable plants grew to abundance, but many of the settlers found only malarial swamps and impenetrable forests. The Trustees' notions and expectations began to be challenged soon after the first settlement of the colony. When the Georgia settlers compared their miserable progress with the apparent prosperity of neighboring low country South Carolina it seemed to them that the environments were similar and only the prohibition of slavery prevented them from emulating the Carolinian experience. They did not acknowledge, and perhaps did not appreciate, that even with the help of slaves it had taken the Carolinians many years to clear their forests and come to terms with their coastal and river swamps. Some Georgians saw slavery as a panacea that would guarantee instant economic success with little or no effort on their part. The great tragedy of the Trustees was that they seriously misjudged the aspirations of those they chose to settle Georgia.

Within two years of the first settlement of Georgia a clearly defined pro-slavery sentiment had emerged in the colony; by the end of the 1730s that sentiment had hardened into a coherent faction. These developments must be seen in the context not only of a clash between the myth and the reality of Georgia but also in that of the early settlers' ability and willingness to execute the Trustees' economic design. It is therefore relevant to ask whether they were equal to the tasks required in the founding of any new colony and, more specifically, to those demanded by the Georgia Board. A secondary question follows: how much did the clamor for slaves reflect deficiencies and inadequacies in the occupational backgrounds of the early settlers?

Although the humanitarian instincts of the Trustees dictated that they aid the "necessitous and starving" without regard to their occupational backgrounds, the need to secure government backing meant that in practice they had to select colonists from among those who were ill able to meet the current requirements of the British labor market. The occupational skills that would have been of most use to Georgia were precisely those upon which a premium was placed in Britain. For example, although experienced agricultural workers would have been of immense value, the Trustees stated that under no circumstances would they recruit settlers from among "husbandmen, or labourers from the country." Indeed, they insisted that they would confine their charity to "such only as fall into misfortunes of trade, and even admit none of these, who can get a subsistence, how narrow so ever it may be."[29]

The Trustees realized that their scheme could, and probably would, be attacked on the grounds that virtually none of the early settlers had any experience of agriculture. How could they expect people "who cannot work with the plough at home . . . to go through the same labour abroad"? Benjamin Martyn thought that the answer was self-evident: Georgia's benign environment and the provisions made for the charity settlers' first year in America would facilitate adjustment to this new way of life. Even more important, these settlers would go to Georgia not as servants but as landowners, and surely men drawn from the lower reaches of British society and offered this unique opportunity for self-improvement and economic advancement would not "repine at any fatigue, when it is on an estate of his own, and his gains . , . will rise in proportion to his labour."[30] Martyn and the Trustees failed to realize that this incentive might be reduced by the restrictive land policy they envisaged for Georgia and, moreover, that landownership would not of itself transform a man into a farmer. Finally, they could not conceive the possibility that for many settlers, and not just those who had paid their way to America, the agricultural capitalism of South Carolina would constitute a model to be emulated rather than avoided.

The Trustees' determination not to deplete Britain's agricultural work force was reflected in the occupational structure of the first settlers.[31] Only three men out of the forty-four whose occupations were recorded admitted to having any knowledge of agriculture. But the dearth of agricultural experience did not necessarily mean a complete absence of useful skills for the initial stages of settlement. The ten colonists who claimed a knowledge of carpentry, joinery, and allied skills could be expected to perform a crucial role, as could the miller and baker, the surgeon, the apothecary, the tailor, and the cordwainer.

Between 1732 and 1742 the Trustees maintained their initial policy. During this decade approximately 1,800 charity settlers were sent to Georgia. The occupational data for just over 800 of them compiled by E. Merton Coulter and Albert B. Saye show that only 55 had experience of agriculture. Another 363 were described as servants or laborers, and some of them may have worked on the land. A similar analysis of the occupations of 528 settlers who went as "adventurers" to Georgia shows that only 29 were farmers.[32]

The utility of securing an appropriate age structure and sex ratio among the early settlers does not seem to have occurred to the Trustees. A quarter of the first embarkation of settlers were aged under ten, and these twenty-nine children were an economic burden, at least in the short term. At the other end of the age scale, twenty-one settlers were aged forty or over, late in life for uprooting and making a fresh start in America.[33] More men in the fifteen-to-thirty age group would have been desirable to tackle the heavy manual labor required during the initial stages of colonization. Although the age data for later embarkations are fragmentary, they suggest that the Trustees continued to disregard this factor.

The question remains as to whether the early settlers were suited to the work demanded of them in Georgia. There is no simple answer; their occupational background was less important than their willingness to adapt themselves and their skills to the possibilities as well as the limitations of the Georgia environment. The dearth of men in the fifteen-to-thirty age group (especially in the first embarkation), the high proportion of children, and the lack of agricultural expertise may certainly be regarded as weaknesses in the Trustees' blueprint. But it is important to bear in mind that agriculture as well as almost every other aspect of life in America would be very different from anything experienced in Europe.

The Trustees were confident that those chosen as charity settlers were, and would remain, fully committed to the Georgia experiment. Their certainty stemmed partly from the opportunity they were offering prospective migrants and partly from the manner in which charity settlers were recruited. The number who could be sent "on the charity" was limited by the financial resources available to the Trustees, and all applicants were subjected to a rigorous screening procedure. According to Francis Moore, the Trustees favored those "who had the best characters, and were the truest objects of compassion." In practice, this probably meant that the Georgia Board was impressed by people who vowed to work hard, who paid lip service to the aims and ideals of the Georgia project, and who showered thanks on their benefactors.[34] Benjamin Martyn felt able to reassure Governor Robert Johnson of South Carolina, who had advised the Trustees to send as settlers "none but People used to Labour and of Sober Life and Conversation," that those selected were "inured to Labour . . . prepared for the hardships they must undergo, and are . . . determin'd cheerfully to support them. All of them likewise have the Characters of Sober, Industrious, and Moral Men."[35]

In view of the subsequent history of Georgia it is highly relevant to ask whether these "Sober, Industrious, and Moral Men" left England with any preconceived ideas about black slavery. Unfortunately, a lack of evidence makes it impossible to do more than speculate on this crucial point. From Georgia they wrote at great length about the African and slavery, but there is no record of their thoughts, if any, on these subjects before their departure. One may surmise, however, that settlers who originated from or who had spent any length of time in London or any other major port town had probably encountered Africans and that at least some of them knew of the existence of chattel slavery in the New World.[36] Ideas and impressions formed in England might have contributed to the later debate on slavery. But there is no suggestion that the first settlers left for Georgia in the hope or expectation of being able to secure black slaves. If anything, the reverse was more likely to have been true.

In November 1732 the Trustees saw off the 114 men, women, and children who made up the first embarkation in the belief that they had provided for every possible contingency. These hand-picked settlers were to be supported from a public store during their first year in the colony; they had been given land and opportunity in what the Trustees sincerely believed to be a well nigh perfect physical environment; and the initial settlement was to be supervised by James Oglethorpe. The Trustees, and at this stage the settlers, too, were convinced that everything augured well for the new colony. Indeed, those on board the *Anne* sent a message to the Trustees thanking them for "all their fvrs. and indefatigable pains" and promising "an intire Obedience."[37] But within weeks the first murmurings of discontent were heard, murmurings that set the stage for the vitriolic debate that erupted after 1735.

The first settlers had been in Georgia for barely a month when Thomas Causton, the keeper of the public store and third bailiff of Savannah, noted that "though we want for nothing we have some Grumbletonians here also." He did not elaborate on the reasons for the grumbling or suggest that the discord was serious; no doubt the rigors of the transatlantic voyage, combined with the first taste of a new environment, created tensions that, although giving rise to a certain amount of carping, did not signify any deep-seated hostility toward the Georgia Plan.[38] If the voyage to America and the first weeks of settlement held any pointer to future developments, it was that the relationship be-

tween Oglethorpe and the settlers would be of the utmost importance. In all his dealings with the colonists Oglethorpe epito-
mized the Trustees' paternalism, which accounted for most of
the strengths and many of the weaknesses of the Georgia
project.[39]

The settlers soon forgot any earlier differences and buckled
down to the hard work involved in the building of Savannah.
The *South Carolina Gazette* was impressed by their attitude and
expressed surprise at "how cheerfully the Men goes to work,
considering they have not beed bred to it." But Oglethorpe did
not find such a rosy picture in mid-1733 when he returned from
a short visit to South Carolina. He was "shocked" to find that
during his absence "the People were grown very mutinous and
impatient of Labour and Discipline." Oglethorpe believed that
there were two reasons for this sorry state of affairs. First, the
settlers were allowed to buy unlimited quantities of hard liquor.
His solution was to destroy all the barrels of rum he could find
and threaten to stop the allowance of provisions to anyone who
sold spirits. Second was the presence of slaves. He might have
added two other considerations: the settlers' reactions to the
heat and humidity of their first summer in Georgia and his own
absence during this critical period for the new settlement.[40]

By mid-1733 Oglethorpe regretted the Trustees' decision (with
which he had concurred) to augment the labor force at Savannah
with slaves borrowed and hired from South Carolina. No doubt
his visit to that colony had made him particularly sensitive to the
subject of slavery. During his stay several South Carolinians who
hoped to establish slave-manned rice plantations in Georgia had
attempted to bribe him into securing a reversal of the Trustees'
land and labor policies.[41] Oglethorpe rejected their advances out
of hand but was persuaded that only a practical demonstration
of the Trustees' determination to exclude slavery would prevent
similar approaches in the future. Just because slaves had been
brought to Georgia for a specific purpose did not mean that the
Trustees would turn a blind eye to any subsequent attempts to
introduce black labor on a more permanent footing.

By the summer of 1733 Oglethorpe was in no doubt about the
nature of the South Carolinian threat to the Trustees' social

design. But he was at least as concerned by the Georgia settlers' reaction to the use of slaves, who "encouraged" the settlers in their "idleness," and therefore must be left in no doubt as to the Trustees' intentions.[42] It was essential that the black work force be returned to South Carolina as soon as possible and the Trustees secure formal legislative backing for their prohibitory policy.

Oglethorpe's analysis of the situation in Savannah was supported by Jean-Pierre Purry, who visited Egmont in November 1733 in search of backing for his settlement at Purysburg. During the course of their conversation, he remarked that some of the Georgia settlers were displeased "that they are not allowed to keep slaves of blacks, as Carolina allows."[43] There is, however, no record that any settlers expressed a wish for slaves. Perhaps Oglethorpe's presence in the colony made them reluctant to voice an opinion that was certain to provoke his wrath.

Although not yet faced with demands from Georgia for slaves, the Trustees were receiving comments about their prohibitory policy from elsewhere in America. Several South Carolinians, including Samuel Eveleigh, a Charles Town merchant, believed that Georgia could not survive, let alone prosper, without the permanent employment of slaves. The nub of Eveleigh's argument was that whites were unsuited to hard, manual labor in the Georgia environment and, moreover, that they were far more expensive to maintain than Africans. But Eveleigh acknowledged that to allow an unlimited importation of slaves would pose grave problems for the defense of Georgia, and he suggested that the Trustees follow the "Golden Mein" and allow each family to own a maximum of two slaves.[44]

In mid-1735 Benjamin Martyn informed Eveleigh that the Trustees had no intention of relaxing their prohibition and advised him to recruit German servants, "a Sober Strong laborious People," for his Georgia enterprises. Martyn agreed that white workers might be faced with the "Danger" of illness during their first few months in Georgia, but he pointed out that against this must be set the "ignorance" of the "New Arrived Negro." Time might be lost because of the indisposition of white servants, but time would have to be spent training Africans for agricultural labor. Martyn was assuming that blacks would be imported directly from Africa rather than from elsewhere in the Americas and that they would be immune to the seasoning process and ignorant of the agricultural practices employed in Georgia. He was also implying that white migrants would be familiar with these practices, a notion at odds with the emigration policy outlined in his *Reasons for Establishing the Colony of Georgia.*

Although Martyn believed that white servants would prove more profitable than blacks, he conceded that "the Right of Inheritance" might induce a colonist to make a heavier capital investment in order "to have a Man and his whole Posterity for ever." But this would necessitate the purchase of female slaves who "cannot do so much Work as a man." Moreover, masters would have to maintain nonproductive black children and must also expect to lose the value of the mother's work during her pregnancy because only "a very cruel" or "a very imprudent" owner would "force a Woman that is pregnant to work equal to another Slave." These were some of the reasons why the Trustees had banned slavery but there was another, more important reason: they preferred to "lay out their Money in sending over and subsisting poor white men than in buying of Slaves."[45]

In September 1735 Eveleigh answered Martyn's letter. He reported that the unanimous opinion of those whom he had consulted was that without slaves "Georgia can never be a Colony of any great Consequence," and surely the colonists were "better acquainted in these Affairs than the Gentmn. in Engd."[46] But Eveleigh did not persist: he seems to have believed that in view of the Trustees' intransigence there was little point in saying more. His writing, however, contains one of the earliest references to the existence of a pro-slavery sentiment in Georgia.

In October 1734 Eveleigh drew Oglethorpe's attention to a group of settlers who met regularly at John West's house in Savannah to discuss what they believed to be the defects of the Trustees' scheme. According to Eveleigh, they were "dissatisfied That they have not Liberty of getting Negroes."[47] Although such comments intensified after 1734, the growing disappointment over the economic condition of Georgia and the consequent clamor for slaves must be set in the context of social and political tensions that were threatening to tear the colony apart. The demand for slaves was closely related to a more broadly based campaign waged by a group of settlers who were determined to secure greater autonomy over local matters. The deteriorating social and political atmosphere in Savannah gave rise to a rash of complaints that served only to persuade the Trustees that any settler who made even the mildest criticism of life in Georgia must be a troublemaker bent on destruction.

In mid-1733 Oglethorpe established the civil government of Savannah along the lines stipulated by the Trustees. There was to be no elected assembly; executive and judicial authority would rest with a town court composed of the three bailiffs and the recorder of Savannah, men appointed by the Trustees. Many difficulties soon arose because the powers and responsibilities of the persons appointed to office were not clearly defined. While Oglethorpe remained in Georgia this question was of little consequence because he assumed the ultimate responsibility for the day-to-day management of the colony. But when he left for England early in 1734 he bequeathed a social and political vacuum with a strong potential for disaster. The inexperienced local officials had been given virtually no instruction for the tasks that now confronted them, and, just as important, it was not clear why particular persons had been singled out to hold office.

Peter Gordon, a charity settler who had worked as an upholsterer in England, was made first bailiff of Savannah, but ill health forced him to travel to South Carolina and then back to Britain in search of medical treatment. In Gordon's absence Thomas Causton assumed the responsibilities of first bailiff. Many people felt that once Causton assumed the mantle of authority he became tyrannical, and they accused him not only of taking the law into his own hands but also of inflicting brutal corporal punishment on offenders.[48] For many of Causton's critics the final straw was his handling of the Watson case. Joseph Watson, a somewhat disreputable settler engaged in the Indian trade, admitted responsibility for the fact that an Indian companion had drunk himself to death. But soon there were rumors in Savannah of poison, and Causton, who hoped to avoid a confrontation with the Trustees' Indian allies, sentenced Watson to be jailed as a lunatic. Some settlers believed that, as he had on many previous occasions, Causton was acting too harshly. At this juncture, when tempers were running high, Peter Gordon returned to Savannah. Gordon was still first bailiff, and, predictably, Causton's opponents looked to him for support. Gordon sympathized with them and agreed that Causton's high-handed behavior must be reported to the Georgia Board.[49]

Conflicting accounts of these disturbances reached London, and the Trustees came down firmly on Causton's side. They believed that the attacks on him were no less than indirect criticisms of themselves and that unless they supported him "the unruly people . . . would grow more insolent." They informed Causton that he had acted properly in jailing Watson, dismissed Gordon, and promoted Causton in his place.[50] The Trustees had decided that they must adopt a hard line: any complaints from Georgia, however politely phrased, were interpreted as insolence. It was into this increasingly fraught atmosphere that Gordon injected his criticisms of the Georgia Plan.

By the end of Georgia's first year some settlers were complaining that the "comfortable subsistence" promised by the Trustees had failed to materialize. The Trustees had anticipated that after their first harvest the charity settlers would be able to fend for themselves, but many people argued, and the Trustees were forced to concede, that this was far from being the case. Yielding for the first time to pressure from Georgia, they found they must continue to provision the charity settlers.[51] Although this decision was warmly welcomed in Georgia, some settlers believed that far more drastic changes would have to be made before the colony could prosper, and by the end of 1734 they were citing three main reasons for Georgia's unsatisfactory economic performance: a shortage of labor, an environment that was unpleasant and unhealthy for white workers, and a land policy that provided little incentive to improve grants which under certain circumstances might revert to the Georgia Board.[52] The first two of these assumptions soon led certain settlers to the conclusion that Georgia's economic growth depended upon the employment of slaves.

Early in 1735 Elisha Dobree, a South Carolinian who had

moved to Georgia the previous year, reported to the Trustees that some settlers had asked him to help them draw up a petition asking for slaves. He did not reveal the names of those concerned, and there is no evidence to suggest why they approached him. But Dobree wanted the Trustees to know that he had declined the commission because he felt that he might "Incur your Displeasure in a Work of that Nature." His suspicions were confirmed when Benjamin Martyn informed him that the Trustees, who were "determined never to tolerate Negroes in Georgia," were "well pleased" with him.[53] No petition like that mentioned by Dobree ever reached the Trustees; possibly it was never written. His letter suggests, however, that by early 1735 an embryonic pro-slavery faction, as opposed to a vague pro-slavery sentiment, had emerged in Savannah.

Although certain settlers moved inexorably to a pro-slavery position, others, including Dobree, believed that black slaves were not necessarily the answer to Georgia's economic difficulties. Dobree conceded that the economic condition of Georgia was unsatisfactory, but he disagreed with those who held that the climate precluded the profitable employment of white workers. He suggested that instead Georgia's development would be greatly enhanced were the Trustees to send twenty-five hundred white servants to the colony. These workers could be recruited from among "Vagabonds Idle Vagrants etc who would be put in a way to Live in plenty & with Expectation of lands after their Servitude."[54] But other settlers believed that some of Georgia's problems stemmed from the fact that the Trustees had already sent this class of person to the colony. The behavior as well as the expense and low productivity of white servants was to figure prominently in the pro-slavery argument.

By the end of 1734 discontent in Georgia was appreciable. Social and political conditions in general, and Causton's behavior in particular, combined with a languishing economy to form the grist for the dissidents' mill. Within months Peter Gordon, the first major spokesman for the complainants, returned to England and related their grievances to the Trustees. He asserted that the dissidents were not an unruly mob but, on the contrary, people of "credite and reputation" who faced many difficulties:

uncertainties regarding their land grants, "the tedious and frequent holding of Courts," which forced men to take time off work, and the "feastings and Clubs . . . caryed on and encouraged by the Magistrates," which pushed up prices in Savannah. Gordon argued that unless decisive action was taken by the Trustees settlers would leave Georgia in droves, and if that happened the consequences would be catastrophic.[55]

The Trustees' reaction to Gordon's comments was entirely predictable. Despite Gordon's insistence that his sole concern was to set Georgia more firmly on the road toward the attainment of those economic goals so ardently desired by all the participants in the project, the Trustees regarded him as a disloyal and possibly unbalanced man who was determined to wreck their scheme. They believed, moreover, that there was every reason to doubt his analysis of the economic condition of their colony.[56]

Significantly, not all of those who settled in Georgia during the 1730s became malcontents upon their arrival in America. On the contrary, some colonists insisted that all was going well in Georgia, and their reports were vital in shaping the Trustees' attitude toward the complainants. These favorable accounts ranged from the supremely optimistic to the opinion that the colony was doing as well as could be expected. Joseph Fitzwalter, the accountant at the Trust Garden in Savannah, who perhaps was telling his employers what he thought they wished to hear, spoke of Georgia as "the Promised Land," and William Bateman claimed that "Philadelphia was 10 or 12 years before it could boast of such a Towne as Georgia at present."[57] The Trustees continued to receive glowing reports of the amount of land that had been cleared and planted, the health, and, as important, the attitude of the settlers. Even Samuel Eveleigh was forced to concede that many settlers were coping reasonably well with the difficulties that confronted them.[58]

Some of those who penned favorable accounts suggested that the complainants were simply lazy. Thomas Christie, who claimed that the achievements of the Georgia settlers had "never yet been paralled [sic] by any people under the sun," and Elisha Dobree referred to the dissidents as "drones," but they emphasized that those "whose heads are turn'd no way but to the Ale House" were the exceptions.[59] Such reports, regardless of the motives of their authors, bolstered the Trustees' confidence in their scheme, and, even before Gordon returned to England, all the complainants were being tarred with the same undiscriminating brush: they were dismissed as "malcontents," "drones," and "idlers," men who preferred a life of ease to the hard but rewarding work involved in implementing the Trustees' design. Through no fault of his own Gordon found himself appealing to men who saw no reason to accept or even to discuss his account of conditions in Georgia. This unwillingness to listen to what were often expressions of genuine concern did not bode well for the future.

CHAPTER TWO

THE MAKING OF A PRESSURE

GROUP, 1735–1740

*B*etween 1735 and 1740 a clearly defined and increasingly articulate pro-slavery faction emerged in Georgia. The most prominent spokesmen for this group were four Lowland Scots, Patrick Tailfer, David Douglass, Patrick Houstoun, and Andrew Grant, and an English merchant, Robert Williams. These "adventurers," men who had paid their own way to Georgia and taken servants with them, insisted that if prosperity did not materialize under the Trustees' scheme, that scheme must be rejected as impracticable.

Tailfer and his friends arrived in Georgia in 1734 and were soon firing off letters to the Trustees. Early in 1735 they protested Causton's behavior and the distance of their land grants from Savannah; within weeks they had decided that the location of their farms was of minor importance when compared with other disadvantages that were impeding Georgia's economic development.[1] Specifically, they demanded permission to employ slaves. The Scots put their case in a letter, probably written by Tailfer, which reached the Trustees in August 1735.

Tailfer alleged that Europeans were unaccustomed to Georgia's hot climate and if forced to work during the summer months they would succumb to "Distempers which render them useless for almost one half of the Year." In addition, white servants were more expensive to maintain than slaves. Tailfer, like Gordon, had a low opinion of the Europeans available as indentured servants, and he feared for the future of Georgia. Were "parcels of hardn'd abandoned Wretches, perfectly Skill'd in all manner of Villany" permitted, let alone encouraged, to settle in the colony, they would not only form "treasonable Designs" against the colonial authorities but would most likely try to escape from Georgia. They would probably be successful in the latter endeavor because there was no law to stop "White People who are travelling." Africans would constitute a more secure work force by virtue of their color. Having established the case for slavery to his own satisfaction, Tailfer proposed that a clearly defined limit be imposed on any slave element introduced into Georgia; he agreed with Eveleigh that a fixed, low ratio ought to be established between the races. But Tailfer also suggested that Africans should be employed only as unskilled agricultural workers.[2] Perhaps he sensed the danger implicit in using slaves as domestic servants or teaching them skills that demanded an ability to read or write. He might also have felt that the use of blacks as skilled workers would threaten the economic security of Georgia's white craftsmen and, for that reason, deter potential migrants.

Tailfer and his friends argued their case honestly, but, as with Gordon, their motives were immediately called into question. Thomas Jones, one of the Trustees' most ardent supporters, believed that the Scots had in mind private gain rather than the public good, and he suggested that Tailfer and Williams hoped to monopolize the slave trade to Georgia and for that reason stirred up "discontents among the Drunken Idle part of the Inhabitants."[3] Once more the Trustees' suspicions were confirmed by a report from Georgia, and they merely noted that they had no intention of modifying their labor policy. At this stage the Trustees were under no real pressure to alter their scheme, and this remained the case until Thomas Stephens's entry into the political arena in 1739. But the essential ingredients of the pro-slavery argument were outlined in Tailfer's original letter. What changed after 1735 were not the malcontents' arguments but their political stratagems.

The Georgia settlers were comparatively silent on the subject of slavery between mid-1735 and late 1738. The deterioration of Anglo-Spanish relations may have given the malcontents pause for thought, but such an argument is not wholly convincing because it does not take into account the renewed activity of the pro-slavery faction in 1738, well before the Battle of Bloody

Marsh. Similarly, there is little evidence that Georgia's economic condition improved enough in these years to persuade the dissidents that the Trustees' plan could succeed. Probably the reverse was true: by the end of 1738 some settlers believed that their situation was so desperate that their only recourse was yet another round of appeals to the Trustees. It might also have been relevant that the indentures of many of the servants brought to Georgia in 1734 and 1735 were beginning to expire and that replacements were hard to come by.[4]

During this lull in the slavery debate the Trustees continued to receive comments about their prohibitory policy from elsewhere in America. Eveleigh had argued that it was unrealistic; William Byrd of Virginia adopted a different stance. He lavished praise on the Trustees and expressed the wish that his own colony would follow Georgia's example.[5] Byrd's remarks were of the utmost significance because they confirmed the tensions and difficulties and, not least, the threat to white manners and morals posed by the unlimited importation of slaves.

Although the Georgia settlers marked time on the question of slavery, they continued to disagree about the economic progress being made in the colony, and in this sense the debate continued. The Trustees' supporters attributed such economic ills as beset Georgia to indolence and the appeal of nonagricultural labor; their opponents blamed the environment and the Trustees' land and labor policies rather than their own failings for the colony's poor economic performance.[6] These conflicting accounts, a continuation of the argument that had been raging since 1734, finally persuaded the Trustees of the need to appoint a resident secretary whose sole function would be to send regular reports to London.

As early as September 1733, the Trustees had concluded that they must take steps to ensure more frequent reports from Georgia. Oglethorpe tried to keep his colleagues informed but found his time increasingly taken up with military matters. Back in London some of the other Trustees complained that he was a negligent correspondent, and in 1734 they asked him to appoint someone "to correspond constantly . . . and keep a Journal of all remarkable transactions." The Trustees were hard-pressed to provide the Board of Trade with accurate information, without which they feared Parliament might withhold its annual appropriation for the colony. In January 1736 they asked Thomas Causton to "keep a constant Diary of what happens," but his correspondence must have left something to be desired because by the end of the year they had decided to appoint a resident secretary. Early in 1737 James Vernon, who had been highly critical of Oglethorpe's tardiness as a correspondent, informed his colleagues that "Willm. Stephens Esq. . . . had offer'd his Service to go to Georgia, and be our Secretary." Egmont was impressed by Stephens and confident that he could be relied upon to send back "constant information about the State of the Colony concerning which hitherto we have been kept too much in the dark."[7] His confidence in Stephens was to have important implications for the slavery debate.

What kind of man was this William Stephens whom the Trustees held in such high regard? First and foremost he was a "gentleman." He was born at Bowcombe on the Isle of Wight in 1671, the son of the island's lieutenant-governor. Educated at Winchester and Cambridge, Stephens was elected member of Parliament for Newport, Isle of Wight, in 1702 and served in that capacity for twenty years. Between 1722 and 1727 he sat as the member for Newtown. Although Stephens's parliamentary career was uneventful, his business ventures proved disastrous until, in 1736, he was hired by Colonel Samuel Horsey to survey some land in South Carolina. During his stay in South Carolina he visited Savannah. The Trustees were delighted by his firsthand knowledge of Georgia but even more so by the journal he had kept for Horsey: it was precisely what they had in mind for their colony.[8]

Considering his advanced age, the terms of employment offered to Stephens were extremely generous. He was given five hundred acres of land, the use of ten Trust servants during his first year in Georgia, unlimited access to the public store, the cost of his passage to America, and £100 to cover his immediate expenses. The Trustees thought that he might welcome secretarial assistance and suggested that his son Thomas might accompany him to Georgia—an offer they were soon to regret.[9]

Stephens reached Savannah on 1 November 1737 and on his

first evening in Georgia was approached by the malcontents. Although he had no executive power, Stephens had the ear of the Trustees, whom the Georgians were certain would set great store by his reports. A few weeks after this initial encounter Stephens sent his first detailed report on the malcontents to his employers. He identified the Lowland Scots as the ringleaders but suggested that although they complained about life in Georgia they made "profession of all good Will to the Colony, and ready Obedience to the Civil Power," an opinion he was soon to revise. Stephens admitted that he was concerned that many people were leaving Georgia, but he argued that most of them were "Idle, and of no use to ye Community." As many able-bodied men as possible would be needed to defend the colony against Spain, and Stephens preferred that the defense of Georgia be entrusted to those who believed they had something worth fighting for. Stephens ended his letter with a passing reference to slavery. He suggested that the consequences of introducing slaves would be "very pernicious" but did not explain why.[10]

How much reliance may be placed on the accounts Stephens sent to London? Soon after he arrived in Georgia, Stephens realized that he was in an unenviable position. He was paid by the Trustees to report on conditions in Georgia and to suggest possible improvements in their scheme. But he was rebuked when he proposed alterations in their land policy and thereafter seems to have been afraid the Trustees might think he was siding with their opponents. If they ever came to that conclusion and dismissed him his career would be over. Georgia was his last chance in life, and he was determined not to squander it. It is difficult to ascertain whether his official reports reflected his personal opinions or whether he acted out of a sense of duty tinged with self-preservation. But whatever his motives, Stephens assumed a central role in the slavery debate. After 1738 no one, with the possible exceptions of Oglethorpe and Johann Martin Bolzius, pastor of the Salzburger settlement, did more than he did to reinforce the Trustees' faith in their design for Georgia.

The malcontents hoped that Stephens's appointment would herald the dawn of a new era in their relations with the Trustees.

But Stephens soon let them know where his allegiance, if not his personal sympathies, lay. Far from being the malcontents' friend or even a neutral observer, he would do his utmost to thwart them. The malcontents in turn recognized the need to alter their tactics and, more specifically, to organize themselves.

On 9 December 1738 Tailfer told Stephens that he and his friends had just put the finishing touches to a petition demanding extensive alterations in the Trustees' scheme and that it was supported by "almost every Body" in Savannah.[11] The petition, which was signed by 117 settlers, contained little that the Trustees had not heard before. The authors explained that they were sending the document because they had not received any reply to their earlier missives; they then outlined the progress, or in their view the lack of it, made in Georgia since 1733.[12]

The petition of 1738 is of value less for the arguments it presented than for the insights it offers into the extent of discontent in Georgia. Most of the petitioners lived in Savannah, which is not surprising given the distribution of population. Of more import is that, although the document had been inspired by Tailfer and Williams, two "adventurers," such settlers did not monopolize discontent. Almost as many charity settlers (forty-five) and servants (nine) as adventurers signed the petition. But the social mix was not paralleled by an ethnic or national mix; all but about a dozen of the petitioners were English or Lowland Scots. The Salzburgers and Highland Scots were notably missing and, within weeks, were to send counterrepresentations to the Trustees. Most of the petitioners had spent at least three years in Georgia (only four are known to have arrived after 1736), which lends weight to their argument that they had tried over a number of years to implement the Trustees' plan.

Finally, almost half of the petitioners did not endorse any of the formal protests sent from Georgia in 1740 and 1741. Their absence at that time may be explained partly, but not entirely, by death and desertion. A settler's decision to leave Georgia did not necessarily mean that he was thereby obliged, or wished, to opt out of the slavery debate, for subsequent protests were sent to the Georgia "exiles" in South Carolina before being forwarded to England. Settlers who chose to petition the Trustees in 1738 might have been unwilling to sign these later representations because of an antipathy toward their content, a dislike or distrust of those who were soliciting their signatures, a fear of further antagonizing the Trustees, or a belief that the Trustees were so intransigent that further complaints would be futile. Alternatively, but less likely, some might have felt that conditions were improving and that there was no longer any cause for complaint.

The petition of 1738 provoked a response from the Salzburgers, the Highland Scots, and James Oglethorpe. The Salzburgers opposed the introduction of slavery on the grounds that the institution was both undesirable and unnecessary. The Highland Scots, writing from the exposed outpost of Darien, emphasized the pragmatic, and especially the military, arguments in favor of the ban but also spoke out against slavery for reasons and in a language that, as a recent historian has stated, "would reverberate through the anti-slavery movement and culminate in Lincoln's Second Inaugural Address."[13] Thus the unknown author of the Scots' petition declared: "It's shocking to human Nature, that any Race of Mankind and their Posterity, should be sentenced to perpetual Slavery; nor in Justice can we think otherwise of it, than they are thrown among us to be our Scourge one Day or another, for our Sins; and as Freedom to them must be as dear to us, What a Scene of Horror it must bring about! And the longer it is unexecuted, the bloody Scene must be the greater."[14] The Trustees anticipated the later antislavery movement by drawing attention to the adverse effects of slavery on white manners and morals; the Highland Scots did likewise by emphasizing the natural rights of the African and suggesting that sooner or later the sin of slaveholding would be punished.

The third, and in the short term most influential, reply came from Oglethorpe. He informed his colleagues that the pro-slavery petition had been inspired by a small group of selfish men who had completely misrepresented conditions in Georgia. Other settlers had signed the document because their servants' indentures had expired and they hoped "to get a new credit for Negroes [and] live upon their labour as they did upon their Servants." These men exemplified the "idleness" and "luxury" which the Trustees were determined to eradicate; if they had their way the "labouring poor white Men would be starved." In a second letter Oglethorpe rejected the argument that a plantation economy would benefit both Georgia and the home country. On the contrary, if Georgia duplicated the Carolina economy the British market would be glutted "with more of the present American Commodities, which do already but too much interfere with the English produce." Rather more interesting, however, was Oglethorpe's professed concern for the African. The legalization of slavery in Georgia would "occasion the misery of thousands in Africa . . . and bring into perpetual Slavery the poor people who now live free there." The Trustees must resist all demands for black workers; the "idle" settlers would then leave Georgia and the agitation for slaves would subside.[15]

Oglethorpe's letters confirmed the opinion of the other Trustees and, not least, of Egmont. His insistence that the condition of Georgia was nowhere near so serious as the malcontents claimed (and of course he was regarded as a reliable witness) reinforced the Georgia Board's determination to persevere with their scheme. They decided, however, for the first time, to reply formally to the malcontents. Benjamin Martyn, who wrote on their behalf, argued that far from benefiting South Carolina, slavery had pushed that colony to the "Brink of Ruin." Did not the Stono Rebellion demonstrate the "inconvenience and danger" that accompanied the use of slaves? Martyn scorned the petitioners' "Appeal to Posterity," saying that time would show that the Georgians' best friends had been those who "endeavoured to preserve for them a Property in their land" rather than those "few Negro merchants [who] would become the Sole owners of the Province, by introducing their banefull Commodity." Martyn castigated the Savannah magistrates for having permitted the dissidents to send such a petition and was particularly severe on the signers of the document. The Trustees were not surprised to find "unwary People drawn in by crafty men" but were appalled that their own officials should "so far forget your duty as to put yourselves at the head of this Attempt." They had seriously miscalculated if they believed that the Trustees would be swayed by "such a irrational Attempt" to alter a plan that had been drawn up "with the greatest Caution for the Preservation of Liberty and Property."[16]

As the summer of 1739 drew to a close the Trustees were hopeful that they would receive an accurate account of Georgia when Thomas Stephens returned to England.[17] But they were in for a rude shock: Stephens soon declared his intention of joining forces with the malcontents. In fact, his arrival in London marked the beginning of the most vital phase of the slavery debate. In 1739 the Trustees were under no real pressure to modify their labor policy; by 1743 they had all but conceded defeat in their attempt to exclude slavery from Georgia. This remarkable turnabout is to be explained primarily by the campaign waged by Thomas Stephens on behalf of the malcontents.

Until 1739 the condition and likely future of Georgia were matters for discussion between the Trustees and the settlers and, occasionally, interested parties in South Carolina. Thereafter, mainly because of Stephens, Parliament took a much keener interest in Georgia. By 1739 it was abundantly clear to the Trustees that if they wished to maintain the integrity of their scheme they would have to demonstrate beyond any shadow of a doubt that financial support for Georgia was very much in the national interest.

Thomas Stephens arrived in Savannah in December 1737 to act as his father's assistant, but within two years he had emerged as the malcontents' most important spokesman and strategist. How is this dramatic change of heart to be explained? In his published works Stephens cited various reasons why Georgia could never prosper under the Trustees' plan, and the points he isolated were not unfamiliar: the climate, a restrictive land policy, a corrupt and inefficient local administration, Oglethorpe's often arbitrary behavior, and the prohibition of slavery. By the winter of 1738–39 his disenchantment with Georgia was almost complete.[18] William Stephens, who commented that his son was "under sad apprehensions of future Misery," tried to reassure him that the Trustees would never abandon those settlers who "acted an honest & diligent part."[19] But a few weeks later the last tenuous link of Thomas Stephens's attachment to the Trustees' project was severed when Oglethorpe accused him of trying to embezzle the regimental store in Savannah and told him that he "deserved to be sent home to England" to be tried as a felon. William Stephens was thankful when Oglethorpe said that out of "Tenderness" toward the Stephens family he would "pass it over"; his son was "shocked at the Imputation of so vile an Act." The affair did not end there, however, for two months later Thomas was involved in a contretemps with Thomas Jones, Causton's replacement as the Trustees' storekeeper. Stephens refused to give Jones the keys to a wine cellar under the Trust house in Savannah on the grounds that he had not been authorized to do so; Jones, like many local officials, was jealous of his authority and complained to Oglethorpe. The matter was brought before the Savannah magistrates who, much to Stephens's dismay, found against him. Rightly or wrongly, he felt that he had been victimized by Oglethorpe. Although these two incidents seem trivial, they provided Stephens with a private grievance which he nursed for the next five years.[20]

Although it is tempting to assume that Thomas Stephens joined forces with the malcontents early in 1739 there is no evidence that he did. Indeed, according to his father's later reports Thomas thought that the complainants were "the Pest of the place" and often argued with them "even to excessive heat, against the use of Negroes." But William thought that in view of his son's illness and clashes with Oglethorpe it would be wise for him to return to England for "a short Season." After a period he would come back to Georgia "restored to bodily ease and Strength" and prepared to see the colony in a better light.[21]

Thomas Stephens arrived in England in October 1739 and, on the tenth of that month, gave the Trustees "a tolerable account" of Georgia. But three days later he met Egmont privately and "unfolded . . . the true state of our colony, after a different manner than he acquainted the Trustees."[22] Stephens visited Egmont again on 5 November and told him that the antislavery petitions sent from Georgia were worthless because the signatures had been obtained under duress by officers of Oglethorpe's Regiment. He implied that at best Oglethorpe had turned a blind eye to these methods and at worst had inspired them. Egmont was surprised by these comments but did not object when, two weeks later, the Georgia Board awarded Thomas £50 as payment for his secretarial work in Savannah. Perhaps he believed that this sum would secure the young man's silence.

On 16 November Stephens intimated that he intended to return to Georgia in the not too distant future, but a week later he presented the Trustees with his first written analysis of conditions in the colony, a piece entitled *Thoughts on the Colony of Georgia*. Stephens argued that most of Georgia's problems stemmed from the Trustees' land and labor policies and the behavior of the local officials, but he added that the situation had been exacerbated by the offhand manner in which the Georgia Board had rejected the petition of 1738. He admitted that the petition had been "drawn up in a most Shamefull manner" but expressed his confidence that the Trustees' "Compassion for the Poor will not be obstructed thro' the Misbehaviour of the Proud." Although he asserted that the petition contained "nothing false," Stephens doubted the wisdom of allowing an unlimited importation of slaves into Georgia. But he offered no suggestions as to how the size of the colony's black element might be contained within acceptable limits.[23]

Although Stephens's actions down to the end of 1739 may be ascribed to "youthful exuberance,"[24] his attitude hardened during the months that followed. Given that he believed Oglethorpe was responsible for many of Georgia's problems, it is not surprising that he looked to Egmont, together with Oglethorpe the most influential of the Trustees, for support. But Egmont was disinclined to believe him and made it clear that he would not be a party to any campaign against Oglethorpe. Stephens soon realized that unless additional pressure could be exerted on the Trustees they would never change their scheme. He appreciated that his main hope lay with the House of Commons and, after January 1740, geared his campaign to take advantage of the Georgia Board's financial vulnerability.

It was not for want of trying that the Trustees lacked a cast-iron guarantee of continuing financial support. In 1737 they had proposed that Parliament finance Georgia's military establishment and underwrite the colony's civil expenses to the tune of £4,000 per annum. The House of Commons agreed to the first request but stipulated that the Trustees must continue to apply annually for any additional funds.[25] As Stephens and the Trustees appreciated, the Georgia project would stand or fall by this financial arrangement.

By 1740 the parliamentary Trustees had lost much of their earlier effectiveness as a lobby. Interest in the Georgia experiment had diminished, but the main reason, according to Richard S. Dunn, was that parliamentary Trustees were "too heterogeneous to make possible the existence of a bloc of Georgia voters, unless loyalty to Georgia came before loyalty to party."[26] For only a handful of Trustees did loyalty to Georgia come first. Moreover, Egmont's decision in 1734 to stand down from his Harwich constituency in favor of his son had serious implications for the Georgia Board. Much to Egmont's surprise, his son was defeated. Egmont believed that the machinations of the Walpole ministry were responsible, and after 1734 he was convinced that Sir Robert Walpole was implacably opposed to the Georgia project. In fact, this was not entirely true. Egmont's resignation as a member of Parliament and Oglethorpe's absence in Georgia meant that at a time of mounting opposition two of the Georgia Board's most committed and influential spokesmen were unable to participate in the parliamentary debates that would have a profound bearing upon the fate of the Georgia Plan. Significantly, by his scarcely disguised hostility to Walpole Egmont made it difficult for himself to exert an informal influence on the ministry. John Laroche, who became the Trustees' main spokesman in Parliament, was to face a great many difficulties, not least of which was the apathy if not the outright opposition of certain of his colleagues on the Georgia Board.[27]

Although he took no part in the parliamentary debates, Egmont planned the Trustees' strategy. In December 1739, partly to counter Stephens's *Thoughts* and partly to provide the parliamentary Trustees with ammunition, he prepared a brief account of the state and importance of Georgia.[28] Egmont emphasized the advantages that would accrue from the new colony. He admitted that Georgia had not yet realized its full potential but suggested that in the long run it would become one of Britain's most valuable American possessions. He reminded his readers that Georgia promised to become a major supplier of silk and wine, but he might have strengthened the Trustees' hand had he also mentioned the colony's potential as a producer of timber and furs. The importance of his papers was they took a realistic line in contrast to the Trustees' promotional literature, which had suggested that Georgia would prove an instant economic success. He conceded that there had been difficulties associated with the settlement of Georgia but pointed out that new colonies always faced problems. He was belatedly pleading for time as well as money for the Georgia project.

At the same time as Egmont was organizing the Trustees' defense, Thomas Stephens was writing a paper designed to assist their parliamentary opponents. In this piece, *Observations on the Present State of Georgia,* Stephens admitted that the colony's "languishing condition" was partly the result of the "mistaken Notices and precipitate Actions" of the early settlers, but he argued that the Trustees must shoulder some of the blame because of their stubborn refusal to modify their plan. Aiming the tract at members of Parliament, he added the observation that Georgia's "arbitrary Government" was financed by funds voted for by the House of Commons, a theme he was to elaborate in his later works.[29]

Stephens did not mention slavery in his *Observations* but more than made up for this omission in February 1740 in a paper devoted to an analysis of the comparative profitability of black and white labor. Here, for the first time, an attempt was made to quantify an argument that previously had been expressed in essentially qualitative terms. Stephens concluded that "a Man at the end of 8 years, who plants with white men is £715.9.9 worse, than he would be were he to use Negroes: and Such at present is the difference in planting on the North and South sides of the River Savannah."[30]

But how accurate was a computation described by Egmont as "partially made in favour of negroes"? A recent analysis of Stephens's paper has suggested that although "his case for slavery looks to be sophistry of the most flagrant variety . . . he was culpable for reasons related to his naivete rather than chicanery." Where his data were patently inaccurate Stephens erred in opposition to his case at least as often as in favor of it. More-over, the "unsophisticated accounting techniques and manage-rial analysis of the day" help to explain why "his analytical techniques and accounting procedures seem designed to produce the desired end result." Although none of the other malcontents produced such a sophisticated attempt to demonstrate the profit-ability of slavery, their qualitative arguments were economically sound.[31]

Egmont was not convinced by Stephens's calculations and ex-pressed his anger at the fact that this young man, who had received favored treatment at the hands of the Trustees, should choose to ally himself with their parliamentary opponents. But although Egmont believed that Stephens was a "rash vindictive fool" he continued to meet with him. Egmont was anxious to discover the charges that might be leveled against the Trustees in the House of Commons; Stephens, who still hoped to secure Egmont's support, was eager to talk about such matters. But once Egmont and the Trustees realized the extent to which Stephens had primed their opponents, they decided to have noth-ing more to do with him. Stephens retorted that if the Georgia Board refused to give him a hearing he would *"justify myself in print."* The Trustees soon discovered that this was no idle threat.[32]

The House of Commons debated the Trustees' money petition in February 1740 and immediately the parliamentary Trustees came under attack from members who, for different reasons, wanted an inquiry into the condition of Georgia. Thomas Gage pressed for more information about the colony and argued that although the Trustees were "Men of the strictest honour" they had mangaged to "put [Georgia] . . . upon so wrong a foot, as must absolutely ruin it." But Gage and the Trustees were thwarted by Walpole, who considered that Gage's proposal came dangerously close to reopening the Spanish Convention issue. Many members were unhappy at having to vote on the Trustees' money petition while the condition of Georgia was largely unknown, but eventually it was agreed to appropriate £4,000 for a project that had already "cost the nation a vast sum."[33]

Although the Trustees had secured a year's breathing space they still did not have a guarantee of continuing support. Moreover, threats such as that made by Captain John Mordaunt, the member for Whitchurch and "a constant enemy to the colony," to the effect that if the Trustees "came next year for more, there would not be a man for giving a farthing" were not lost on the Trustees.[34] During the rest of 1740 they prepared for the next parliamentary debate on the financing of Georgia. Their strategy was two-pronged: first, they explored the possibility of framing a compromise that would be acceptable to the malcontents but would not necessitate the introduction of slaves and, second, they decided to press for a parliamentary inquiry into the importance of Georgia.

In June 1740 a group of Trustees, including Egmont, Vernon, and Laroche, met to discuss the advisability of allowing the Georgia settlers to employ blacks "in some shape or other."[35] Some of those present were opposed to making any concessions, but Vernon, with Egmont's backing, persuaded the meeting to consider a novel proposal that sought to differentiate between slavery and the African. It was the former, rather than the latter, which posed such a potent threat to the Trustees' social design.

According to Vernon, the Act of 1735 prohibited slavery but did not ban the employment of free blacks in Georgia. The malcontents based their incessant clamor for slaves on the grounds of the Africans' alleged suitability for hard manual labor in the Georgia environment rather than on any benefits that would accrue from slavery per se. Indeed, they accepted that the unlimited importation of slaves would pose a threat to their security. Surely, argued Vernon, Georgia's labor requirements, and the malcontents, would be satisfied and the problems of defense posed by slavery circumvented by the employment of free blacks. Egmont and Laroche saw both advantages and disadvantages in Vernon's suggestion. Laroche thought that the presence of free blacks would make it difficult to detect runaways from South Carolina and seems to have been more concerned with the preservation of slavery in that colony than with the implications of Vernon's proposal for Georgia. Egmont added a second reason why free blacks might prove disadvantageous: he believed, for reasons that were never stated, that free blacks would work for lower wages than white workers. If that happened, the latter, who were essential for the defense of Georgia, would leave the colony. If free blacks would work for the same wages as whites, the problem could be avoided. Egmont did not consider the possibility of calling upon free blacks to defend Georgia, but he did see one great advantage in Vernon's scheme: free blacks would constitute a secure and docile labor force because they "could not better themselves" by running away or rebelling.

The Trustees did not contemplate the source of such a work force. Would they have purchased slaves elsewhere in the Americas and given them their freedom in Georgia? The financing of such a scheme, also not mentioned by the Trustees, raises intriguing possibilities. How would a British government, committed as it was to the African slave trade, have reacted to the use of public money for such a purpose? Could funds have been raised from those private benefactors who were willing to subscribe to charitable projects designed to educate and Christianize the African? How would the Georgians and slaveowners elsewhere in the mainland have responded to such a proposal? Apparently, the Trustees did not concern themselves with these vital questions but decided that their first step must be to secure a ruling as to the legality of introducing free blacks into Georgia. Dudley Ryder, the attorney general, dashed their hopes when he declared that whatever the "general Intent" of the Act of 1735, it prohibited "the using of Negroes in any manner or way whatsoever in the province." Blacks might not "be used as common servants hired for terms of years nor can they Settle in the Province." The Trustees did not appeal this ruling but abandoned a unique proposal that might have found favor with the malcontents and fell back on a do-or-die defense of their prohibitory policy. But this episode is of significance because it suggests that in 1740, and possibly thereafter, the Trustees would have allowed the Georgians to employ blacks "in the same manner as they have White Servants."[36] Such a scheme, if followed through, would have had far-reaching consequences for the subsequent development of Georgia.

During 1740 the Trustees also contemplated the problem of how they might demonstrate to the satisfaction of Parliament that Georgia was not in the desperate straits portrayed by the malcontents, and they decided to ask for a detailed report from William Stephens. But before Stephens could put pen to paper an event occurred that raised his and the Trustees' hopes that peace and quiet might at last descend on Savannah: Tailfer and his cronies made good their threat and left Georgia. Realizing by mid-1740 that although the Trustees were willing to tinker with their land policy they had no intention of permitting slavery, these malcontents decided that under the circumstances there was little point in remaining in Georgia. But their most important contribution to the slavery debate, a tract entitled *A True and Historical Narrative of the Colony of Georgia,* was written shortly after their arrival in Charles Town. The Trustees' hopes that the clamor for slaves would cease with the departure of the Lowland Scots were soon to be dashed.

Shortly after the Scots departed, Stephens complied with the Trustees' request and penned *A State of the Province of Georgia.* The main thrust of his report, endorsed by twenty-four settlers, was that the condition of Georgia was infinitely better than alleged by the malcontents. Stephens admitted that several settlers had left the colony, but he insisted that those who remained were "the most valuable people, that find means to live comfortable." He agreed that Georgia suffered from a shortage of labor but advocated the sending over of "English or Welch servants, such as are used to hard labour in the country, and strangers to London." In effect Stephens was rejecting the Trustees' argument that the settlers' occupational backgrounds were irrelevant.[37]

Stephens showed his report to Andrew Duche and John Fallowfield, two settlers who had signed the petition of 1738, and they recorded their astonishment that he intended to send such a mendacious account to the Trustees. They realized that the affidavits of those few settlers who concurred with Stephens's analysis would stiffen the Trustees' resolve and decided to send a counterrepresentation to London. Stephens was alarmed by a rumor circulating in Savannah that their petition included a scathing attack on him, and, no doubt under the impression that attack was the best form of defense, he launched into a bitter assault on the malcontents. He claimed that although only a handful of men had signed his report they had at least been prepared to swear oaths attesting to the truth of their statements. Duche and Fallowfield, on the other hand, had spent days drumming up support for their petition, and most of those who had signed the document had little idea of what they were endorsing. Some had been "seduced by repeated perswasions, against their own Will, to sign what was promised would make them all happy," and others had been plied with so much alcohol that they had been willing to "write their Names to they knew not what." Stephens concluded by observing that most of the petitioners were acting out of spite toward him and the Trustees rather than out of a genuine concern for Georgia.[38]

Duche and Fallowfield finished collecting signatures on 22 November 1740. The document they sent to London began by mentioning that the Trustees had often invited the settlers "to set forth their Miserys, Hardships, and Difficulties," and because Stephens had sent false reports they felt they must set the record straight. They denied that Georgia's agriculture was as prosperous as Stephens claimed and maintained that the silk industry, which he depicted in glowing terms, was so insignificant as to be scarcely worth mentioning. If Georgia was flourishing, why had so many settlers left the colony? Those that had left were not "the Idle, the Drunken, and the Lazy" but the most industrious settlers who, after long and bitter experience, had come to appreciate the "Impossibility, and Improbability of living in this place."[39]

The petition was sent to the Georgia exiles in Carolina, and they added one or two comments before forwarding it to London. They noted that the Trustees' belief that Augusta was the most flourishing settlement in Georgia merely confirmed their argument that slave labor was essential for the economic well-being of the colony. The settlers at Augusta, they alleged, were sufficiently removed from Savannah and close enough to Carolina to be able to employ "at least" one hundred slaves with impunity.[40] When the petition was finally sent to the Trustees, it had been signed by seventy-six people, including thirteen exiles. As a group they included twenty-one charity settlers, thirty-nine adventurers, nine men who had gone as servants to Georgia, and seven men whose status cannot be determined.

On 29 December 1740 a second petition, signed by sixty-seven settlers, was sent from Savannah to London. This document, however, was addressed not to the Trustees but to "his Majesty, or to the Parliament," the recipient to be selected by the malcontents' "Agents in England."[41] The malcontents were determined to do all they could to assist Thomas Stephens and, like him, they were now prepared to bypass the Trustees and appeal directly to the British government.

The petitioners claimed that the Trustees had cited two reasons for prohibiting slavery: the physical threat posed by slaves and the opposition of many settlers to the institution. They agreed that on the face of it these were good reasons for maintaining the ban but suggested that a deeper analysis revealed a different picture. In their view, the Stono Rebellion could be attributed to the serious racial imbalance that had been allowed to develop in Carolina and the employment of slaves "in all manner of handycraft and household Business." The Georgians had requested the importation of a strictly limited number of slaves who would be used only as unskilled agricultural workers. On the Trustees' second point, the malcontents merely repeated the charge that the Salzburgers and the Highland Scots had been bribed by "the promise of a few cattle" to "Act Inconsistent with their own or Posterity's Interest." For their part, they had not been misled by slave merchants but, on the contrary, their own unhappy experience of Georgia had persuaded them of "the Impossibility of White men being able to Work here and live." Africans were not only physically suited to hard work in the Georgia environment but positively reveled in conditions whites found intolerable. Indeed, blacks were "far more happy here than in their own Country." In Africa they were "abject slaves"; in America they might be called slaves but were certain "of being fed and Cloathed, it being their Masters Interest to take the utmost Care of them." The petitioners wondered whether there was any real difference between the lot of the indentured servant and that of the slave. The Trustees might boast of having excluded black slavery from Georgia but seemed oblivious to the fact that they were forcing their fellow countrymen to endure an equally harsh form of servitude. "How shocking," they declared, "must it be even to a person of the least humanity to See his own Countrymen, perhaps his own Townsmen, Labouring in the Corn or Rice feild, Broiling in the Sun, Pale and Fainting under the Excessive heat."[42] They conveniently forgot to mention that, however hard their lot, indentured servants enjoyed the prospect of freedom.

A third petition was sent to the Trustees by certain "Residents, Inmates and Others not Being Landholders" in December 1740. This document was signed by twenty people and contained arguments similar to those in the representations forwarded to London during the previous six weeks. Egmont believed that these petitioners must "have been Spirited up by their Run away Masters," the Lowland Scots, because why else should such "a low Set of Men" petition for slaves? No doubt they had "been promised to be made Overseers" of any slaves brought to Georgia.[43]

The three petitions sent from Georgia in November and December 1740 brought to an end a year of unadulterated anxiety for the Trustees. The most worrying and potentially the most serious developments had been Thomas Stephens's return to England, the opposition their money petition had encountered in the House of Commons, and their failure to secure a parliamentary inquiry into the importance of Georgia. The Trustees were only too well aware that in securing their appropriation for 1740 they had won only a battle and not the war; they knew that their next money petition would meet with a hostile reception. By the end of 1740 the scene was set, in Britain and America, for the struggle that would determine the fate of the Trustees' social design.

CHAPTER THREE

THE STRUGGLE FOR

GEORGIA, 1741–1743

*T*he year 1741 was marked by two important developments in the slavery debate: Thomas Stephens returned to Savannah with the avowed intention of welding the malcontents into an effective pressure group and the Lowland Scots published their *A True and Historical Narrative.* But these occurrences were preceded by an event the Trustees had been anticipating with mixed feelings for the best part of a year: the next parliamentary debate on their money petition.

As the date of the debate drew closer and there was still no sign of William Stephens's report, the Trustees asked Benjamin Martyn to prepare an account that could be presented to the House of Commons if necessary. Martyn obliged by writing *An Impartial Inquiry into the State and Utility of the Province of Georgia,* one of the opening shots in what became a pamphlet war between the Trustees and their critics.[1]

Martyn began by listing the five main charges that had been leveled against the Trustees' scheme: that Georgia's climate was unhealthy for Europeans, the soils were barren, the colony had produced no exportable surpluses, the Trustees' land policy was restrictive, and Georgia could not prosper without black slaves. He then launched his attack on the malcontents by claiming that most of them were not charity settlers but "others of a superior rank, who went [to Georgia] at their own expense" and who imagined that they could make their fortunes "without any labour or toil." Those who alleged that Georgia's soils were infertile were those "who would not take any pains or labour to make [them] fruitful." Similarly, much of the ill health experienced in the colony had nothing to do with the climate but reflected the settlers' failure to "regulate their diet and manner of living" in accordance with their new surroundings. Martyn replied to the charge that Georgia had not produced any items for export by repeating Egmont's argument that such results were scarcely to be expected from such a young colony. The only drawback to the realization of Georgia's economic potential would be the "impatience and diffidence" of the settlers; if they cooperated with the Trustees and if the latter continued to receive funds from Parliament, Georgia would soon emerge as one of Britain's most highly prized colonies. But Georgia's prosperity would not be conditional upon the introduction of slavery: slaves were not only "needless for the produces which are to be raised there" but also "absolutely dangerous to Georgia in its present situation, as well as to the adjacent provinces." If Georgia was to function successfully as a buffer it could ill afford to admit "secret enemies . . . ready to join with her open ones upon the first occasion."[2]

In 1735 Martyn had attempted to persuade Eveleigh of the profitability of white servants; now he emphasized the economic and social disadvantages of slavery. He denied that parallels could be drawn between Georgia and South Carolina for the simple reason that the two colonies had been founded upon very different principles. Rice cultivation might necessitate slaves, but the crops to be produced in Georgia did not. The Trustees, who had no intention of competing with Carolina, anticipated that their plan would provide the settlers with a "comfortable subsistence." One of the implications of this aim was that whereas the Carolinians could afford as many field hands as they required, together with female slaves "whose increase adds to [their] property," the Georgians would be unable to meet the cost of "the negro, his wife, and the child or children, when perhaps the first is the only one from whom he receives any profit."[3] This was a rare mention in the slavery debate of the possibility of securing a self-perpetuating labor force, but, as in 1735, Martyn did not develop the point.

Martyn argued that even if the Trustees allowed each settler to own just one slave, it must be remembered that at current prices a male slave cost around £30 sterling, and he doubted whether many Georgians could lay their hands on such a sum. Tailfer had suggested that the Trustees bear the initial cost of supplying slaves, but Martyn foresaw enormous difficulties were such a scheme adopted. Parliament was unlikely to approve an appropriation for such a purpose, and, even if it did, the settlers would have no incentive to take care of slaves bought with other people's money. But the purchase of slaves was only the first step. They would have to be supervised, and, assuming that the Georgians would be unable to afford overseers, much time would have to be spent "in watching them, in order to oblige them to work, to prevent their running away, or to secure himself and his family from danger against them." The settlers would also have to be wary of chastising their bondsmen. Blacks would be quick to respond to harsh treatment but, on the other hand, there was little likelihood of converting the slave by kindly treatment into "a trusty servant." The malcontents claimed that they had more to fear from unruly white servants than they had from black slaves, but Martyn doubted that this was so.[4]

Martyn concluded by discussing the probable implications of slavery for the poorer white settlers, men whom the Trustees believed were being duped by the likes of Tailfer. He warned that if the ban on slavery was lifted slave merchants and wealthy planters from South Carolina would amass enormous estates in Georgia. Many of the less well-off settlers would be deprived of their economic independence and left with little choice but to work as hired hands or overseers. Surely they had more to gain by hiring white workers, for whose upkeep they would have to pay, but this "need not be costly."[5]

Although the Trustees were pleased with Martyn's tract, they took additional steps to try to ensure the smooth passage of their money petition. The task that confronted them was hinted at by Thomas Stephens early in 1741 when he visited Egmont to make one final appeal for changes in the Trustees' scheme. Stephens repeated his earlier allegations against Oglethorpe and insisted that the Georgia Board must send "an honest man over of character to view the situation . . . and bring us a faithful report." Egmont was adamant: as long as William Stephens remained in Georgia the Trustees could be certain of receiving reliable information.[6]

The final breach between Egmont and Thomas Stephens occurred a few days after this exchange and shortly before the appropriations debate. Apparently Stephens had just supplied certain members of Parliament with yet more written ammunition and Egmont felt that he had gone too far. And he was not alone among the Trustees. Lord Sidney Beauclerk threatened to resign unless the Trustees defended themselves, and Alderman George Heathcote insisted that the Georgia Board should either sue Stephens for libel or vindicate themselves before the House of Commons.[7] The Trustees decided upon the latter course. For good or ill, the fate of their project would be decided on the floor of the House of Commons.

The appropriations debate of 1741 was similar to that of the previous year. Gage launched the attack by saying that he "wondered that any gentleman should think of giving a farthing more to support a colony where there is not a man left to be supported," and Sir John Cotton suggested that those settlers who remained in Georgia should be moved to South Carolina "to strengthen that province." But the Trustees had some friends in the House. Horatio Walpole spoke on their behalf, emphasizing the military arguments that demanded the preservation of Georgia. The Trustees believed that a parliamentary inquiry would clarify the situation and vindicate their reputations, and they were delighted when Thomas Carew, the member for Minehead, intimated that he would propose an inquiry. They were horrified when Carew moved that they be asked to submit an account of the present condition of Georgia; they had expected him to ask for a report on the colony's importance to Britain, which would have enabled them to repeat the familiar arguments about the colony's economic and strategic importance.[8] Without William Stephens's report they felt unable to supply information that would stand up to close scrutiny by members who had been primed by Thomas Stephens.

Carew's motion was not seconded, and Edward Hooper, appointed a Trustee in 1739, proposed that £10,000 be appropriated for Georgia. His proposal was seconded by Horatio Walpole, and, although they had to force a division, the parliamentary Trustees carried the day by a vote of 115 to 75. Carew reintroduced his motion, but, thanks to Laroche, the House agreed to accept "an account . . . of the colony, from its first settlement" rather than demand a report on its present condition.[9] The Trustees were elated at the prospect of being able to vindicate themselves, but their joy was short-lived: they were opposed by a Walpole ministry that did not wish for a full-scale inquiry, allegedly because "a motion would follow for declaring the utility of the province, which would render it more difficult for their giving it up to the Spaniards for facilitating a peace." The debate was adjourned, and, as Egmont wryly remarked, the Georgia Board was "liable to be attacked again every session."[10]

Egmont was not alone in bemoaning this decision. Thomas Stephens was bitterly disappointed when the House of Commons voted the Georgia appropriation without making its support conditional upon the outcome of an inquiry into the present state of the colony. Although he had vowed not to return to Georgia "unless Negroes are allowed," he decided that his best course of action would be to go back to the colony. He left England in April 1741, and the Trustees were convinced that his sole purpose was "to work more mischief."[11] Their expectations were soon fulfilled.

The petitions sent from Georgia in 1740 began to arrive in London shortly after the appropriations debate. From the Trustees' standpoint they were important not because of what they said but because of what they signified. Any lingering hopes the Georgia Board might have entertained that discontent in their colony depended upon the stimulus provided by the Lowland Scots were shattered. But worse was to follow. The Trustees were shortly to discover that Tailfer and his friends had every intention of continuing with their campaign.

On 30 January 1741 William Stephens recorded in his journal that the *South Carolina Gazette* was advertising the imminent publication of a work entitled *A True and Historical Narrative of the Colony of Georgia*, which had been written by some of the Georgia exiles in Charles Town. When he saw the tract shortly after its publication in June 1741, he informed the Trustees that never before had he seen "Such an Heap of

Malicious Calumny and vile Falsehoods." He promised to send them a copy of this "Infamous" work by the next ship to England, but the Trustees obtained the tract well before Stephens's letter reached them.[12]

On 25 July 1741 Captain Patrick Tailfer, father of the "late troublesome surgeon and Landholder at Savannah," called on Egmont at his Charlton home. He had just received a copy of *A True and Historical Narrative* from David Douglass, one of the co-authors, with the request that he publish the work in London and send any profits to "the distrest Georgians" in Charles Town. Tailfer had browsed through the pamphlet, and its contents sent him scurrying to Egmont for advice. Egmont, gratified to hear Tailfer say that he had shown the work "to no man living," played on his financial fears and, in a scarcely veiled threat, warned him of the possible consequences of vilifying such an influential group of men as the Georgia Trustees. Tailfer promised Egmont that he would "reprehend his son by letter," but the latter was soon to discover that he had succeeded only in delaying, and not preventing, the publication in England of *A True and Historical Narrative.*[13]

Egmont admitted, albeit only to his closest confidantes, that although it was "very partially drawn up" Tailfer's tract contained much truth. Although *A True and Historical Narrative* contained information hitherto unavailable to a wide audience in England, its style and tone, rather than the thesis advanced, made it a potent work. The singling out of Oglethorpe for particularly vicious treatment was part and parcel of a searing attack on the Trustees' scheme. The Scots claimed that Georgia was on the point of collapse and that Oglethorpe must bear a great deal of the blame. Such accusations were familiar to the Georgia Board, but now the malcontents added an explanation to the British public as to why "so pleasant and temperate climate, so fruitful a soil; such extensive privileges . . . and such considerable sums of publick and private benefactions have not . . . enriched us." Their American readers would "be equally surprised to find that such numbers have been so fooled and blindfolded, as to expect to live in this part of America by cultivation of lands without Negroes, and much more without titles to their lands." The authors then reiterated all of the points made by the malcontents since 1735.[14]

Soon after he saw a copy of the tract Egmont remarked that "dirt will stick to the whitest hand till wash'd away," and he advised the preparation of "some Remarks . . . which may make us . . . the better and readyer to answer to the Complaints, and justify our Conduct if call'd on."[15] Egmont was prepared to fight tooth and nail to preserve both the integrity of the Georgia Plan and the Trustees' reputation.

In December 1741 Egmont informed the Georgia Board that the "scandalous Carolina pamphlet" was on sale in London and that he had ordered the publication of William Stephens's *A State of the Province of Georgia* as an "Antidote." Every member of Parliament would be sent a copy so as to be able to form "a right impression" of Georgia.[16] Some of the Trustees thought that Egmont was overreacting, but he persisted: unless the Trustees came to their own defense the "false Facts" presented by the Scots might be taken seriously. But although, thanks to Egmont, the Trustees tried to neutralize this latest attack, their efforts were to no avail: the Scots' pamphlet soon became an important weapon in their parliamentary opponents' armory. Moreover, while they were trying to ward off this assault, the Trustees came under renewed attack from a familiar enemy: Thomas Stephens. By the end of 1741 it was abundantly clear to them that Stephens had every intention of involving himself in the next parliamentary debate on the Georgia appropriation.

Thomas Stephens arrived back in the colonies in August 1741, and the day after his return to Savannah he arranged a meeting at which the settlers could air their grievances and discuss their tactics.[17] Stephens rehearsed the hardships he believed stemmed from the Trustees' policies and promised that if appointed the Georgians' agent he would work "without any Expence or Charge" on their behalf in England. The meeting duly took advantage of this generous offer and, on Stephens's advice, appointed a five-man committee of correspondence to act as his assistants in the colony.[18] At a second public meeting these assistants pointed out that an effective lobby would be expensive and that most of the necessary funds would have to be raised in Georgia. About £60 was collected before Stephens returned to England, and South Carolinian sympathizers donated "a much larger Sum."[19] Several settlers were willing to give money but would not sign Stephens's commission as agent; no doubt Oglethorpe's presence in Georgia made many reluctant to endorse such a document. Nevertheless, 120 people signified their support for Stephens.

The drawing up of Stephens's commission marked the high-water mark of formal discontent in Georgia, and it would therefore be appropriate to assess the extent and nature of the opposition to the Trustees' scheme.[20] The petitions of 1738 and 1740 and Stephens's commission attracted 212 different signatures. But the question arises as to the proportion of the population these signatories represented. The incomplete, and in many cases probably biased, data available for the years between 1738 and 1741 suggest that Georgia's population totaled no more than about 1,500 persons of which a maximum of around 800 or 900 were men. Of this number, roughly a quarter signed at least one of the four documents.[21]

One of the most salient characteristics of the protesters was their nationality: the vast majority were English or Lowland Scots. Only in this respect, however, is it possible to say that protest was the prerogative of particular groups within Georgia society. With the notable exception of Thomas Stephens, the leaders of the malcontents and their most consistent supporters were adventurers. But the same pattern was not so evident among the rank-and-file dissidents: fractionally over 44 percent of the malcontents were charity settlers or had gone as servants to Georgia. By the end of the 1730s differences in original status counted for very little. Finally, the personnel of the pro-slavery faction was fluid. As we have seen, half the petitioners of 1738 did not endorse any of the subsequent protests, thirty men made their first protest in November 1740, and sixty did so a year later. But the fluidity of the movement is balanced by the existence of a hard core of men whose names appeared on more than one document. Just over 40 percent of the petitioners of 1738 also signed the petitions of 1740 and Stephens's commission. Twenty-nine men signed all four protests and another nineteen (who were augmented by the three settlers who endorsed the petitions of 1740 and Stephens's commission but not the petition of 1738) signed two of the three later protests. These malcontents tended to be recruited from among the adventurers: twenty-nine had paid their own way to Georgia, thirteen were charity settlers, six were former servants, and the status of three is unknown. As we shall see, one of the ironies of the post-Trustee period was that those who had lobbied so hard for slavery were not among the major beneficiaries of the economic growth experienced by Georgia after 1750.

Thomas Stephens left for England on 28 October 1741, the day after he had received his instructions as the "Agent for the People of Georgia." He was given a free hand to "apply, petition, and solicit for redress of grievances, in such manner as you shall think most advisable" but was forbidden to make any further appeals to the Trustees.[22] The debate with the Trustees was over; from now on the malcontents would concentrate all their efforts on securing the support of a majority in the House of Commons.

The Trustees awaited Stephens's return with apprehension, not least because of the possible implications for the Georgia project of Walpole's recent fall from power. As Richard Dunn has pointed out, Walpole's removal had the effect of weakening the Trustees' position vis-à-vis the House of Commons. Ten of the parliamentary Trustees had not been reelected at the general election, and, although the Trustees immediately appointed six other members of Parliament to their Board, only six of the sixteen parliamentary Trustees took an active interest in Georgia.[23]

Early in 1742 Egmont visited the Earl of Wilmington in an effort to ascertain his attitude toward Georgia. The two men discoursed at some length on "the peoples desire of Negroes," which Wilmington saw as a clear-cut question: could the settlers "cultivate their lands as cheap with out Negroes as with them?" Egmont admitted that they could not but insisted that this was not the main point at issue. Georgia was intended "to form a frontier" and the Trustees "dared not" introduce slaves as long as Spain offered "liberty, protection and . . . lands" to black

runaways. The time would have been right for Egmont to have
raised the question of employing free blacks in Georgia, but he
did not, nor did he defend the Trustees' policy on social or moral
grounds. Instead he said that the Trustees would not permit
slavery because to do so would be to "venture the hazard" of a
colony "committed to our care." If Parliament was prepared to
accept the responsibility for the "mischief" that would stem
from the repeal of the prohibitory legislation, then so be it, but
the repeal of the Act of 1735 would be against the Trustees'
advice and without their consent.[24]

Two months later the Trustees presented their money petition
to Parliament. Again they emphasized the military function of
Georgia, the fact that during the previous year they had sent to
the colony "a considerable number of Saltzburghers and other
German Protestants," and the significance of the "steady friendship" that had been forged with the "neighbouring Indians." But
their effort was to no avail because the motion that their petition
be referred to a Committee of the Whole House was defeated by
the narrow margin of 194 votes to 181.[25] Why the House should
have voted in this way is difficult to explain. Egmont could not
account for the summary rejection of the petition at the first
hurdle. But Thomas Stephens was equally dissatisfied because
the House had not intimated that the Trustees' land and labor
policies should be revised. He decided to petition the Commons
on the malcontents' behalf and simultaneously to publish a tract
that would explain and justify their demands.

On 26 April 1742 Stephens's *The Hard Case of the Distressed
People of Georgia* was published in London.[26] Stephens de-
nounced the Trustees' design as "utterly impracticable" and
claimed that ever since the first settlement of Georgia the colonists had "pursued the very *Miseries and Wants,* which they
were here placed to extricate themselves out of." That the introduction of slavery would result in the "destruction" of Georgia
he dismissed as an "idle Insinuation." It was patently obvious
that "the Colony is already ruined . . . and it can't be said, that
the Introduction of Negroes has brought this about." Stephens
accepted that the Trustees had not conspired "to ruin so many
People," but he held that they must be faulted for their obstinacy

in supporting Georgia's local officials "against the Complaints of the People." In addition, they had authorized the publication of "false Accounts, both of the State and the Expences of the Colony" and "wickedly impugned ... honest Men's Characters ... *designedly* to weaken their Authority and Evidence in these matters."[27]

The Trustees decided that Stephens's allegations were so serious as to warrant a formal complaint to the House of Commons. They were confident that they would be able to vindicate themselves and, in the process, regain financial support for their colony. They therefore asked Edward Digby, one of the parliamentary Trustees, to complain about Stephens's "virulent Libel." Digby's ineffectual performance gave the Trustees' critics an opportunity they were quick to grasp. As soon as Digby sat down, Walter Carey, the member for Dartmouth, presented Stephens's petition to the House. The document was short and to the point, stating that the Trustees had mismanaged Georgia's financial affairs and permitted "many abuses in the Civil power." Moreover, the colony was so depopulated "as to be incapable of fulfilling His Majesty's gracious Designs in establishing it." Carey proposed that the petition be dealt with by a private committee but, after some discussion, it was agreed that an inquiry into the condition and importance of Georgia was a matter that warranted "the attention of the whole house."[28]

In May 1742 the Trustees were ordered to present to the House copies of their regulations governing land tenure in Georgia as well as of all the representations they had received from the colony. A few days later Thomas Stephens gave evidence and, according to Viscount Percival, Egmont's son, he "made great Impression on the house." Percival thought that there was considerable parliamentary support for persevering with Georgia but also for relieving the Trustees of their responsibility. The Committee of the Whole House promulgated six resolutions which emphasized the economic and military value of Georgia and thereby more than vindicated the Trustees. Some members, headed by Sir John Barnard, tried to introduce an additional resolution calling for the introduction of black slavery but were defeated by a vote of 35 to 18. An attempt was made to revive this resolution when the House formally considered the committee's recommendations but, after a three-hour debate, the motion was lost by 43 votes to 34. Those members who voted in favor intimated, however, that unless changes were made in the Trustees' labor policy they would be opposed to the continued financial support of the colony.[29] This was precisely what Thomas Stephens had hoped to hear.

The committee's sixth resolution, that Stephens's petition contained "false Scandalous and Malicious Charges, tending to Asperse the Character of the Trustees," met with no opposition, and Stephens was ordered to attend at the Bar of the House of Commons, there to be reprimanded by the Speaker. Fortunately for him, *The Hard Case* was not read formally to the House; many members believed that had this been done Stephens would probably have ended up in Newgate Prison rather than on his knees before the Speaker.[30]

Despite his reprimand Stephens had reason to believe that his endeavors had not been in vain. Most significantly, his campaign was decisive in bringing about Egmont's resignation from the Common Council of the Trustees in July 1742. Egmont cited ill health as the reason for his resignation, which was probably true, but he also hinted that the events of the past few months had led to his decision. Indeed, he advised his colleagues to surrender their charter because it was obvious that "the New Ministry as well as the old were resolved to have the power of disposing of the Colony as they please." The Trustees, who had been refused permission to vindicate their reputations by publishing the details of Stephens's reprimand, had gone to a great deal of trouble to secure such "a slight punishment of a malicious Vilain." They still lacked financial support, and if they continued to labor selflessly in the face of all these rebuffs "the World will believe [we] receive some private advantage . . . which makes [us] cling so close to [Georgia]."[31]

Benjamin Martyn, on the other hand, believed that Stephens's campaign had worked to the Trustees' advantage. Stephens had managed to secure a parliamentary inquiry into the importance of Georgia, which the Trustees had been unable to achieve, and this investigation had not only "ended in his own confusion" but also amply demonstrated the utility of Georgia.[32] But in the final analysis Egmont's assessment was more realistic. Over a three-year period Stephens had spearheaded the resistance to the Georgia project and, despite his reprimand and the resolutions adopted by the House of Commons, his campaign had left the Trustees in an unhappy position. Without financial support, and now without the wholehearted commitment of Egmont, they had little hope of continuing their scheme in its original form.

Although Parliament had not recommended the repeal of the Act of 1735, the Trustees, beginning in mid-1742, took steps that suggested a move to revise their labor policy. Their earlier categorical statements that they would never permit slavery in Georgia were replaced by an apparently more flexible attitude: they appointed a committee of their Common Council to consider the advisability of introducing slave labor and, at the same time, asked William Stephens to gauge the opinion of the Georgia settlers.[33]

Why the Trustees should have opted for this course of action is far from clear. One likely explanation is that, as in 1740, they believed that such concessions might persuade the House to renew its financial support and placate the malcontents. But they were certainly not committing themselves to any one course of action. Indeed, it was to be another seven years before they finally abandoned their prohibitory policy.

Unwilling to wait for the outcome of the Trustees' deliberations, Thomas Stephens again petitioned the House of Commons on the malcontents' behalf early in 1743. Percival opposed the petition on the grounds that the House had already given its verdict on Georgia, and the Speaker ruled that because it contained "nothing . . . contrary to the Resolutions" adopted in 1742 "it would be sufficient to order it to ly on the Table." The Trustees presented their annual money petition to the Commons in January 1743. They reminded members of the resolutions adopted the previous year and argued that without financial support they were "utterly incapable of further settling and improving" Georgia. In the absence of Sir John Cotton and Gage, the Trustees' "most inveterate enemies," Walter Carey spoke out against the petition and reaffirmed that unless changes were made in the Trustees' land and labor policies he would "be ever against giving any money." But Carey's threats fell on deaf ears, and the House agreed by a vote of 136 to 60 that "a sum not exceeding twelve thousand pounds" should be set aside for Georgia.[34] At last the parliamentary tide seemed to be turning in favor of the Trustees.

Thomas Stephens made one final effort to secure changes in the Trustees' plan by publishing a work entitled *A Brief Account of the Causes that have Retarded the Progress of the Colony of Georgia.* In this tract, which was intended as a rebuttal of his father's *A State of the Province of Georgia,* he pointed out that despite the enormous public expense involved in the founding of Georgia the colony was "in a more indigent condition than any of those which were settled at the expense and risk of private adventurers." This unhappy situation was partly the result of the Trustees' land policy and partly of the fact that the settlers were "totally prohibited the importation, use, or even sight of Negroes." In what became one of the best-known comments of the entire Trusteeship Stephens alleged: "In spite of all endeavours to disguise this point, it is as clear as light itself, that negroes are as essentially necessary to the cultivation of Georgia, as axes, hoes or any other utensil of agriculture." He agreed that it would be inadvisable to introduce slaves before the war with Spain had been concluded but argued that this had not been a consideration in 1735 when the Trustees had imposed their prohibition.[35]

A Brief Account, which said little that the Trustees had not heard before, was Stephens's last contribution to the slavery debate.[36] In mid-1743 he left England for South Carolina and is not known to have taken any further part in Georgia affairs. Although it is not clear why he abandoned his campaign while the outcome of the slavery debate was still uncertain, several explanations are possible. First, he might have felt that the Trustees had all but conceded defeat and intended to introduce black slaves into Georgia once peace had been concluded with Spain. Alternatively, the renewed financial support for the Trustees might have persuaded him that because they were under little parliamentary pressure to modify their scheme they would not do so. Finally, it is possible that Stephens, who apparently had no regular employment between 1739 and 1743, was unable to bear the financial burden of carrying on the battle. He had married in 1742 and, although his wife brought a substantial dowry, he may well have found it difficult to finance both a household and a political campaign. To add to his worries, he received news that his father had disinherited him. Nor was Stephens's financial situation helped by his constituents, who, after the first flush of enthusiasm, became increasingly unwilling, or perhaps unable, to supply him with funds.[37] In 1761 Stephens petitioned the Georgia Commons House of Assembly for redress, an action that implied that he felt he had been let down by the malcontents. His petition was referred to a select committee but, for reasons that were never stated, Stephens withdrew his application before the committee arrived at any decision. Little is known of his career after 1743. Apart from his appeal to the Georgia Assembly, Stephens made only one other appearance in Georgia affairs. In 1755 he applied for a land grant, but his petition was postponed and he apparently never secured his claim.[38]

Thomas Stephens was one of the most controversial figures of the Trusteeship, and the Georgia Board did not mask their view that he was a major threat to the integrity of the Georgia Plan. Stephens achieved what earlier leaders of the malcontents had failed to do: he organized the dissidents into a coherent pressure group which the Trustees ignored at their peril. In the absence of personal papers, his motives must remain debatable. Was he, as Egmont believed, only a scheming, unprincipled opportunist? This thesis is not supported by any neutral evidence. Egmont and Oglethorpe had a very real interest in portraying Stephens in the worst possible light, and against their interpretation must be set Stephens's own claim that his sole concern was with the welfare of the Georgians. Although Stephens's motives are uncertain, it is clear that he was unflinching in his willingness to argue the malcontents' case and prepared to accept the potentially serious consequences of confronting such an influential group of men as the Georgia Trustees.

CHAPTER FOUR

THE SALZBURGERS AND

SLAVERY, 1734–1750

own to the end of the 1740s the Trustees received important support for their land and labor policies from Georgia. Some settlers reported that their own experience justified the Trustees' claim that the Georgia Plan would prove viable and that at all costs slavery must be excluded from the colony. This body of opinion, which goes a long way toward explaining the tenacity with which the Trustees clung to their prohibitory policy, has been virtually ignored by historians. It is, however, of such significance as to demand separate and detailed analysis.

The Trustees' labor policy was vigorously defended by two communities: the Highland Scots at Darien and the Salzburgers at Ebenezer. Although the former proved loyal supporters of the Trustees, their most important contribution to the slavery debate was their reply early in 1739 to the pro-slavery petition sent from Savannah in December 1738. In general, however, the Trustees were not bombarded with antislavery literature from Darien. The Salzburgers, on the other hand, assumed an active role. From the time of their arrival in Georgia they sent a steady stream of letters to the Trustees urging them to stand firm and to resist any and all attempts to undermine their prohibitory policy.

The Salzburgers made little mention of the moral and religious issues posed by chattel slavery but instead emphasized the practical problems that would accompany the use of black workers. Like the Trustees, they were deeply concerned by the impact of slavery on white society. The crux of their antislavery argument was that their own agricultural ventures demonstrated that Georgia could prosper without slaves and that any relaxation of the Trustees' prohibitory policy would pose an intolerable threat to the physical and psychological security of the entire white community.

The Trustees always expressed interest in settling foreign Protestants in Georgia, and the persecution of the Salzburgers during the late 1720s suggested an opportunity for such an undertaking.[1] In mid-1732 they asked Samuel Urlsperger, pastor of the Lutheran Church of St. Ann in Augsburg, whether the Salzburgers would be interested in moving to Georgia. The Trustees offered extremely generous terms of settlement. The Salzburgers would be conveyed at the Trustees' expense from Rotterdam to Georgia, and once in the colony each family would receive fifty acres of land. Free goods and provisions would be made available to tide over the community until its first harvest. In addition, and crucial for the Salzburgers, complete religious freedom was guaranteed. Finally, the community would be granted all the civil and political rights of British subjects.[2]

The Salzburgers quickly declared themselves satisfied with these terms, and in December 1732 the Trustees intimated that they "would engage to convey 50 Saltsburg Families to our Colony." In the spring of 1733 Parliament appropriated £10,000 for the use of the Trustees, and this sum, together with private donations in excess of £3,000, provided the resources necessary to execute the scheme. In July of that year James Vernon informed his colleagues that he had arranged for "Seventy Head of Saltzburghers . . . to be settled in Georgia," and three months later the Trustees warned Oglethorpe that he might "expect sixty Salzburghers very soon."[3]

In October 1733 seventy-six Salzburgers, led by Baron Georg Philip von Reck, left Augsburg for Rotterdam on the first stage of their journey to Georgia. They reached the Dutch port on 27 November, where they were joined by Johann Martin Bolzius and Israel Christian Gronau. Pastor Bolzius, who had been employed as the superintendent of the Latin Orphan House at Halle, soon emerged as the spiritual and temporal leader of the community. His reports from Georgia and his secret diaries provide an invaluable commentary on life in the colony during the Trusteeship.[4]

The Salzburgers landed at Dover in December 1733 and, after taking an oath of allegiance to the British crown, embarked for America on board the *Purisburg*.[5] Their arrival in Charles Town two months later coincided with that of Oglethorpe, then on his way home to England, and he insisted upon changing his plans so that he might escort the new settlers to Savannah.

The Salzburgers' brief stay in South Carolina enabled them to see something of a slave society, and neither von Reck nor Bolzius was very impressed. Both were shocked by the irreligion of the black population and believed that the colony's slaveowners must be held responsible for this sad state of affairs. Although they appreciated that it must be "a great convenience to have many slaves to do the work," they recognized, even at this early stage, that this economic advantage was "coupled with great danger." Already it was clear to the Salzburgers that Carolina's blacks were "not faithful to the Christians and are very malicious."[6]

The Salzburgers arrived in Savannah on 12 March 1734 and were greeted warmly.[7] The community had every reason to be pleased: their escape from religious persecution was assured; they had promises of religious liberty, free lands, and provisions; Oglethorpe had gone out of his way to help them; and the British settlers at Savannah had given them a rousing welcome. There can be no doubting the Salzburgers' gratitude to their benefactors or the strength of their attachment to the Trustees' scheme. These sentiments were to become increasingly apparent and important during the late 1730s.

The site eventually chosen for the Salzburger settlement was about twenty-eight miles to the northwest of Savannah, and in April 1734 the community, together with a dozen slaves loaned to them by a South Carolinian benefactor, began work on a village which they named Ebenezer.[8] This firsthand experience with black workers, together with the impressions formed during their stopover in Charles Town, played a vital part in shaping the Salzburgers' attitude toward the Trustees' prohibitory policy.

Some of the slaves employed at Ebenezer tried to run away
and received what Bolzius and Gronau referred to as "their regular punishment."[9] They were "tied to a tree half naked and . . .
badly beaten with long switches while having to suffer from
hunger and thirst most of the day." The black workers were
superintended by a South Carolinian overseer, a carpenter by
trade, but it is clear that he regarded Bolzius and Gronau as
being responsible for determining the type and amount of punishment meted out to offenders. It is also clear that the two
Salzburgers agonized every time they were asked to prescribe
punishments. More often than not they relied on the judgment of
the overseer. Thus on one occasion, when the slaves "would not
work well" and were taken to task by the overseer, one of them
threatened him with an ax. Gronau was asked by the overseer to
name a suitable punishment, and he freely confessed (in his journal if not to his congregation) that he "did not know what to do
with the poor people. After the affair had been investigated long
enough I called the carpenter and asked him what was to be
done so that the people would not get too much or too little
punishment. I suspected various answers, but he immediately
told the people to go back to work, and he whipped the one that
had threatened him. I thank God for having arranged it in this
manner for the poor people could easily have been given too
much punishment, which might have made them run away."

The ax incident and a later attempt to burn down the Salzburger settlement testified to the "great danger" that accompanied the use of slaves. Gronau believed that if these workers remained at Ebenezer the community would continue to suffer the
less serious but nonetheless irksome problem of theft because "the
Negroes are very bad, always happy when they can steal this or
that in the way of meat or other things." After the slave work
force had been returned to South Carolina, Bolzius commented
that "the departure of the Negroes has deprived us of some advantage but it has also freed us of much disquietude and worry," a
remark that aptly summarized the Salzburgers' feelings about
slavery.

Bolzius and Gronau did not simply report the behavior of
those blacks brought to Ebenezer but, unlike most of the colonial participants in the slavery debate, sought to explain it.

Whereas Benjamin Martyn ascribed such "misconduct" as running away to a natural craving for liberty, the Salzburger leaders suspected that the "misbehavior" they had witnessed was due mainly to "the bad treatment [slaves] receive [in Carolina]." Their suspicions were confirmed while Bolzius accompanied von Reck on the first leg of a return trip to Europe. They were forced by bad weather to land in South Carolina, "where we found a colony of blacks with whom we had to spend the night." The two Salzburgers took this opportunity to learn as much as they could about the slavery experience.

According to von Reck, these blacks "complained a great deal about their masters as, to be sure, most Negroes have good cause to." They claimed that an owner expected his slaves "to earn for him a certain amount each day" and, if they did not, demanded that they "bring in double the amount on the next day, or triple on the third." Thus slaves might be "led to steal, but this seems to satisfy the master as long as he gets the required amount." Another owner was said to whip his slaves "nearly to death" but "not to punish even the greatest misdeed with death because that would make him lose a slave." Von Reck believed that this frequent punishment was one reason why blacks were "easily given to knavish tricks."[10] But although he and Bolzius considered that masters must be held mainly responsible for the behavior of their slaves, they, like Benjamin Martyn albeit for rather different reasons, did not believe that kindly treatment would transform a slave into a "trusty servant." While in Savannah Bolzius had heard about two slaves who "had strangled and drowned their sick master even though he had always been very kind to them," and he suspected that similar episodes would characterize slavery in Georgia. He and Gronau had tried to deal as fairly as they could with the slaves brought to Ebenezer, but they had run away, fought with one another, and almost burned down the Salzburger village.

Although von Reck had helped to select the site of Ebenezer, the community's experience there was most unhappy. Within a year of their arrival the Salzburgers had cleared and planted "100 Acres . . . with Corn, Pease and Potatoes" but were dissatisfied with the quality of their lands. Thomas Causton tried to persuade them that the soils around Ebenezer were fertile but found "Their Prejudice is strongly raised."[11] Unrest simmered and finally erupted in the spring of 1736 when von Reck arrived with another embarkation of settlers. He was shocked to discover the "pitiful condition" of Ebenezer and alleged that the settlement was "without tools, without houses, and without lands." In his attempt to rectify matters von Reck clashed with John Vat, the storekeeper at Ebenezer, and their argument was settled only by the personal intervention of Oglethorpe.[12]

But if the community was torn by the disagreement between von Reck and Vat it was united in outright opposition to remaining at Ebenezer, and in 1736 the Salzburgers asked permission of Oglethorpe to relocate their settlement. Oglethorpe could not understand why they should wish to abandon the site at which they had worked so hard but, after visiting Ebenezer, he concluded that they "were only ignorant & obstinate and without any ill Intention" and allowed them to move five miles to New Ebenezer.[13] This settlement also had troubles. The Salzburgers continued to complain of a shortage of tools and provisions but, taking everything into account, Bolzius felt able to reassure the Trustees that "there is noe body in my Congregation, that is sorry for having resolved to come to this . . . Colony." Indeed, the difficulties being encountered "were profitable & wholesome to their spiritual Welfare & Increase in true Christianity."[14] The hard work envisaged by the Trustees and endorsed by the Salzburger leaders would result in both the spiritual and the secular redemption of the settlers.

During the winter and spring of 1736–37 the Salzburgers worked at clearing land and planting crops, and by early 1738 sixty-five land grants had been taken up and 180 acres were under cultivation. In mid-1737 John Wesley visited Ebenezer and reported that "the industry of this people is quite surprising." He found it hard to believe that "a handful of people" had achieved so much in the space of a year. Three years later George Whitefield, soon to disagree violently with Bolzius over the question of slavery, commented that "all other places of the colony seem to be like Egypt where was darkness but Ebenezer, like the lands of Goshen, wherein was great light."[15] Progress continued apace, and in 1742 the Salzburgers produced "3048 bushels of corn, 537 of peas, 566 of potatoes, 733 of Rice, 92 of wheat and 11 of Rye and barley." More would have been produced, explained Bolzius, but for the fact that the Mill River burst its banks and flooded some of the fields.[16]

The Salzburgers' agricultural achievements were matched by their industrial ventures. They began to produce raw silk in 1736 and, despite early setbacks, by 1749 had produced 732 pounds of cocoons and just under 51 pounds of raw silk. The community also took advantage of the pine lands around Ebenezer and by the mid-1740s was exporting red pine to South Carolina and the West Indies. But unlike the North Carolinians, the Salzburgers did not engage in the manufacture of by-products from their timber. Although James Habersham suggested that they send some of their number to North Carolina to learn the techniques of tar and pitch production, they did not do so during the Trustee period.[17]

It is not too much to suggest that the Salzburgers were by far the most industrious and successful of the Georgia settlers, although in view of the slight economic progress made by the colony this is not saying a great deal. Indeed, summing up the community's experience at the end of the Trusteeship, Bolzius remarked that its achievements had been secured at the cost of great hardship and that most of his congregation "still belong among the poor who have always been in need of support from Europe."[18] Nevertheless, the Salzburgers were convinced that the progress that had been made more than demonstrated the fallacy of the argument that Georgia's economic survival depended upon the employment of slaves.

The Salzburgers' antislavery sentiments were usually articulated by Bolzius, and he was responsible for the petition sent to the Trustees in March 1739. This document, which urged the Trustees not to abandon their labor policy, questioned some of the economic assumptions at the heart of the malcontents' proslavery argument. Thus the Salzburgers drew attention to the fact that shortly after their arrival in Georgia they had been told that "it proves quite impossible and dangerous for white people to plant and manufacture rice, being a work only for negroes." The petitioners thought this an absurd proposition, not least because they had secured "in the last harvest, a greater crop of rice than they wanted for their own consumption."[19]

Bolzius believed that the malcontents exaggerated the unpleasantness and unhealthiness of the Georgia climate. In his view, Georgia summers were no worse than those experienced in parts of southern Germany or elsewhere in the mainland colonies. But Bolzius agreed that unless sensible precautions were taken, the climate could pose problems, and he suggested that the settlers would be well advised to imitate the Salzburgers and avoid working out of doors during the hottest part of the day. Once the Salzburgers had grown accustomed to the Georgia climate they found it "tolerable, and for the working people very convenient, setting themselves to work early in the morning, till ten o'clock and in the afternoon, from three to sunset. And having business at home, we do them in our huts in the middle of the day." Bolzius doubted that it was necessary to work at the more strenuous agricultural tasks during the summer: were there not "9 Months in the Year time Enough to prepare the Ground for European & Countrey Grain"? The pastor concluded that the malcontents were using the climatic argument as an excuse for introducing slavery into Georgia. The "idle and delicate" settlers were deluding themselves when they claimed that the climate was unbearable and for that "unreasonable Reason [would] like it mighty well . . . to imploy Negroes." The Salzburgers had "not the least reason to make any Complaint about the Hot Season of the Country."[20]

Bolzius disputed Whitefield's argument, which was largely ignored by the malcontents, that Africans should be brought to Georgia to expose them to the spiritual benefits of Christianity. He was appalled by the irreligion of South Carolina's slaves and suggested to Whitefield that if he wished to undertake missionary work he had "a Large Field" in the neighboring colony. The pastor expressed the hope that "first the White people . . . may be brought to the Saving & Experimental Knowledge of Christ." Bolzius feared that were Africans brought to Georgia under a religious pretext the situation would soon resemble that of South Carolina, where "Very few, perhaps not any, have been baptized" and most "live like animals, with respect to the Sixth Commandment and in other ways."[21] He was convinced that, whether in Carolina or in Georgia, the conversion of Africans must be accompanied or preceded by the conversion of their owners. Bolzius did not explore the relationship between Christianity and bondage or suggest that the acceptance of Christianity necessarily altered the relationship between master and slave.

Bolzius also used South Carolina as an example of the social and economic relationships that were likely to materialize in Georgia were the Trustees to lift their ban on slavery. Whereas the pro-slavery faction saw in Carolina an economic and social system that, in some respects, ought to be emulated, Bolzius saw a system that must at all costs be avoided. He believed that Carolina offered a perfect example of the likely fate of those Georgians who were unable or unwilling to buy slaves. In that colony, "a Common white Labourer . . . of the meaner Sort can get his & his Family's Livelyhood honestly . . . except he embraces the Sorry Imploy of a Negroe Overseer. A Common white Laborer in Charles-Town . . . has no more Wages, than a Negroe for his work . . . for which it is . . . impossible to find Victuals, Lodging & washing much Less Cloaths." Because Carolina masters taught their slaves "all Sorts of trade," the lot of skilled white workers in that colony was scarcely better than that of unskilled laborers and the outlook for those who aspired to the ownership of land and slaves was grim. "Merchants & Other Gentlemen" had taken up "all good & Convenient Ground at the Sea Coasts & Banks of Rivers," and the less well-off were "forced to possess Lands, remote from the Conveniency of Rivers & from Town."[22]

The Trustees' argument that slavery would threaten the physical as well as the economic security of the white community was not lost upon Bolzius. He thought that it would prove impossible to regulate the growth of any slave element introduced into Georgia for the simple reason that owners would have a vested interest in securing slave children, and, as in Carolina, it was likely that Africans would be encouraged to "breed like animals." Before long "you would meet in the Streets . . . many Malattoes & many Negroe children." These blacks would pose a "great danger" to the Georgia settlers, who would have to be on their constant guard against "the Robberies of Fields and Orchards, that must be expected from these savage & hungry Creatures." Bolzius agreed that the Spaniards would do their utmost to incite Georgia's slave population to disorder, and he feared for the future of the colony should it ever be placed in the position of "having such Cruel Enemies within & without." Given the amount of money that had been spent on Georgia and the selfless endeavors of the Trustees, it seemed to Bolzius that "the Lord . . . has something better for us in Store, than the Introduction of Black Slaves & their Cruel Usage."[23]

Bolzius accepted that the economic condition of Georgia left room for improvement, but he disputed the proposition that slave labor was the only answer to the colony's problems. In his view, many of the malcontents' arguments reflected the primitive condition of Georgia agriculture, and he believed that if more efficient agricultural techniques could be devised there would be no need even to think of employing slaves. Thus although it was wholly inadequate for most farm needs the hoe was the most commonly used agricultural implement in Georgia. Bolzius thought that if the settlers could be "Supply'd with a Horse each or 2 families, or a Couple of broken Oxen, or with Convenient tools for Agriculture . . . they would not make Complaints of the great Heat of this Climate."[24] The pastor was not alone in bemoaning the lack of suitable and sufficient tools. Thomas Causton thought it was "practicable and therefore wish, that the Plough would in a few years supply the place of the Hoe," and another settler, Isaac Gibbs, was even more explicit about the connection between a deficient agricultural technology and the demand for black slaves. In 1738 he reported to the Trustees his

> Dispair of Ever Doeing any Great matters by pecking with a
> hoe for where it there be two or three hands they have
> Cleared 5 or 6 acres it is as much as they can well manage by
> way of Planting or tilling without Goeing on with Clearing
> any more . . . I Propose to have a Plow if I Can Possibly for it

is a hard thing to Come att in this Place for I have heard of
nor Seen but one . . . for here is Scarcely any that Understands to make them or husbandry Either and what they Do
in Carpentry is So very Chargeable that it is hard to Come att
on that account itt might be of very Great Service to the Col-
lony if your Hons. would Please to assist them with a few
English Plows for I am Sure that one man and a boy with but
a Couple of oxen or horses Shall Do more than ten men with
their hoes and much Better Done and I think would be better
also than that Inhumane and Abominable useing of Negroes.[25]

Bolzius tried to keep abreast of current European agricultural
theory and practice and did his best to apply the relevant portions of what he learned to the Georgia environment. In 1744,
for example, he acquired a copy of Jethro Tull's *Horse Hoeing
Husbandry* (1731), which he "perused with great Pleasure." He
thought that some of Tull's techniques might be applied to the
lands around Ebenezer and, with this in mind, read extracts of
the work to "several Meetings" of his congregation. According
to Bolzius, the Salzburgers were "intirely convinced, that their
pine Land will be changed by Degree, into fruitful Acres." The
pastor saw an additional advantage from a more mechanized
agriculture: more time could be given over to silk production.[26]
But for Bolzius the important point was that a more efficient
agriculture would nullify the supposed need for slaves, and it is
entirely possible that he was correct. Yet a more mechanized
agriculture might well have hastened the progress toward the
agricultural capitalism the Trustees were determined to avoid.
The prospect of more acres cleared and planted would have been
hard to resist.

Although Bolzius rejected the argument that slaves should be
brought to Georgia, he was acutely aware that the colony suffered from a serious shortage of labor that could be compensated
for only in part by the mechanization of agriculture. But he
believed that if appropriate inducements were offered, Georgia
would soon be "Settled better with white people, than Pennsylvania," and, not surprisingly, he regarded those Salzburgers who
remained in Europe as likely migrants.[27] As was to be demon-

strated in the late 1730s and 1740s, however, Georgia experienced great difficulties in building up its white population. Heavy mortality rates, disenchantment with the Trustees' policies, and the likely consequences of war with Spain acted as a brake upon population growth. The late 1740s and 1750s witnessed a reversal of this trend, but, as we shall see, the increase in the size of Georgia's population was to be intimately bound up with the development of the colony's slave-manned plantation economy.

The malcontents viewed the relative success of Ebenezer and Bolzius's staunch support for the Trustees as bolstering his determination not to permit slavery, and they did their best to dissuade and discredit him. Indeed, some of their most vicious accusations were reserved for the man whom they saw as an extremely influential stumbling block to the accomplishment of their objectives. The most serious charge brought against Bolzius was that he misrepresented the sentiments of his congregation. The malcontents claimed that he used his position to enforce his own point of view and to suppress that of any Salzburger who disagreed with him. There can be no doubting the fact that Ebenezer was a theocracy in the broadest sense of that term and that in the final analysis the formulation of community policy rested with Bolzius. But the pastor often approached the Salzburger elders in Europe for advice and instructions, and to say that he was responsible for decision making at Ebenezer is not to agree that he coerced the fifty-nine Salzburgers who signed the 1739 petition. Yet no doubt the arguments against slavery and the reasons for supporting the Trustees were put very forcefully by the pastor, and it must have been an extremely strong-willed Salzburger who refused to sign the document. But the Salzburgers were exposed to the malcontents' arguments in October 1741, when Thomas Stephens visited Ebenezer.[28]

It was probably as a result of this visit that Stephens accused Bolzius of exercising a "spiritual tyranny" over his congregation. He managed to find four men, Christopher Ortman, John Michael Spielbiegler, Thomas Bicher, and John Spielbiegler, who were willing to sign affidavits to the effect that most of the Salzburgers "would yet sign a petition for negroes, were it not that Mr. Boltzius . . . who exercises an arbitary power over us, might make them uneasy." Ebenezer, they claimed, was not in the flourishing condition depicted by the pastor but, on the contrary, the Salzburgers "had never corn, and rice, or any sort of bread kind sufficient for the use of their families from crop to crop." Spielbiegler swore that it was only by working as a laborer in Savannah that he had managed to survive.[29] Bolzius was taken aback by these accusations. He held that Stephens had not one shred of evidence to substantiate his allegations and reiterated his opinion that the Salzburgers "had not much reason to complain of Hardships" and absolutely no desire to become associated with the "self interested dangerous Contrivances" of the malcontents. But he was far more pleased to be attacked by Stephens than had the "Enemies of this Colony" found any reason to commend him.[30]

The closely allied charges of misrepresentation, "spiritual tyranny," and coercion were the main weapons employed by the malcontents in their continuing campaign against Bolzius. Thomas Stephens believed that if the pastor could be forced out of the slavery debate the Trustees might reconsider their labor policy. The logic behind this approach was impeccable. Bolzius's belief that Georgia could prosper without slave labor established a firm base of support within the colony for the Act of 1735. The evidence he supplied to the Trustees helped to shape, and indeed to confirm, their opinion that their plan could succeed, and it was reasonable to expect that were he removed from the scene the malcontents would enjoy more success. As the demands for slavery became more strident after 1738 so did the accusations made against Bolzius. According to the pastor, the malcontents not only cursed him "in a very scandalous manner" but also threatened him with physical harm. He was at a loss to explain why they should have adopted such a hostile attitude. After all, he was only trying to execute the Trustees' scheme to the best of his ability. Yet the more he defended his benefactors "the more increases the jealousy & wickedness of all sorts of people in & about Savannah."

By the mid-1740s Bolzius found his position intolerable, and he complained to Benjamin Martyn that it was "inexpressible, under what reproaches & contempts I lye herein." Whatever the Trustees might say about continuing with their labor policy, Bolzius was convinced that the malcontents would not be satisfied until they had forced him out of the slavery debate and "gain'd their point with respect to Negroes." He told Martyn that he was under such pressure that he could no longer assume responsibility for both temporal and spiritual affairs at Ebenezer and that his spiritual duties must take precedence over all else.[31] He therefore resigned his post as conservator of the peace at Ebenezer, a minor victory for the malcontents. But Bolzius did not lose interest in the outcome of the slavery debate; he remained firmly committed to the Trustees' labor policy.

Bolzius was so concerned that he might be mistaken in his assessment of the Salzburgers' feelings about slavery that in 1747 he asked one of his congregation to undertake an independent investigation and promised that if any of his community expressed a wish for slaves he woud gladly report this change of heart to the Trustees. But after the inquiry had been completed he was pleased to be able to report that "not a man . . . shew'd not an abhorrence for Negroes," and he pleaded with the Trustees not to permit slavery but to recruit white servants in Germany.[32] By 1748, however, the Trustees were consulting with the Savannah authorities about the most appropriate conditions under which slavery might be permitted in Georgia, a development that placed Bolzius in a grave dilemma. Since his arrival in America he, and through him the Salzburger community, had accepted the Trustees' authority without reservation. Now that they seemed likely to rescind their labor policy, should he lend his support and thereby his prestige to any slave code they might devise for the colony? Bolzius was adamant that slaves would not make Georgia "flourish," and as late as May 1748 he asserted that he would "rather . . . suffer hardships heinous reflectings revilings reproaches and I don't know what else [than] lend the least finger to promote the Introduction of Black Slaves to the apparent destruction of our Well Situated and fertile Province." But Bolzius realized that he had virtually no support outside Ebenezer. If only, he lamented, "one single person in Authority and power . . . would agree with me in the wise scheme of their Honrs. it would give me comfort and encouragement." But "all from the highest to the lowest" favored slavery and saw him "as a Stone in their way towards which they direct all their Spite."[33]

The fact remained, however, that the Trustees were soliciting advice as to the rules and regulations that ought to govern slavery in Georgia. Although he was bitterly opposed to such a move, Bolzius remained faithful to the Trustees and offered them his advice if not his wholehearted support. In mid-1748 a Grand Assembly was convened in Savannah to discuss a possible slave code for Georgia. One problem that faced the meeting, which Bolzius attended, was that of devising an appropriate numerical ratio between the races. The pastor was skeptical of the malcontents' willingness to abide by any legislation that sought to govern the size and distribution of Georgia's black element. Some slaves had already been brought to the colony "at this dangerous time of War," and it was too much to expect that the dissidents would adhere to any controls imposed by the Trustees. Bolzius believed that his main objective must be to ensure that the spiritual needs of Georgia's slaves were catered to, and he was gratified when the Trustees incorporated many of his suggestions into their code. Following the meeting, Bolzius felt able to reassure the Trustees that "all is done to my great satisfaction" and, despite his earlier remarks, he ventured the opinion that the proposed legislation was "so much liked and unanimously agreed upon as Salutary restrictions for the security and well being of the People . . . that I don't doubt any more but they will be as strictly observed as they were willingly consented to." The pastor still believed that the "Black Faces of Negroes" were "disagreeable," but he was as confident as he could be that slavery in Georgia would be regulated by the most humane and sensible laws that could be formulated. The Salzburgers would continue to support their benefactors and "rely intirely upon God's & their Honours favours being in confidence, that merciful God will protect & bless us notwithstanding."[34]

CHAPTER FIVE

SLAVERY PERMITTED,

1743–1750

*I*n July 1742 the Trustees asked William Stephens whether he agreed with "some Gentlemen of Eminence in Trade" who had advised them that slavery "under proper Limitations and Restrictions" ought to be permitted in Georgia. Stephens, perhaps for once being completely honest with his employers, ruled out the introduction of slavery as long as England and Spain remained at war because even the indefatigable Oglethorpe would be unable to prevent black runaways from reaching St. Augustine. If Florida remained in Spanish hands after the war, the British government must take care to negotiate terms that would prevent slave fugitives from "being receiv'd or entertained" by the Spaniards. The continuance of a sanctuary at St. Augustine would have an unsettling effect on Georgia's blacks, which would be serious enough in peacetime but potentially disastrous in the event of another war.[1]

The rest of Stephens's reply dealt more directly with the question asked of him by the Trustees: what rules and regulations ought to govern slavery in Georgia? Stephens insisted that the size of the colony's black element must be limited, and he agreed with the malcontents that Georgia's "safety" necessitated the imposition of a clearly defined numerical balance between the races. He thought one white man would be needed to superintend every four slaves. These men must "constantly inspect" the slaves under their charge and, it went without saying, take "strickt care" to ensure that "Arms of all kinds be kept out of [their] power."[2]

Stephens next contemplated the most appropriate modes of employment for slaves. The malcontents based their pro-slavery case on the alleged need for a work force capable of arduous agricultural labor, and Stephens suggested that the implications of their argument were twofold: that slaves "are not wanted on any other occasion" and that they "are not to be allow'd in Towns." The malcontents would not have disputed the first of these points; they had not pressed for the employment of slaves in nonagricultural capacities and, moreover, were dubious of the South Carolinian practice of using blacks as domestic servants. Stephens's second point was merely a rephrasing of the first. He was not, at least not explicitly, suggesting that urban slavery posed peculiar problems of racial control but was equating the word "town" with skilled labor. The gist of his argument was that skilled or even semiskilled slaves would threaten the economic security of many whites already in Georgia and almost certainly discourage white migration to the colony. Finally, Stephens expressed the hope that the Trustees would persevere with their attempt to exclude idleness and luxury from Georgia. Some settlers hired out their white servants and lived off the resulting income, and Stephens believed that they would do the same with their slaves. In his view, the Trustees would be well advised to prohibit the hire of slaves "for wages."[3]

Stephens's comments confirmed the Trustees' opinion that, despite Bloody Marsh, there were still strong military reasons in favor of retaining their ban on slavery. It was only when these arguments diminished in force and the situation in Georgia left them with no alternative that they agreed to press for the repeal of the Act of 1735.

Thomas Stephens continued with his anti-Trustee activities until mid-1743 but then abandoned his campaign and took up a life of comparative obscurity in America. The malcontents did not replace him, and after 1743 they no longer had an agent in London; neither did they embark on a fresh round of tracts and petitions. But they had not given up all hope of securing slaves. Far from it. In July 1743 the Trustees were informed that "Negroes, nothing but Negroes," was the constant refrain in Savannah and, three years later, that the Georgia settlers were "still stark Mad after Negroes."[4] But why did the malcontents abandon their formal lobby? It is possible that they could no longer afford to finance their campaign but just as likely that they believed money spent on supporting an agent in London was money wasted. The Trustees' consultations with William Stephens and Oglethorpe's triumph at Bloody Marsh must have suggested to some of the more optimistic malcontents that the Act of 1735 would soon be repealed. But at the same time, certain other developments persuaded them that they should no longer be denied the economic benefits of slave labor. Indeed, after 1743 the dissidents were struggling to secure the legal recognition of an institution that was already beginning to exist in practice.

By the mid-1740s Georgia's local officials were forced to admit that slaves were being employed in the colony. It is uncertain when the first blacks, excluding those employed in the construction of Savannah and Ebenezer, were brought to Georgia. But slaves could not have been used in Savannah or Frederica without the knowledge of the colonial officials or Oglethorpe, and mainly for this reason infringements of the prohibitory legislation were few and far between.[5] The willingness of some settlers to inform on their neighbors and of the local officials to enforce the law constituted important deterrents.

The situation in the more remote parts of Georgia was different. Regardless of their other disagreements, the Trustees and the malcontents did agree that Augusta was "the most flourishing town in Georgia."[6] But whereas the Trustees believed that Augusta demonstrated the economic progress that could be achieved under their scheme, the malcontents held that the main reason for the town's success was the illicit use of slaves smuggled across the Savannah River.[7] Much to the Trustees' surprise, William Stephens admitted that there was a grain of truth in what the malcontents were saying. But he dismissed their allegation that large numbers of slaves were being employed in Augusta as yet "another Instance of their Labour to Magnify Molehills into Mountains," and he assured his employers that all attempts to evade their ban on slavery were "discountenanc'd [and] also strictly forbidden, by those in Authority here."[8]

Yet despite Stephens's assertion it is obvious that some local officials disagreed with the labor policy they were required to enforce. The first major spokesman for the malcontents had been Peter Gordon, the first bailiff of Savannah; John Fallowfield, the third bailiff, and Andrew Duche, a constable, had signed the petition of 1738 and drafted that of November 1740; and although not a local official per se, Thomas Stephens had gone to Georgia in the Trustees' employ. These men were not afraid to let the Trustees know where they stood. But there was one factor that worked to secure a semblance of loyalty on their part: Oglethorpe's presence in Georgia.

Dissident officials were reprimanded by the Georgia Board, a punishment so slight as to be meaningless. No argument or verbal abuse the Trustees could present was likely to dissuade them. The only other choice open to the Trustees was to dismiss all recalcitrant officials, but they never employed this option in a systematic manner.[9] Thus the extensive reorganization of Georgia's local government in 1741, which was designed to trim Oglethorpe's power rather than to grant more self-determination to the settlers, did not result in the wholesale dismissal of local officials. Under this new scheme, proposed by James Vernon, Georgia was divided into two administrative districts based on Savannah and Frederica. Each district was to be under the charge of a president and four assistants, who would be appointed by and answerable to the Trustees. William Stephens, a logical choice, was made president of the District of Savannah, a post he occupied until 1751. But three of his first four assistants, John Fallowfield, Henry Parker, and Samuel Mercer, who previously had served as bailiffs, had publicly sided with the malcontents. Only Thomas Jones had proved unswerving in his loyalty to the Trustees. After 1741 there was to be some doubt about the loyalty of Georgia's civil establishment and the vigor with which it enforced the Trustees' labor policy. By the mid-1740s, however, those officials who, sometimes in direct opposition to their own hopes for Georgia, endeavored to comply with the Trustees' wishes found themselves in an increasingly untenable situation.

The factors that had served as a check on the malcontents disappeared in rapid succession after mid-1742, but one development in particular, Oglethorpe's victory at Bloody Marsh and his subsequent return to England, was of decisive importance in hastening the demise of the Trustees' labor policy. Although Bloody Marsh did not end the Anglo-Spanish rivalry over the borderlands, it virtually guaranteed the survival of Georgia.[10] Moreover, the stunning victory generated a new mood of confidence in the colony. Ever since the early 1730s the Trustees had argued, and few disagreed, that it would prove dangerous to introduce slaves into Georgia as long as the colony was faced with the prospect of imminent invasion. With the waning of the Spanish threat the Trustees' argument lost much of its force; Oglethorpe's departure meant that those settlers who wished to run the risk of using slaves could do so without incurring the wrath of the man who had done as much, if not more, than anyone else to maintain the ban on slavery. But by the mid-1740s the Georgians were not alone in believing that there were few remaining obstacles to the employment of slaves.

From an early date many South Carolinians had cast envious eyes on Georgia's potentially rich rice lands and, soon after the first settlement of the colony, had offered Oglethorpe a bribe to secure a reversal of the Trustees' land and labor policies. Oglethorpe's contemptuous rejection of their overtures, the enthusiasm with which the Georgia Board pursued its labor policy, and the prospect of a Spanish invasion dampened but did not eradicate the Carolinians' interest in establishing slave-manned rice plantations in Georgia. The rapidly changing situation after 1742 revived their hopes that such a course might prove possible in the not too distant future, and during the last five years of the Trusteeship around sixty Carolinians petitioned for lands in Georgia.[11] Their interest in employing slaves added to the pressure on the Trustees, and, as we shall see, their arrival in Georgia marked the beginning of a migration that was to exert a profound influence on the development of slavery and race relations in that colony.

By the mid-1740s the Trustees' supporters were claiming that the Act of 1735 was being evaded and that the local officials must be held responsible. It seemed to some as if the entire civil establishment was "in eager pursuit of a Scheme directly opposed to that of the Trustees." Local officials not only spoke "contemptuously" of the Georgia Board but did their best to "weaken the Hearts and Hands of all those, who are faithfully attach'd to the Interest of the Trustees." By 1746 many settlers had succumbed to their threats and blandishments and there were "very few . . . whose minds are not more or less tainted with what they call 'Liberty and Property without restrictions' an eager Desire of Negroes and other unreasonable Things."[12] According to Alexander Heron, a member of Oglethorpe's Regiment, the "constant toast" of the local officials was "the one thing needful by which is meant Negroes." He added that it was "well known to every one in the Colony that Negroes have been in and about Savannah for these several years" and that "the Magistrates knew and wink'd at it."[13]

In 1748 John Dobell, a faithful supporter of the Trustees, made one last appeal to the Georgia Board. He insisted that the Georgians could "live prosperously" without slaves and pleaded with the Trustees to encourage white migration to the colony. Bolzius had suggested that enough white workers to satisfy Georgia's needs could be recruited in Europe; Dobell believed that the northern colonies could be tapped for settlers.[14] But Bolzius and Dobell were soon to discover that far from exploring the possibility of attracting white settlers the Trustees were in fact contemplating the problem of devising an appropriate slave code for Georgia.

Although the Trustees had asked William Stephens to suggest regulations that might govern the use of slaves in Georgia, this apparent willingness to reappraise their labor policy by no means prejudged the final outcome. The rejection of their money petition was a bitter blow to the Trustees, and especially to Egmont, but even so they stubbornly refused to concede defeat on the slavery issue. Egmont's resignation from the Common Council and Oglethorpe's failure to play an active part in Georgia affairs after 1742 might have encouraged evasions of the Act of 1735 but did not noticeably diminish the Georgia Board's determination to preserve its prohibitory policy and thereby the integrity of its social design. In 1746, for example, Benjamin Martyn reassured Bolzius that slavery would never be permitted in Georgia, and two years later he was directed to inform the settlers that because slavery was "inconsistent with the Intent of His Majesty's Charter" and "directly contrary to an express Act approved of by His Majesty in Council," the Trustees were "surprised that any Expectations of Negroes can yet remain." Those settlers who wanted slaves ought to migrate "to any other Province, where they will be freely allow'd the Use of Negroes."[15] But by mid-1748 the Trustees were forced to admit that such defiant words were falling on deaf ears, that they no longer exercised the necessary authority, in either England or in Georgia, to enforce a total ban on slavery. The reports they received from America left them in no doubt that their prohibitory policy was in tatters. But even now their defeat would not be unconditional; they were determined to salvage something from the situation. James Vernon and the Earl of Shaftesbury, now the effective leaders of the Trustees, were adamant that the repeal of the Act of 1735 would depend upon the formulation of an appropriate slave code. Even at this late date they were determined to exclude from Georgia the worst excesses of an unbridled agricultural capitalism.

The decision to exclude slavery had been taken without regard to advice from America; the formal ending of the prohibition came only after protracted discussions between the Trustees and their officials in Georgia. The Trustees' initial approach to Stephens and his assistants took the form of a series of questions regarding such fundamental points as the most appropriate size, distribution, and employment of any slave work force introduced into the colony. The questions asked and the answers given indicate that the Trustees and their officials were in broad agreement on one crucial point: slavery in Georgia must be made subject to rigid controls. Both sides in the slavery debate acknowledged that slaves would threaten the physical, if not the psychological, security of Georgia's white inhabitants and, down to the late 1740s, the Trustees had insisted that the Georgians' security could be guaranteed only by the total exclusion of slaves. Their opponents had argued that the colony's and their own personal security would not be jeopardized but that economic growth might be achieved by the limited importation of slaves and the imposition of a clearly defined ratio between the races. Although the Georgia Board would not contemplate such a proposal as long as Spain challenged the very existence of Georgia, it was one which they were keen to incorporate into their slave code.

The Trustees asked their officials whether any limits ought to be imposed on the size of individual slaveholdings. Although such a restriction would have served the purpose of establishing a rough numerical balance between the races, it is possible to place a different interpretation on the Trustees' question. Since the inception of the Georgia project they had been highly critical of the "luxury" and "idleness" of America's plantation societies and at the same time had pointed to the unenviable lot of land-less, nonslaveholding whites in such societies. Apparently they still held out the hope that the emergence of a planter elite in Georgia might be prevented while safeguarding the interests of those whites who were unwilling or unable to invest in slave labor.

Stephens and his assistants suggested that any limitations on the size of individual slaveholdings would pose "many and great inconveniences," not for masters but for Georgia's slaves. If, for example, an owner was restricted to a maximum holding of ten slaves it was likely that sooner or later he would have to dispose of some of his bondsmen and possibly split black families. For this reason the colonial officials declared themselves opposed to the restriction proposed by the Trustees. They agreed, however, that there ought to be a fixed, and low, ratio between the races and proposed that of one white man for every five "Working Negroes." Mainly for the reasons outlined by William Stephens in 1742, they agreed that slaves ought to be confined to "the necessary Work of Plantations and for Exporting the Manufactures of the Colony."[16]

The Trustees' next question focused on the relationship between master and slave. More specifically, they asked whether "it is just and Equitable that the Proprietors of Negroes should have an unlimited power over them?" Stephens and his assistants declared emphatically that they should not. In their opinion, any owner who "wilfully and maliciously Murders Dismembers or Cruelly and Barbarously uses a Negro" should be dealt with in precisely the same way and made subject to precisely the same penalties as if the offense had been committed against a white person. They did not discuss, perhaps because they had not been asked to, the legal rights, if any, to be enjoyed by the slave.

Finally, the Trustees inquired whether slaves ought to be made to work on Sundays. The colonial officials endorsed the theory, if not always the practice, operative in the other plantation colonies by saying that they should not. They added that they wished to "make the condition of Slavery as easy as may be consistent with the Safety of His Majesty's Subjects" and hoped that their proposals would shame the other colonies into following Georgia's humane example.[17]

Although some of the Trustees' supporters were skeptical of the malcontents' willingness to abide by any rules and regulations governing the employment of slaves, the Trustees were persuaded of the settlers' good intentions and, in May 1749 they agreed to press for the repeal of the Act of 1735.[18] Events moved forward in rapid order. In July of that year, replying to the proposals submitted from Georgia, the Trustees suggested that one white man, aged between twenty and fifty-five, would be needed to superintend every four, rather than every five, working blacks. They also argued that slaves must be exposed to all the spiritual benefits of Christianity; that miscegenation ought to be forbidden; that the silk industry would benefit were slave women trained in the techniques of silk production; and, finally, that a duty ought to be levied on slave imports.[19] Although in close agreement with the Trustees, Georgia's officials asked that the lower age limit on white males be reduced from twenty to sixteen years because slightly younger men made "better Servants": they were "more docile, healthier, and sooner reconciled to this Climate as well as more alert in Arms than those of more advanced Years." Otherwise they merely repeated their request that coopers and sawyers be allowed to take on black apprentices.[20]

The Trustees received these comments in the spring of 1750 and referred them to the relevant committee of their Common Council for consideration. By August they were ready to submit proposals to the Lords Justices in Council. They began by explaining why they wished the Act of 1735 to be rescinded. In 1735 there had been every reason to "apprehend a Rupture with the Spaniards," but since "a General Peace" now obtained there was no longer any pressing military need for them to persevere with their prohibitory policy. The Trustees declared themselves satisfied that the introduction of slaves would be consistent with the "safety" of Georgia and, moreover, finally admitted that the institution of slavery would "conduce to the Prosperity" of the colony. They therefore wished to permit the Georgia settlers to employ slaves from 1 January 1751.[21] They included with their petition a draft copy of an act that not only lifted the ban on slavery but also stipulated the conditions under which the institution would be permitted in Georgia. As Benjamin Martyn remarked to William Stephens, the Trustees' slave code was virtually identical to that proposed by the Georgians.[22]

The Trustees did not limit the size of individual slaveholdings but imposed a ratio between adult male slaves and white men aged between sixteen and sixty-five of four to one. But it was one thing to formulate such a ratio and another to enforce it. The Trustees believed that the desired racial balance could be maintained through a system of fines of up to £10 sterling for every slave held in excess of the permitted number and £5 sterling per month for as long as the offense continued. There were readily apparent reasons for wishing to ascertain the size and distribution of Georgia's blacks and, in order that this might be done regularly, the Trustees incorporated a census mechanism into their slave code. They were also concerned to ensure the health of the black, and thereby the white, population, and to prevent the introduction of "contagious Distempers (particularly the Yellow Fever)" by the opening of the slave trade they devised a comprehensive set of quarantine regulations for slave ships.[23]

The remainder of the code was concerned with the employment, religious welfare, and treatment of Georgia's slaves. On the matter of employment the Trustees followed the advice given by their officials: coopers and sawyers could take on black apprentices, but otherwise slaves were to be used only for unskilled plantation work. Two other regulations formulated by the Trustees suggest that they still held out high hopes for silk culture in Georgia. They decreed that at least five hundred mulberry trees must be planted on each five-hundred-acre land grant "and so in proportion" and that slave women must be sent to Savannah "at the proper Season in every Year" to learn the techniques of reeling and winding silk.[24]

The Trustees did not deal with the punishment of slave offenders; their main concern was with whites who maltreated their black workers. They emphasized the duties and responsibilities of the white community, and, in effect, their slave code amounted to a rigorous code of behavior for Georgia's whites. The Trustees' humanitarianism now found an important expression in a concern for the welfare of Georgia's black element. It is important to emphasize that their proposals were very similar to those submitted by the colony's local officials. Any white who inflicted physical punishment "endangering the Limb of a Negro" would be fined "not less" than £5 sterling for the first offense and at least £10 for any subsequent infringement. No mention was made of the judicial procedures that would obtain in such cases. For example, would blacks be allowed to testify against whites? The Trustees gave no guidance, although they included a regulation in their code to cover the murder of a slave by a white person. Any white so accused would "be tried according to the Laws of Great Britain" and, one assumes, if found guilty be liable to the same penalty as that which obtained in the home country.[25]

The only detailed reference in the slave code to the punishment of slaves was in the brief section dealing with miscegenation. The Trustees' thoughts on this subject were in keeping with those reflected in the slave codes of the other plantation colonies: interracial marriage was forbidden, and any such unions already entered into were declared "absolutely null and void." In cases of interracial fornication the Georgia Board drew no distinction between male and female offenders. Blacks would be subject to "Corporal Punishment" of a type and amount left to the discretion of the courts; whites would be fined £10 sterling and might also receive such corporal punishment as the courts deemed appropriate.[26]

Finally, and of paramount importance in the Trustees' scheme, masters were required to attend to the spiritual welfare of their slaves. Blacks were forbidden to work on Sundays, and their owners were obliged to see that they attended "at some time on the Lords Day for Instruction in the Christian Religion." Even now the Trustees did not concede that there might be any inconsistency between Christianity and slaveholding. Indeed, at no point had they defended the prohibition of slavery on purely religious grounds. In their slave code they emphasized the religious duty of the Christian master toward his bondsmen.

The sum total of the Trustees' deliberations and consultations with the Georgia settlers was a slave code which in some respects, for example those sections dealing with religion and miscegenation, was not dissimilar to those of the other southern colonies. But in other respects, and most notably in the absence of regulations that sought to govern the behavior of slaves, it was unlike any other colonial slave code. It had two primary aims: to permit slavery and to attempt to curb white behavior. Neither the Trustees nor the Georgians explained why the code did not address itself to the practicalities of slave management. It is difficult to believe that the failure to include provisions designed specifically to regulate slave behavior was an oversight on the part of men, on both sides of the Atlantic, who were coversant with the practices of the other mainland colonies. Two other explanations are more plausible. First, the Trustees, who for many years had tried to control every facet of life in Georgia, might have decided that those who would operate the system were in the best position to draft such ordinances as might prove necessary to prevent slave misconduct. Second, they and their officials might have believed that it would prove possible to avoid certain of the regulations in force elsewhere in British America. The malcontents had always held that as long as a strict racial balance was maintained the risk to masters and to the white community at large from slaves would be minimal. Perhaps they and the Trustees also thought that a ratio of one white male to every four working blacks, significantly lower than any found in the other plantation colonies, would be sufficient to minimize black resistance. But the colonial officials had also stated that they wished to "make the condition of Slavery as easy as may be consistent with the Safety of His Majesty's Subjects." They might have simply been saying what they thought the Trustees would like to hear; alternatively they might have meant it. That is, they might have believed that a combination of white firepower and humanitarian treatment would serve the purpose of containing black misconduct within acceptable limits. In a sense the situation was reminiscent of that a decade earlier when the Trustees had contemplated the employment of free blacks in Georgia. Then a prime consideration had been that free blacks would have no reason to misbehave because nowhere else in British America could they hope to find such a favorable situation. Possibly the Trustees and their officials believed that an essentially similar argument could now be applied to the conditions under which black slavery would be permitted in Georgia.

In launching the Georgia project the Trustees had attempted to stamp a clearly defined pattern of social and economic development on the southern borderlands, but their scheme was based on a serious misconception of the region's environment and, more seriously, of the settlers' aspirations. Moreover, there was a fundamental conflict between the Trustees' military and economic objectives. On one level, of course, a closely knit settlement pattern would enhance Georgia's role as a military buffer and, at the same time, fifty- and five-hundred-acre land grants were adequate for the crops that were to form the basis of the settlers' comfortable subsistence. But as Ralph Gray and Betty Wood have argued, "The example set in the other American colonies suggests that subsistence-level mixed farming is not the key to rapid settlement." The Trustees were in a cleft stick because "a colony based on indentured white labor that was large enough to serve as a military deterrent to the Spanish could not be economically viable in its own right; a colony whose workforce was dominated by black slaves could not serve as an effective military buffer."[27]
In withdrawing from direct participation in Georgia affairs the Trustees attempted to bequeath a legacy of continuing influence

over subsequent events such that Europeans and Africans alike might be protected from the worst manifestations of the agricultural capitalism that characterized the plantation societies of British America. The economic pattern they now envisaged differed markedly from those of the other southern colonies, but it was a continuation of their original concept. Silk would remain Georgia's most important staple, thereby achieving the initial objective of securing for Britain a singularly valuable member of its colonial system. The difference now was that this objective would be attained through the employment of slaves. In their first formulation the Trustees had blithely assumed that inexperienced Europeans could be instructed in the techniques of silk culture; now they transferred that same assumption to slaves in general and to slave women in particular.

It would be pointless to speculate on the consequences for the future of Georgia, and thereby possibly of all the southern colonies, had the slave code drawn up at the end of the 1740s been persevered with. In fact, it survived for only five years before being rewritten by the Georgia Commons House of Assembly. Once again, and given the South Carolinian domination of the assembly predictably, Georgia turned to South Carolina for its model. The Trustees' attempt to influence events and the good intentions of their officials were thwarted by the realities of the situation and the personalities involved. As we shall see, the result of this assertion of home rule was the abandonment of a unique experiment in the history of British North America.

CHAPTER SIX

THE MAKING OF A

PLANTATION ECONOMY,

1752–1775

*A*lthough it would be fallacious to suggest that the ending of the Trusteeship marked a sharp break in the economic and social history of Georgia, the years of royal government witnessed far-reaching changes in the economic fortunes as well as in the economic and social structure of the colony. Despite the assurances and the tangible support given by the Trustees, but mainly because of the restrictions they imposed on land, labor, and credit, the Georgia of the late 1740s scarcely ranked as a producer, major or otherwise, of the commodities the Trustees had assumed would not only form the basis of a comfortable subsistence for the settlers but also make their colony an invaluable addition to Britain's old colonial system. Although, as Egmont appreciated, the Trustees might have erred in promising too much too soon, the fact remains that they "not only decreed the least remunerative labor system, but from a profit standpoint specified an inferior farming model."[1] For most of the Trustee period the overriding concern of the Georgia settlers had been economic survival.

The malcontents had argued vigorously that a free land market and the employment of slaves would remedy Georgia's economic ills, and on one level they were to be proved correct—but not immediately. The decade of the 1750s was one of economic and social adjustment and modest economic growth, made all the more difficult by the outbreak of the Seven Years' War and renewed anxieties about the future of Georgia. After 1763 and a war that finally eradicated the Spanish menace, the pace of

Georgia's economic life quickened. Finally, the settlers began to enjoy the fruits of the malcontents' victory. But for many whites those fruits were to prove very bitter indeed.

Before 1750 the flow of migrants to Georgia was counter-balanced by death and desertion and, after two decades of settlement, the colony contained fewer than 3,000 whites and 600 blacks.[2] After 1750 the population grew, and after 1763 the pace was much more rapid. In 1761 Governor James Wright estimated that there were "no more" than 6,100 "white Persons" and "about 3,600" blacks in the colony; twelve years later Georgia's inhabitants numbered roughly 33,000 and included approximately 15,000 blacks.[3] This impressive rate of population growth was matched by an equally impressive improvement in Georgia's economic health. By the early 1760s important trading links had been forged with Britain, the other mainland colonies, and the West Indies, and between 1761 and 1773 Georgia's exports soared from just over 1,600 tons valued at £15,870 to around 11,300 tons valued at £121,677. In 1763 Georgia's exports to Britain were valued at £14,000; ten years later they were worth almost £41,000. The amount of rice shipped from Georgia increased tenfold between 1755 and 1775, and the colony's other major exports, indigo, skins, timber, and tobacco, showed a comparable increase.[4]

These economic achievements, which made Georgia an increasingly valuable member of the old colonial system, were intimately related to fundamental changes in the colony's social structure. Although the Trustees had been concerned to avoid extremes of wealth and poverty in Georgia, they never intended to establish a society in which wealth was distributed equally. Their main objective had not been the attainment of economic and social equality but the elimination of what they deemed to be the wholly undesirable social attributes of an unfettered plantation economy. They accepted that there would be a degree of economic inequality in Georgia, which in large measure would reflect the settlers' willingness to work, but anticipated that their policies would prevent the emergence of gross inequalities in the distribution of wealth. The abandonment of their plan, which had acted as a brake on economic development, paved the way for the economic growth experienced after 1750. But as the Trustees had feared and predicted, the removal of tight economic controls exerted a profound influence on the course of Georgia's social development. By the early 1760s the colony contained, according to Gray and Wood, "a pyramid shaped distribution of landholders with a handful of large, slave-owning rice planters at the apex and small family farms with one or no slaves at the bottom; precisely the class structure which the Trustees [had been] determined to avoid."[5] Most of those at or close to the top of the "pyramid" were men who had not participated in the slavery debate. The 1750s and 1760s saw not only the creation, virtually from scratch, of a plantation economy which closely resembled that of South Carolina but also, as the Trustees and their supporters had warned, of a plantation economy which to a considerable degree came to be dominated by migrants from that colony.

By 1750 the Trustees had abandoned all their original restrictions on landholding and ceded the right to make land grants to the colony's president and his assistants. In 1754, with the inauguration of royal government, that right passed to the governor and his council. The Georgians now enjoyed the free land market which the malcontents had deemed essential for the economic well-being of the colony. But many of the early settlers soon discovered that such an arrangement did not necessarily work to their advantage.

Although personal wealth derived from various commercial enterprises assumed a growing importance in Georgia, land, whether to farm or as a source of timber and furs, and sufficient labor to exploit that land, remained the key to economic and thereby social and political advancement. But how easy was it to acquire land? Who gained and who lost by the operation of a free land market?

After 1754 there were three main ways of acquiring land: by purchase on the open market or privately, by a deed of gift or a bequest, and, in terms of the acreage disposed of most important, by applying to the colonial authorities for a land grant. The governor and his council met monthly to consider petitions for land, and the acreages allotted depended upon the size of the applicant's household. The Board of Trade's policy, which was closely adhered to by Georgia's royal governors, was that the colony should be settled as quickly as possible but that the number of acres granted should depend upon the "grantee's ability to use the acres he received."[6] Heads of families could petition for one hundred acres of land for themselves and an additional fifty acres for each member of their household, including their servants and slaves. The profitable exploitation of land grants meant that one option open to their proprietors was that of acquiring more labor and, in turn, applying for extra acres. These might be granted or, if the governor and council saw fit, purchased for the nominal sum of one shilling per ten acres.[7] Those who were well placed to take advantage of this system and those who were favored on "Land Days" were applicants who could demonstrate that they had sufficient labor to cultivate the lands for which they petitioned. Many of those who fitted such a description were migrants from South Carolina and the West Indies.

The rice lands to the south of the Savannah River had long held an attraction for the South Carolinians and, even before the end of the Trusteeship, a few migrants from that colony had settled in Georgia.[8] The Trustees' land and labor policies acted as a fairly effective check on migration; the abandonment of these policies revived the South Carolinian interest and, as William G. De Brahm recorded, in 1752 "the Spirit of Emigration out of South Carolina into Georgia became so universal . . . that this and the following year near One thousand Negroes was brought into Georgia." Although the tide of emigration ebbed and flowed, between 1746 and 1766 South Carolina accounted for "more of Georgia's new settlers . . . than . . . Europe or any other American colony."[9]

Beginning in the late 1740s South Carolinian migrants settled in two areas to the north of the Altamaha River, both of which were ideally suited to rice production. Between 1752 and 1754 the Puritan community that had originated in New England and subsequently moved to Dorchester, South Carolina, established itself in the region between the Savannah and Altamaha rivers, which came to be known as the District of Midway. One of the Puritans' main reasons for moving to Georgia was a shortage of lands which threatened "the imminent dissolution of their congregation." Georgia offered the prospect of lands for the younger members of the congregation and thereby promised to ensure the community's continuing coherence. By the time the transfer from South Carolina had been completed 350 whites and roughly 1,500 blacks had settled in Midway.[10]

The increasing cost of prime rice lands in South Carolina explains why men whom David R. Chesnutt referred to as some of the colony's "fairly substantial planters," including Jonathan Bryan, Stephen Bull, and William Butler, as well as a number of "small and middling planters," who believed that the "avenues of mobility in the Carolina social order were clogged," were keen to take up lands between the Savannah and Ogeechee rivers.[11] Georgia held out the tantalizing promise of an upward social mobility apparently denied them in South Carolina, and it was a promise which the likes of Benjamin Farley and William Gibbons were eager to exploit.

Before 1763 the area open to rice cultivation extended only as far south as the Altamaha River. After a considerable amount of wrangling with South Carolina, the lands between the Altamaha and St. Mary's rivers ceded by Spain were annexed to Georgia and thereafter constituted an important focus of settlement.[12] The removal of Spain and the Indian Cession of 1763, which put in excess of 2.5 million acres at the disposal of the Georgia authorities, were of vital importance in shaping both the economic and the social development of the colony during the decade before the War for Independence. Although by no means all of these lands were suited to rice cultivation, their availability for other modes of argicultural production and the generous land policy pursued by Georgia's royal government made settlement in the colony an attractive proposition. There is no suggestion that a rapidly increasing slave element deterred prospective migrants. Indeed, if anything, the reverse was true. Although the possibility of securing land lured many migrants, this would have counted for little had they not been permitted to employ slaves. It was the very fact of being allowed slaves that now made Georgia so attractive to migrants, not least to the South Carolinians.

Although the most important, South Carolina was not the only source of settlers for Georgia. The years after 1750 saw the arrival of other groups and nationalities, including Germans, Scotch-Irish, and the ill-fated Acadians, as well as settlers from the Upper South and the West Indies.[13] In exploiting their land grants, many of the South Carolinians enjoyed an initial advantage over most of these other newcomers, which the notable exception of those from the West Indies, and over the majority of those who had settled in Georgia before 1750 because they often brought slaves with them to the colony. Thus around 41 percent of the Carolinians who applied for lands in Georgia between 1747 and 1765 held slaves (the average holding was fourteen slaves) at the time of making their first application to the Georgia authorities.[14] The labor that made slaves so attractive in the allocation of land grants also gave them an important head start in the process of plantation building. Of course, many of the early settlers had cleared and planted some land, owned livestock, and constructed houses and outbuildings, but as of 1750 few of them possessed the labor and capital available to the Carolinians. A second advantage enjoyed by these newcomers, who were moving into an environment that was well known to them, was their close familiarity with the techniques of rice and indigo production. Rice had been produced on a very limited scale in Georgia before 1750, and few of the early settlers had any practical experience of its cultivation and preparation for the market.

Although the Carolinians enjoyed certain advantages, this is not to say that they all became eminent planters or that none of the early settlers or migrants from elsewhere could compete with them. But the fact was that many of those who had arrived in Georgia before the mid-1740s faced certain problems that made it difficult, but not altogether impossible, for them to climb to the very top of the economic ladder during the years of royal government. These problems stemmed partly from the terms under which they had settled in Georgia and partly from the difficulties they encountered once in America.

Those who went as charity settlers to Georgia had been recruited from the lower echelons of British and European society, and they arrived in the colony with virtually no agricultural experience, little or no capital, and no more labor than could be provided by themselves and their families. Initially, adventurers were in a somewhat stronger position because they were accompanied by servants. But as the experience of Tailfer and others demonstrated, the possession of labor was no guarantee of economic success. Many adventurers complained bitterly that they had exhausted their capital on futile attempts to develop their lands along the lines envisaged by the Trustees. Their servants had been taken ill, died, run away, or come to the end of their indentures and proved impossible to replace. They claimed, moreover, and with some justification, that even were more labor available it would prove impossible to wrest a living from some of the lands assigned on an arbitrary basis by the Trustees. Although the malcontents might have been guilty of wishing for instant prosperity, the fact was that however hard they worked they could do little more than break even as long as they were forced to rely exclusively upon white labor.[15]

Some settlers believed that given the dire straits in which they found themselves they had no option but to leave Georgia, and many of those who had been in the forefront of the struggle to secure a plantation economy, including Tailfer and Thomas Stephens, turned their backs on the colony; others stayed on and tried to carve out a living. Predictably, some did better than others and by the end of the 1740s were poised to take advantage of the economic opportunities presented by the abandonment of the Trustees' plan. Three such were James Habersham, Noble Jones, and Francis Harris, perhaps the most successful of the early settlers. They had arrived in Georgia at different times and under different circumstances: Jones, then aged thirty-two, was included among the first embarkation of settlers; Habersham began his career in Georgia in 1738 as a schoolmaster but in 1747 joined forces with Francis Harris to establish what soon became the colony's leading merchant house.[16] At the time of their arrival in Georgia there was nothing to mark them as men who were likely to achieve a prominent position in that colony's society; by 1750 they were leading members of Georgia's first elite. The three men owed their success partly to their own abilities and initiative but in large measure to the assistance, both material and political, which they received from the Trustees. In this context it is relevant that although sympathetic to the aims of the malcontents none of these three played an active part in the slavery debate.

Jones was employed by the Trustees as a surveyor, and his fees supplemented the income he earned as a carpenter and doctor and derived from his agricultural operations. On the political front he was appointed to serve as one of William Stephens's assistants. During the latter part of the Trusteeship the firm of Harris and Habersham assumed the major responsibility for handling the Trustees' business affairs in Georgia and benefited accordingly. Both partners were held in high regard by the Trustees and were also appointed as assistants to Stephens. In this capacity they enjoyed a significant say in the allocation of land grants. The three men continued in public office after 1752. Harris was the Speaker of Georgia's first General Assembly and made a member of the first Royal Council; Jones and Habersham were also appointed councillors in 1754. Jones also occupied the post of colonial treasurer for many years, and during the early 1770s Habersham served as the acting governor of Georgia while James Wright was away in England.[17] The economic, social, and political progress achieved by the clerk, the carpenter-cum-doctor, and the schoolmaster before 1750 was the all-important platform upon which they were able to build during the years of royal government. But they were the rare exceptions. Their less favored and less successful compatriots who, often through no fault of their own, had little to show for their time in Georgia faced irresistible pressure from the South Carolinian newcomers.

Some indication of the initial advantage enjoyed by those South Carolinians and West Indians who brought even a few slaves with them may be gathered from contemporary accounts of the amount of capital required to establish a slave-manned rice plantation. The estimates compiled by Bolzius and De Brahm reveal that regardless of the scale of the operation envisaged, labor was by far the most expensive item in the would-be planter's budget. During the 1750s and 1760s prime rice lands could be had for a modest sum; the labor required to cultivate those lands was a different matter. Bolzius estimated that "a newly established plantation with 10 Negroes and one boy" would necessitate an outlay of £456 "in the first year" and that 60 percent of this sum would go for the purchase of the black workers. De Brahm believed that roughly 72 percent of the £2,376.16.0 which he thought would be needed to start and operate a two-hundred-acre plantation for a year would have to be spent on "40 Working Hands."[18]

The cost of a slave varied according to the origin, age, sex, skill, and health of the African concerned. In the early 1750s, the critical time for plantation formation in Georgia, a newly imported male slave cost between £28 and £32 and a woman "is about £3 cheaper." Country-born or acclimatized slaves were more expensive than "New Negroes," mainly because it was feared that the latter might succumb during the seasoning period. Owners could not insure their slaves and had to bear any financial loss that might be incurred by the ill health or death of their bondsmen. A country-born or seasoned slave could be had for between £28 and £36; a female slave of similar origins who was required for "field work" cost between £26 and £33 and if she was "useful in the house" as much as £57. Children under the age of about eight were usually sold with their mothers. But as with adults, and for the same reason, there was a price differential between slightly older children. A newly imported boy aged between eight and fifteen cost between £10 and £25, whereas a country-born boy would fetch "from £14 to £35 according to whether he looks well and has good expectations." Girls brought slightly less; regardless of their origins they were priced at between £10 and £21. Although they had to be fed, clothed, and otherwise maintained, children did not necessarily constitute a heavy financial burden on their owners because depending upon their age they could be used for "various small jobs," which might include "hoeing the potatoes, feeding the chickens, [and] shooing the birds from the rice and grain."[19] Of course, in the long term they represented not only potentially valuable workers but also highly lucrative capital assets.

Partly because of the savings that could be effected by using their own slaves and partly because of the income that accrued from their hire, the most highly prized slaves were those who possessed skills. Coopers cost upward of £50 and a carpenter could fetch over £100.[20] Although slave prices increased after the mid-1760s, differentials remained fairly constant. During the late 1760s and early 1770s prime field hands brought around £60; slave women cost at least £30 and usually closer to £50; and slave children upward of £25.[21] But throughout the period some slaves, the old and the infirm, had little or no market value.[22]

The prior possession of, or ease of access to, the capital needed to start a rice plantation, and by definition this included slaves, played a decisive part in shaping the social and economic structure of late colonial Georgia. Any settler who wished to buy slaves to begin or expand a plantation could pay cash and secure his hands "more cheaply" or seek credit from local or South Carolinian merchants. The chances of securing credit and the sum advanced depended upon the security that could be offered and the ability to repay the debt. As Lachlan McIntosh's career demonstrates, close personal contacts with a South Carolina merchant, in this case Henry Laurens, could greatly enhance a settler's prospects of securing a loan.[23] If credit was arranged the borrower could expect to pay an interest rate of at least 8 percent per annum on his outstanding debt.

Even with an interest rate that hovered around 8 percent, rice planters were likely to recoup a handsome and speedy return on their initial capital investment. Obviously, productivity and profits varied from plantation to plantation and from year to year; much depended upon commodity prices, the plantation's crop and livestock mix, the composition of the work force, the owner's expertise, the vigor with which he or his overseer worked the slaves, and the amount of money spent on the upkeep of the black work force. Most masters worked on the assumption that a slave could plant up to ten acres of corn, peas, and potatoes and around three acres of rice a year. The amount of rice produced per hand varied from the 0.57 barrels complained of by William Knox in 1771 to the 3.5 barrels produced on James Habersham's Silk Hope plantation in 1765 "without hurry and too much driving."²⁴ But taking everything into account, it is evident that considerable profits were made from rice cultivation and, as was the practice on most estates, from the sale of the timber and timber products that derived from the continuing process of land clearance. Recent research has shown that depending upon the value of the implicit managerial wage, the proprietor of a hundred-acre plantation manned by eleven slaves could expect to recoup an internal rate of return of between 37 and 43 percent, and a two-hundred-acre estate employing forty hands "would have yielded almost 25% per annum on invested capital."²⁵ In purely economic terms there was every incentive to establish slave-manned rice plantations even if this meant, as it often did, going deeply into debt in order to secure slaves. Obviously, those who already possessed labor and capital, in effect the South Carolinians and West Indians, were at a distinct advantage.

Although slavery was officially sanctioned in Georgia from 1 January 1751 it was not until the mid-1760s that the colony began to import slaves directly from West Africa. As Robert S. Glenn, Jr., has observed, Georgia "approximated the pattern of the other southern colonies in that it did not develop a direct slave trade with Africa until its economy was advanced enough to absorb cargoes of 150 to 200 slaves at a time."²⁶ Between 1751 and 1766 Georgia looked to the other American colonies, but especially to South Carolina and the West Indies, not only for settlers and financial capital but also for the bulk of its slaves. Although at least nine hundred slaves were shipped from the West Indies for sale in Georgia, most of the Africans who arrived in the colony before 1766 either came with their owners or were purchased in the slave markets of South Carolina. The South Carolinians and West Indians who applied for lands in Georgia between 1750 and the mid-1760s held upward of two thousand slaves and, as mentioned above, in 1752 and 1753 alone around a thousand slaves were taken to Georgia from South Carolina. Unfortunately, the records reveal nothing about the origin, sex, ages, or skills of these slaves, although contemporary reports suggest that the majority were African-born.²⁷

The purchase of slaves in South Carolina took one of two

forms: they might be bought privately or selected from among the "New Negroes" landed at Charles Town. South Carolina's merchants were keenly aware of the Georgian demand for slaves and, often acting in close collaboration with Savannah's merchants, they might consign parcels of slaves for sale in that colony. Alternatively, the Georgians visited Charles Town and made purchases on their own behalf.[28]

Before 1766 Georgia's involvement with the African slave trade was indirect; thereafter slaves from several regions of West Africa, including Gambia, Angola, Sierra Leone, Senegal, Guinea, and Nigeria, were shipped directly to Savannah. Although slave traders sometimes negotiated directly with potential customers, the main responsibility for the marketing of slave imports was assumed by local merchants, who included among their number men such as James Habersham and John Graham, whose economic interests embraced both planting and commerce. Georgia's planter-merchants and the firms with which they were associated—Telfair, Cowper, and Telfair (founded in 1767 by three migrants from Antigua), Clay and Habersham (a partnership between cousins), Inglis and Hall, and John Graham and Company were among the most prominent—played a vital role in every sector of the colony's rapidly developing and increasingly complex commercial life and not least in the organization of the African slave trade.

It was usual for slave shipments, which could consist of as many as two hundred slaves, to be consigned to a particular merchant or merchant house in Savannah. The human cargo might be sold at public auction, in which case details of those on offer would be advertized in the *Georgia Gazette,* or privately. New imports, who had to be fed and sheltered and who sometimes required medical attention, were usually sold off as soon as possible after their arrival, but if a merchant believed that they would not fetch an acceptable price because of their health or the state of the market, he would hold them back and await a "Better Market."[29] Merchants were willing to accept payment in cash or commodities and to extend credit for varying lengths of time. Indeed, it was not unusual for several different credit arrangements to be entered into for slaves drawn from the same cargo.[30]

Although the Georgians began to import slaves straight from West Africa in the mid-1760s this did not mean that the slave trade with South Carolina, in all its aspects, ceased to be of consequence. After 1766 slaves were still purchased in Carolina and, as had been the case since the early 1750s, a deed of gift, a bequest, or a marriage settlement could result in the transfer of slaves across the Savannah River. Some Georgians, but notably the larger planters, continued to bid for slaves in Charles Town, and their willingness and often eagerness to do so reflected a business acumen which was greatly assisted by the regular reports they received from their contacts in South Carolina about the quality of the Africans on offer and the state of the market.[31] Some indication of the continuing importance of the Carolina market may be gathered from the report in the *South Carolina Gazette* of 26 July 1773 that "at least 1,000" of the 6,471 Africans imported into Carolina since 1 November 1772 had been purchased by Georgians.

Although Georgia was the net gainer, the slave trade with South Carolina was not a one-way traffic. Deeds of gift, bequests, and private sales could take slaves out of as well as bring them into Georgia. Indeed, when in 1766 the Carolina authorities introduced an extra levy of £100 on slave imports the Charles Town merchants took advantage of their Georgia connections and consigned slave cargoes destined for their own colony to Savannah. But occasionally the usually excellent and mutually beneficial relations between the Georgians and South Carolinians were strained almost to the breaking point. Thus the former had no compunction in flouting the nonimportation agreement drawn up by the Carolinians in mid-1769 and, according to the *South Carolina Gazette,* the "unfeeling Georgia merchants," who were "dead to every Thing but their own Interest," brought slaves to their own colony and introduced them "over Land into This," even though they knew that "Every Slave so introduced is liable to Seizure and Forfeiture." In December 1770 South Carolina's nonimportation agreement was declared to be at an end and, as far as the Carolinians were concerned, it was back to business as usual with the Georgians.[32]

When it came to the purchase of "New Negroes" the Georgians had clearly defined preferences and, of course, local merchants knew precisely which slaves would fetch the best price in the Savannah market. For most owners the slave's sex was less important than his or her age, health, and place of birth. That the Georgians appreciated the potential value of slave children cannot be denied, but there is no suggestion that they viewed black women primarily as "breeders." Although masters recognized that women were physically unable to undertake some of the heavier tasks associated with plantation agriculture, the amount and type of work demanded of them during the planting season and at harvest time were similar to that required of their menfolk.[33]

Obviously, the age and health of a slave had a direct bearing on his or her capacity for work, and the Georgians' opinion about the significance of the former was summed up by Telfair, Cowper, and Telfair in 1773 when they complained that a slave cargo that had been consigned to them was "in no way calculated for this market, and great number being old *Men &* *Women & Boys & Girls* added to this unfortunate circumstance." They believed that the slaves that would "prove exceeding advantageous" in the Georgia market were "prime Men & Women, with a few Boys & Girls, the Men & Women not exceeding twenty five years of age."[34]

During the Trusteeship the malcontents had claimed that Africans were far more resilient than whites to the diseases encountered in the Georgia environment, and although this argument did not change appreciably after 1750 the Georgians expressed fears about the health of slave imports. First, they believed that unless effective quarantine regulations were put into force various contagious diseases would be introduced into their colony as a direct consequence of the slave trade. Their second and not entirely unrelated fear concerned the Africans' resilience during the seasoning period, especially if this coincided with the winter months. The weakened physical condition of many "New Negroes" raised the very real possibility that they might fall ill or die before their owners had seen any return on their investment.

The conditions under which Africans were transported to the

Americas and the mortality rates on the Middle Passage can only be described as horrific, and that portion of the slave trade which involved Georgia was no exception. In 1774, for example, "thirty two new Negroes" were consigned to Telfair, Cowper, and Telfair, but ten died before the slave ship docked "at Cockspur, & during Quarantine there" and four more succumbed "coming up the River." The Savannah merchants ascribed this heavy loss to the ship's "long passage added to the severity of the Weather on this coast." Those blacks who survived were "of so mean an appearance, as had not been exposed to Sale in Savannah this Season." Earlier that year the same merchant house had anticipated the arrival of sixteen Africans from the West Indies, but only seven were delivered alive to Savannah and "one died the next day." Although Savannah's merchants bemoaned the financial losses occasioned by such high mortality rates—Telfair, Cowper, and Telfair reported the loss of £2,000 sterling on a single cargo[35]—the appalling human cost of the trade provoked no comment in Georgia. The Georgians' main concern was not with the mortality of Africans en route to their colony but with the physical condition of those who survived the passage to Savannah.

Unfortunately, the evidence is so sparse as to preclude any firm conclusions about the precise mortality rates among Africans during their first few months in Georgia. It is apparent, however, that the experience of certain slave cargoes only reinforced the Georgians' anxieties about the susceptibility of "New Negroes." In 1774, for example, Telfair, Cowper, and Telfair remarked on the "daily Complaints" they were receiving from their customers about "the Great Mortality" of the slaves they had purchased from among a consignment of 211 Africans shipped from Sierra Leone. The merchant house was not unduly surprised by these complaints: "It was evident that such would be the case from the amazing Loss, in the course of the few days [the ship] was in port previous to the sale[.] this proceeded from an inveterate Scurvey, in a Great measure owing to the Long destination."[36] Telfair, Cowper, and Telfair had no compunction about selling slaves in such a condition; to them it was a case of caveat emptor. But for their customers each slave represented a significant capital outlay, and few were in a position to shrug off a speedy loss of their investment. For this patently obvious reason, the Georgians took a keen interest in the health of the slaves on offer in Savannah and Charles Town and merchants emphasized the good physical condition of those on sale.

The Georgians also attached a good deal of significance to a slave's origins. Particular modes of behavior, including an aptitude for work, were associated with particular regions and tribal groupings. Even before the opening of a direct slave trade with West Africa the stark, uncomplicated view of the African held by the early settlers had given way to a very different set of impressions. By the end of the 1750s the Georgians were differentiating among blacks in a way which, given the early settlers' lack of familiarity with Africans, could not have been the case during the Trusteeship. This changed perspective is nowhere more evident than in the writings of Pastor Bolzius. During the 1730s and 1740s he made sweeping generalizations about the character and conduct of Africans; by the early 1750s he was asserting that black behavior varied according to tribal origins. Thus "the best Negroes came from the Gold Coast in Africa, namely Gambia and Angola. The Hipponegroes are the worst nation, stupid and bloodthirsty, and [they] often kill themselves."[37]

This complicated assessment was essentially South Carolinian in origin. As Elizabeth Donnan, and more recently Daniel C. Littlefield, have pointed out, the Carolinians had "decided preferences as to the source of their labor supply. . . . The favourite negroes were those from Gambia and the Gold Coast . . . [and] . . . To describe new arrivals as 'Gambia Men and Women' or 'Gold Coast Negroes' was a guaranty of high quality." These preferences were imported wholesale into Georgia and played an important part in shaping the pattern of slave purchases that characterized the 1760s and early 1770s. Three-quarters of the twenty-five hundred slaves shipped to Georgia from West Africa between 1766 and 1771 came from Gambia (40 percent), Sierra Leone (16 percent), Angola (10 percent), "Gambia and Sierra Leone" (6 percent), and Senegal (3 percent). Of the remainder, 6 percent were said to come from "Africa," 14 percent from the "Rice Coast," and 5 percent from the "Grain Coast."[38]

Georgia masters appear not to have subscribed to the belief that their attempts to secure the good behavior of their slaves would be facilitated by the separation of Africans from the same region, tribe, or family. The positive attributes they ascribed to particular Africans, especially a propensity for work, outweighed fears that a common background, and not least a common language, would enhance the opportunities for successful resistance. Indeed, many owners believed that the separation of Africans would actually prompt such modes of misconduct as running away. They appreciated the strength of the ties that united black families and freely admitted that slaves would run away in order to be reunited with their loved ones.

One sector of the slave trade to their colony, that with the West Indies, proved increasingly unsatisfactory to the Georgians. Their dissatisfaction stemmed not from the tribal origins, health, or ages of the slaves being shipped from the Caribbean but from the conviction that the West Indians were using Georgia as a dumping ground for their "Rebellious Negroes." The potentially "dangerous Consequences" of such a practice were clear enough to the Georgians: the "Felons" and "Convicts" being sent from the West Indies were so incorrigible that they would do their best to foment disorders. They believed that the only way to rid themselves of this problem was to levy a duty on slaves imported from the West Indies, and this they duly did in 1767.[39]

Between 1751 and 1773 Georgia's black population grew from around five hundred to approximately fifteen thousand and, as may be surmised from the foregoing, much of this increase was accounted for by slave imports. In addition to the slaves brought to Georgia by their South Carolinian and West Indian owners and those purchased in South Carolina, at least forty-four hundred blacks were shipped to the colony from West Africa (57 percent), from or via the West Indies (37 percent), and from the other mainland colonies (6 percent) between 1755 and 1771.[40] It is difficult to ascertain the precise contribution made by natural increase. Georgia's first slave code made provision for annual "Inquisitions" of the black element (a requirement not written into subsequent codes), but if censuses were taken after 1750 they have not survived. Contemporary estimates usually made no reference to the sex ratio or age structure of the colony's slaves. The fragmentary evidence that is available, notably inventories and lists of slaves compiled for purposes of taxation, make it possible to arrive at some tentative conclusions.

An analysis of 202 inventories and lists that span the years between 1755 and 1777 and include holdings of all sizes indicates that men heavily outnumbered women.[41] The ratio of slave men to women on all estates was in the region of 146 to 100, but it appears that the larger the holding the greater the imbalance. Thus on estates with more than twenty slaves the ratio was around 135 to 100 and on those with more than forty slaves roughly 152 to 100. On estates with fewer than ten slaves the ratio dropped to 119 to 100. On almost half the estates surveyed men outnumbered women; the reverse was true of less than 20 percent of slaveholdings. These ratios and distributions are very similar to those which characterized Tidewater South Carolina during the 1720s and 1730s, decades in which "rice rose from the status of competing export to become the colony's central preoccupation." Precisely the same was true of Georgia after 1750 and, as Peter H. Wood has suggested, in view of the continuing process of land clearance and plantation formation it is not surprising that "men were in a majority . . . [especially] on the larger plantations."[42]

The comments of merchants and masters, rather than any information included in inventories and lists, suggest that Georgia's black population was young. Merchants recorded the strong preference of masters for slaves under the age of twenty-five, and there is no reason to believe that this preference went unsatisfied. As in South Carolina, however, the importation of young slaves did not result in a substantial rate of natural increase. Indeed, the low birth rate among Georgia's blacks was a matter for comment by their owners. In 1772, for example, Habersham told Knox that he had "been very fortunate in having [his] People preserved, and if I mistake not have lately had two or three Children born—It has not been so with me, and untill [sic] a year or two past, the Births in my Family fell considerably short of the Number I bought and dyed." Habersham's experience was by no means atypical; between 1755 and 1777 the number of children per slave woman in Georgia averaged less than one.[43]

There is no single or simple explanation for the low birth rate. Wood has ascribed that of South Carolina's slaves during the 1720s and 1730s—an average of 1.17 children per woman—to "the general intensification of staple agriculture." Georgia underwent a similar intensification a generation later, a process which as in Carolina resulted in the "arbitrary grouping of slaves to create and maintain plantations in the wilderness." As Wood has suggested, these developments had dire consequences for black family life, not least of which was to impair "the comparative family stability usually associated with a high birthrate." Georgia's low black birth rate cannot be explained solely by physical debility, excessively high rates of infant mortality, or abortion. The colony's slaves, and particulary women of childbearing age, were not grossly undernourished; the diet of most slaves was adequate if monotonous. Neither is there any suggestion that abortion was rife; no contemporary commentator made any reference, however oblique, to that subject. A rate of infant mortality which approximated the 3 percent said by James Wright to characterize Georgia's slave population as a whole would go a long way toward explaining the small number of children recorded in inventories because these, after all, were the children who had survived.[44] There is no evidence that the rate of infant mortality equaled or exceeded that reported by Wright, and in this context it is significant that Habersham was complaining not about infant mortality but about the low birth rate on his estates. Whether out of humanitarian concern, economic self-interest, or a mixture of both, Georgia masters seem to have done their best to safeguard the health of their slave children. It should not be inferred, however, that diet and infant mortality were of no consequence but simply that their significance should not be exaggerated. As important, if not more, in determining the contribution made by natural increase was the social and psychological context in which black partnerships were formed and the pressures confronting every slave couple.

The first, and obvious, point to be made about the distribution of slaves in Georgia is that the colony's rapidly increasing black element and the wealth it both represented and generated were not distributed evenly over region, among the white population or between those who held slaves. Down to the 1770s blacks were heavily concentrated in the Tidewater, a fact that reflected the unsuitability of the interior regions for rice and indigo cultivation as well as the initial and continuing advantage of those Tidewater residents who already held slaves. During the two decades after 1750 the choices facing the nonslaveholder, be he an original settler or a more recent migrant, were stark. According to James Callaway, he "could either starve on the [pine] barrens, waste away in the swamps or else try to compete with large scale agriculture on the only lands left for him, those along stream beds—and even these were often malarial." Nonslaveholders tended to abandon or bypass the Tidewater in favor of "what was then the backcountry, forming settlements such as Queensborough and . . . Wrightsborough. To the larger planter . . . the development of the [lowcountry] was left." Slavery percolated only slowly into the upcountry. Indeed, it was not until the eve of the War for Independence that portions of the upcountry, and especially the "lands around the headwaters of the Rivers Broad and Ogechee," began to be settled by "small farmers from North and South Carolina and Virginia, men with few slaves or none at all."[45] The story of slavery in late colonial Georgia was the story of the Tidewater.

The absence of detailed census and tax schedules makes it difficult to ascertain how many residents of the Tidewater owned slaves. In view of contemporary estimates it may be tentatively suggested that by the early 1760s at least 5 percent of all white Georgians, and probably not less than a quarter of all households, held at least one slave.[46] A survey of the lists and inventories mentioned above suggests that the average size of slaveholdings was roughly twenty slaves but that this figure increased over time from fractionally under eleven slaves between 1755 and 1765 to over twenty-three slaves between 1766 and 1777. But although these averages are of some interest they do not tell us a great deal about the actual distribution of slaves and, more specifically, they do not reveal the extent to which Georgia's slaves and the lands they worked became concentrated in relatively few hands.

By the early 1770s, in the space of twenty years, a clearly defined and increasingly closed planter elite had taken firm root in the Tidewater. Around 5 percent of landowners controlled 20 percent of the lands that had been granted since 1755; sixty Georgians owned in excess of twenty-five hundred acres and twenty held over five thousand acres. Governor Wright owned nineteen thousand acres; James Habersham about twelve thousand acres; and the colony's largest landowner, John Graham, laid claim to roughly twenty-seven thousand acres. Of the masters included in the inventories and lists mentioned above, 6 percent owned more than fifty slaves, and altogether they accounted for roughly 45 percent of the four thousand slaves enumerated in these records.[47] At the other end of the slaveholding spectrum, 43 percent of masters owned between two and nine slaves and 13 percent held just one slave. Or, to put it in a slightly different way, 75 percent of the slaves listed lived on estates containing more than twenty slaves and only 11 percent belonged to owners who held less than ten slaves. This pyramid-shaped distribution of land and slaves, reflecting "a skewed distribution of access to financial capital,"[48] was not unique to Georgia but, on the contrary, closely reminiscent of the pattern that characterized the Tidewater regions of the other plantation colonies. But what is of particular interest is the degree to which the top of the pyramid came to be dominated by South Carolinian and West Indian migrants. Some idea of their preeminent position may be gathered from the fact that they accounted for more than half of the largest slaveholders included in the relevant lists and inventories.

The South Carolinian and West Indian newcomers, who were the main beneficiaries of the economic growth experienced by Georgia after 1750, played a decisive part in shaping many facets of the colony's burgeoning plantation economy. For example, the modes of plantation management which evolved in Georgia were imported, together with a significant proportion of

the black work force, from South Carolina.[49] But also of profound significance for the development of slavery and race relations in Georgia was the fact that the economic affluence of these
migrants was paralleled by an equally important social and political influence. Almost half the members of Georgia's first
Commons House of Assembly were South Carolinian or West
Indian in origin and, although the precise composition of the
assembly varied after 1755, their influence persisted.[50] Slavery in
Georgia did not develop in a legal and political vacuum, and the
public laws of slavery enacted by the Commons House of Assembly between 1755 and 1775 reflected the racial attitudes and
experience of these newcomers. By the mid-1760s, and thanks
mainly to the South Carolinian and West Indian influence, whatever hopes the Trustees and the early settlers might have had that
Georgia's slave system would differ profoundly from those of
the other plantation colonies had been wholly frustrated.

CHAPTER SEVEN

"THE BETTER ORDERING AND

GOVERNING OF NEGROES"

*G*eorgia's short-lived first slave code reflected many of the hopes and most of the fears frequently expressed in the debate on the Trustees' labor policy. Yet this code and the arguments that preceded it clearly demonstrate that the Trustees and their critics were in close agreement about the behavior to be expected from slaves. The main point at issue before 1750 was not the nature of the threat but the definition of an acceptable degree of risk to the white community.

Only rarely did the Trustees, some of their supporters, or seldom the malcontents address themselves to the fundamental question of why slaves behaved as they did. The malcontents suggested that the lax attitudes of the South Carolinians fostered a climate conducive to black "disorder"; the Salzburgers took the view that much of this "misbehavior" stemmed from the mistreatment of the African. Although Bolzius believed that most Africans "like to lie and steal" and that "a faithful and sincere Negro is a very rare thing," he was convinced that the latter "do exist, particularly with masters who know how to treat them in a Christian way." By abusing their slaves, "foolish masters sometimes make disloyal and malicious Negroes," and it was perfectly obvious why "very harsh treatment as regards food and work exasperates them greatly." The Salzburger critique seemed to imply that kindly treatment, including conversion to Christianity, would help to secure a desirably docile slave element. But not even Bolzius believed that this approach would succeed in all cases; some blacks would continue to resist in every way open to them because "eternal slavery to them as to all people is an unbearable yoke." As Benjamin Martyn had opined twenty years earlier, gentle treatment could not be relied upon to transform a slave into a "trusty servant."[1]

Although the participants in the slavery debate emphasized different points in their discussion of black behavior, all were agreed that aggressive responses must be expected from any blacks introduced into Georgia. Indeed, the slave code devised by the Trustees and the settlers had as one of its prime objectives the continuing security of the colony's white inhabitants. By defining a low black-to-white ratio, limiting the employment of slaves to plantation work and one or two skilled and semiskilled occupations, and providing for the slaves' spiritual welfare, the Georgians felt confident that they had remedied the most serious defects of South Carolina's slave system and, moreover, that their code stood as a model the other plantation colonies would do well to copy.[2]

Until the mid-1740s, when slaves began to be imported illegally into their colony, the Georgians based their assessment of the African and African behavior on essentially secondhand reports. Although some of the early settlers had visited South Carolina, most had no firsthand knowledge of the slave systems of the other mainland colonies. In fact, it was not until 1763, with the publication of the *Georgia Gazette,* that they were exposed in any systematic manner to the experience of those societies. But after about 1750 their perceptions of the African and attempts to regulate race relations in Georgia were both reinforced and reshaped by two significant developments. First, of course, was the introduction and rapid growth of a slave element within Georgia, which added a practical experience of the motifs of African behavior to the impressions formed during the Trusteeship. The Georgians' notions of the patterns of black behavior they might expect and their firm belief that the mistakes made by South Carolina could be avoided were put to the test. But a second development assured that this test would be of limited duration. The ideas and experience of the South Carolinian and West Indian migrants had profound, although entirely predictable, consequences for the development of slavery and race relations in Georgia. Part of this experience confirmed many of the hopes and anxieties that had been expressed before

1750; but as the slave code of 1755 demonstrated, these new-comers brought with them different ideas about the management of slaves. By the 1760s many of the features the early settlers had identified as being the most serious shortcomings of South Carolina's slave system had become the established practice in their own colony.

It is impossible to say whether, in the absence of the South Carolinians and West Indians, the Georgians would have persisted with the approach elaborated in the colony's first slave code. Bolzius believed that they would not have done so, a charge that cannot be proved or disproved.[3] All that can be said with any certainty is that from the mid-1730s the malcontents had been consistent in their criticisms of South Carolina's plantation society, and it is hard to believe that they secretly hoped or intended to introduce into Georgia practices they had frequently cited as being the major defects of that society.

After 1750 the South Carolinian and West Indian influence permeated many facets of Georgia life but was particularly evident in the public laws of slavery. In 1755 a new slave code was drafted by the Georgia Assembly and subsequently confirmed by the British authorities.[4] Unfortunately, there is no record of the deliberations that preceded the passage of legislation that was thoroughly in keeping with the South Carolina slave code of 1740.[5] It is likely, however, that the new code was drawn up in direct response to black misconduct, which seemed to be in some danger of getting out of hand. Two months before the passage of the slave code the assembly drafted "An Act for Regulating the Militia of this Province and better Defence of the same," in which it was noted that "many Inland places" were "in Danger of Incursions from Indians, and are frequently infested with fugitive Slaves, whose sudden attempts may prove fatal to many of His Majesty's Subjects."[6] Time was of the essence, and the act stated that militia officers need not obtain the governor's permission before calling out their units to "disperse, suppress, kill, destroy, apprehend take or Subdue" any group that threatened Georgia's security. But the militia would perform a second function: as yet Georgia had no formal system of slave patrols, and it was intended that the militia would assume the main responsibility for policing the colony's slaves. No doubt the continuing fear that their slaves might be recruited as part of the Spanish or French war effort was instrumental in persuading many settlers, and not least the Carolinians and West Indians who already had assumed a significant presence in the assembly, that the approach to slave management outlined in the first slave code left much to be desired.

It is also probable that the first code was posing legal difficulties because, as Kenneth Coleman has noted, it had never been "acted upon by either the Board of Trade or the Privy Council . . . the Trustees allowed slavery upon their own authority."[7] But did legislation authorized by the Trustees and not officially sanctioned by the British authorities have any legal validity after the control of Georgia reverted to the crown? Although there is no evidence that the Georgians addressed themselves to this question, it is possible that legal uncertainties regarding such fundamental points as the rights enjoyed by owners in respect to their human property played an important part in prompting the assembly to draft fresh legislation. Given the experience of the South Carolinians and West Indians, it is scarcely surprising that the assembly took as its model the slave code drafted in the aftermath of the Stono Rebellion. But the South Carolina code was not adopted wholesale; certain of the ideas and practices outlined in Georgia's first code persisted for at least another decade.

The preamble to the new code stated that one reason for this legislation was to ensure that "the owners and other persons having the Care and Government of Slaves may be restrained from exercising too great Rigour and Cruelty over them."[8] The assembly did not suggest that excessive cruelty might prompt slaves to misbehave, and neither did it argue that kindly treatment would ensure a submissive black work force. Rather, the attempt to "restrain and prevent Barbarity being exercised towards slaves," such as murder, castration, cutting out of the tongue, putting out the eye, scalding, and burning, was advocated on the grounds that "Cruelty is not only highly unbecoming those who profess themselves Christians but is odious in the

Eyes of all Men who have any Sense of Virtue or Humanity." The list of unacceptable punishments indicates the behavior the assembly expected some masters to indulge in if left to their own devices. Punishments that were deemed to be acceptable included "whipping or beating with a Horse Whip Cow Skin Switch or Small Stick" and the "putting Irons on or Confining or Imprisoning" slave offenders.[9]

In two clauses that also reflected concern with the likely behavior of owners and overseers, the code paid attention to the maintenance and conditions of employment of Georgia's slaves. Thus it was recorded that some masters worked their slaves so hard "that they have not sufficient time for natural Rest." In view of the code's stipulation that slaves must not be worked for more than sixteen hours a day and in the absence of other evidence, one can only wonder about the work requirements of those owners castigated by the assembly. The new code also required masters, upon the pain of a £3 fine for each offense, to provide their slaves with "Sufficient Cloathing Covering [and] Food." Although it would not have been difficult to draw up general guidelines, the assembly did not specify what was meant by "Sufficient." It accepted that this vague requirement would be difficult to enforce, not least because the dispersed nature of settlement meant that settlers might be unaware of offenses committed on neighboring plantations. It does not seem to have occurred to the assembly that some people might be reluctant to inform on their neighbors. Slaves would not be permitted to testify against their owners, at least not in any recognized manner, but if there was no white witness the owner concerned would be held guilty unless and until he could prove his innocence.[10] In theory, slaves would enjoy a degree of judicial protection against the worst excesses of their owners; in practice, this was seldom the case.

Although the slave code addressed itself to the material conditions of black life, it made no reference to the spiritual condition of slaves. Owners were obliged to recognize the sabbath, in that on that day slaves were forbidden to "Work or Labour (Works of absolute necessity and the necessary Occasions of the Family only Excepted)," but they were no longer required to make provision for the religious instruction of their bondsmen.[11] The slave's religious exposure would depend upon the inclination of his owner. But as we shall see, most owners did not feel themselves obliged to minister to the spiritual needs of their slaves. Indeed, far from looking to Christianity to bolster their efforts to secure a docile slave element, they believed that such exposure might have precisely the opposite effect. The Georgians preferred to rely not on religion but on the rigorous policing and harsh punishment of their slaves.

By 1755 the Georgia Assembly was greatly concerned by the inadequacies of a slave code which, even if it had any legal validity, made no provision for the supervision and punishment of slaves. The legislation enacted that year was designed to remedy the deficiencies of the earlier code in order that black misconduct be made as difficult and as futile as possible. All whites, regardless of whether they held slaves, would be legally bound to assist in the supervision of Georgia's blacks.

Although it was widely accepted that there were practical, and from the owners' standpoint highly desirable, reasons for permitting a degree of slave mobility, it was also acknowledged that once away from their owner's property slaves would have innumerable opportunities to communicate and to plot mischief. Although it would have proved virtually impossible to prevent such communication, especially in Savannah, every effort was made to ensure that when slaves left their master's property they did so only with his permission and that thereafter their behavior would be made subject to the closest possible scrutiny. Slaves could leave their owner's property only with his written permission or if accompanied by a white person, and any white citizen was entitled to challenge a slave. If a ticket from the master was not forthcoming, it was permissible to "Moderately correct such slave," and if any resistance was offered "such Slave may be Lawfully killed." But if physical punishment was inflicted without due cause the white offender was liable to pay compensation to the slave's owner.[12]

Although the movement and misconduct of individual slaves were sources of concern to the white community, far more disturbing was the prospect of "mischiefs" that might be engineered by groups of slaves. These might erupt at any time, but it was widely believed that there were certain occasions, notably weekends "and other Holidays," when extra precautions must be taken to prevent "the Wanderings and Meetings of Negroes." These were the times when whites were likely to be off their guard, and it was feared that slaves would be quick to seize the initiative. Masters were enjoined to keep a particularly close watch on their slaves and, in addition, justices of the peace were instructed to go in person or send constables on their behalf "to dispose any Assembly or meeting of Slaves which may disturb the peace or endanger the safety of his Majesty's Subjects."[13]

It is somewhat paradoxical that, at a time when it was trying to ensure the strictest possible supervision of slaves, the assembly should have relaxed the numerical balance between the races established by the first slave code. The new legislation followed the theoretical requirement in South Carolina and stipulated that masters must employ one white servant "Capable of bearing arms" for every twenty slaves they held. No doubt the Georgians believed that such a relaxation of the black-white ratio, which was very much in the economic interest of masters, would be more than compensated for by the more rigorous supervision of slaves. But in view of the concern expressed at the end of the 1750s about white migration to Georgia, the assembly may have doubted whether the supply of white servants would prove adequate for the maintenance of a lower ratio.[14]

If the slave code was concerned to make it as difficult as possible for slaves to assemble in large numbers away from the direct supervision of a white person, it was also intent upon stamping out another means of communication between slaves: masters were forbidden, upon the pain of a £15 fine, to teach their slaves to write or to "employ any Slave . . . as a Scribe." In theory, all communication between slaves would be by word of mouth, which would make the planning of organized resistance over a large area difficult. But the code also took cognizance of another form of communication that might herald an immediate danger to the white community. The South Carolina experience had shown that slaves used "Drum Horns or other loud Instruments" to "give Sign or Notice to one another of their wicked

Designs" and, for this reason, the beating of drums or the blowing of horns in slave quarters was prohibited.[15]

Predictably, the code also tried to ensure that slaves would be denied access to any materials that might be used to initiate or further violent resistance. That slaves were forbidden "to Carry and make use of Fire Arms or any Offensive Weapon whatsoever" and that justices of the peace were authorized "to Search all suspected places" for illicit arms and ammunition comes as no great surprise. But what is surprising is that the assembly was prepared to tolerate exceptions to this rule. As was the case in South Carolina, necessity explains why some blacks, albeit only in clearly defined circumstances and subject always to the closest supervision, would be permitted to use firearms. The assembly recognized that it might be helpful to masters were certain of their slaves allowed "to hunt and kill game Cattle Mischievious Birds or Beasts of Prey" but, although owners were left to decide which, if any, of their slaves would be allowed the use of a gun, they were required to observe certain precautions. Any slave given a gun must have "a Tickett or Licence" from his owner, which had to be renewed monthly, or be accompanied by "some white person of the Age of Sixteen Years or upwards." Guns must be returned to the owner every evening, and slaves were strictly forbidden to be in the possession of arms at the weekend.[16]

The collective necessity of the white community explains why the militia act of 1755 authorized slaves to be armed for a more important purpose than "keeping off Birds within the plantation." At roughly the same time as it was formulating a slave code based on the premise that slavery in Georgia would be characterized by violent black misconduct, the assembly enacted legislation that provided for the recruitment of Africans into the militia. These black recruits would not be confined to menial roles but, if necessary, would serve as combat troops. This apparently paradoxical situation is explained by the imperial rivalries along the southern frontier in 1755 and the assembly's belief that the white manpower available in Georgia would be insufficient to repel a concerted attack by Spain or France or, if the worst came to the worst, by both powers. However unpalatable it might have been to some Georgians, the only realistic option open to the assembly was to arm a certain number of carefully selected slaves.

Earlier in the century similar considerations to those that now obtained in Georgia had prompted South Carolina to enlist slaves for service in the Yamasee War, and it might have been this precedent which prompted the assembly to declare that "experience" had shown that "several Negro's and other Slaves have in Time of Warr behaved themselves with great faithfullness and Courage in repelling the Attacks of his Majesty's Enemys."[17] By their actions these black combatants had "demonstrated that Trust and Confidence may in Some Instances be repos'd in them."[18] The key words here were "in Some Instances." The qualities of "great Faithfullness" and "Courage" and the "Trust and Confidence" which they might inspire were not considered by the assembly, or the white community at large, to be characteristics common to all Africans. Indeed, the Georgians recognized that some blacks, if entrusted with guns, would prefer to turn their weapons against their owners rather than against "his Majesty's Enemy's." But the important point is that partly as a result of the Carolina experience and partly because of an increasing familiarity with their own African slaves, the Georgians had come to appreciate that there was no single mode of black behavior. They recognized that black behavior was not restricted to the unrelenting and uncompromising aggression predicted by all the participants in the slavery debate. Although the conduct of some slaves conformed to that pattern and had to be guarded against, other bondsmen, for whatever the reason, behaved in a manner that seemed to be deserving of the white community's "Trust and Confidence."

The question remained, however, as to which slaves would qualify for military service should the need for additional manpower ever arise. The militia act did not lay down hard and fast rules but said simply that those Africans "most faithful and fit for service" might be called upon to assist in the defense of Georgia. Obviously, those best qualified to assess which slaves fitted that description were owners and overseers; choices would be based on a close personal knowledge of individual slaves rather than on any personality traits assumed to be characteristic of particular groups of Africans. But in order that the colonial authorities might have an accurate and up-to-date record of the number of slaves theoretically available for service, masters were required to provide annual lists of all their male slaves aged between sixteen and sixty. They were assured that any blacks called up for military duty would serve alongside and under the immediate supervision of whites in regular militia units.[19] There was no question of forming separate black companies; the white community's "Trust and Confidence" did not extend that far. But even so, the willingness to entertain the possibility of using black troops ran completely counter to the arguments which twenty years earlier had prompted the Trustees to exclude black slavery from the colony.

Recognizing that, however serious might be the emergency which confronted Georgia, some masters would be reluctant to lose the services of their slaves, the assembly decreed that owners would receive one shilling per diem for the duration of the bondsman's service. They would be paid "the full value" of any slave killed in action and appropriate compensation for those who were "maimed and disabled." For the slave, however, there was little incentive. Those who survived would not automatically qualify for freedom but would be returned to their owners at the end of their tour of duty. The militia act did hold out the slender possibility of emancipation for some slave soldiers. Those who "Shall Couragiously behave . . . in Battle so as to kill any one of the Enemy or take a prisoner alive or Shall take any of their Colours" and whose action was witnessed by a white officer would receive their freedom. Any slave whose valor fell short of these requirements but who had behaved under fire in such a way as "to deserve public Notice" would receive annually from the colonial authorities "a Livery Coat, and pair of Breeches, made of good red Negro Cloth turn'd up in Blue, and a Black Hat and pair of Black Shoes." The icing on this particular cake was that on every anniversary of his endeavor the slave would "be free'd and exempted from all personal Labour & Service" to his owner.[20]

The slave code of 1755 was concerned not with the freedom

that might be granted to slaves as the result of valiant deeds undertaken in defense of Georgia but with the freedom that might be seized by blacks acting on their own initiative and in defiance of the white community. For the same reasons as those elaborated before 1750, the Georgians were particularly concerned by the fact that the Spaniards persisted with their policy of encouraging slaves to flee to Florida. Although it was anticipated that the ticket system and the other restrictions imposed on slave mobility would limit the opportunities for successful escape, the authors of the slave code took additional steps in an attempt to counter the Spanish threat. Anyone who apprehended a slave runaway would receive a cash payment, and the further south the slave was taken the greater would be the reward.[21] Those who recaptured runaways might also claim "Two pence Sterling" for every mile they had traveled in order to return the fugitive. If the slave's owner could not be identified, and the code required that runaways taken in Georgia must be advertised as widely as possible, he or she would be placed in the custody of a constable and, if unclaimed after eighteen months, sold at public auction. The proceeds of the sale would be applied to the reward and mileage charges due to the slave's captor and to the maintenance costs that had accrued over the previous year and a half.[22] This procedure was modified slightly in the early 1760s when unidentified runaways were sent to the workhouse in Savannah. During the remainder of the colonial period the workhouse served another important function. If all else failed, owners could send their "stubborn obstinate or incorrigible Negroes" to the workhouse, where they would "be kept to hard Labour or otherwise . . . corrected." Owners would be charged for the upkeep of their slaves at the rate of sixpence a day and would pay an additional "one Shilling and four pence for each Chastisement."[23]

The slave code was concerned not only to prevent various forms of black misconduct but also to establish clearly defined judicial procedures for those crimes and misdemeanors deemed serious enough to warrant public attention. The Georgia Assembly ruled out the possibility of condemning slave malefactors unheard. "Natural Justice" demanded that all individuals, regardless of their "Condition," be allowed their day in court.

Slave offenses that would come under the purview of the colonial authorities were divided into two categories: capital and
noncapital. The misdeeds itemized under each of these headings
were broadly similar to those set out in the slave codes of the
other plantation colonies.[24] Capital offenses, which included insurrection, attempted insurrection, murder, the destruction of
certain types of property, and, in some circumstances, striking a
white person,[25] would be tried by two justices of the peace and
"not less than Three or more than five [freeholders] in the District where the Offence shall be Committed." Justice would be
dispensed as speedily as possible: capital courts were required to
sit not later than "three days after" the slave defendant had been
charged. The convening of such courts was not simply a charade.
Some slaves, such as "the negro . . . taken up on suspicion of
being concerned in poisoning Mrs Laroche," were "found not
guilty and acquitted."[26]

Although the slave code specified a range of offenses that were
punishable by death, it did not stipulate the form the death
penalty should take. Instead, courts were instructed to select
"such manner of Death" as would be "most Effectual to deter
others from Offending in like manner." In practice, the courts
always opted for death by hanging or by fire. The same mode
was used to punish offenses of such "an enormous nature and of
the most pernicious consequences" deemed to be "Felony without the Benefit of Clergy." Such a death would be the lot of any
slave who "wilfully" or "Maliciously" destroyed "any Stack of
Rice corn or other grain of the product growth or Manufacture
of this province . . . any Tar Kiln Barrels of pitch Tar Turpentine
or Rozin." Not surprisingly, the items on this list included some
of Georgia's most valuable export commodities—likely targets
of black saboteurs. Two other offenses, the stealing of slaves and
the deliberate poisoning of "any Freeman Woman Servant or
Slave," were also included under the heading of "Felony without
the Benefit of Clergy."[27]

Slaves accused of noncapital crimes would be summoned before a court composed of one justice of the peace and two freeholders. These courts, which met at the convenience of the
whites concerned, were authorized to inflict corporal punish-

ment "not extending to the taking away [of] life or member." If the court believed that the evidence presented suggested an offense more serious than that with which the defendant had been charged, it could summon an additional justice and the requisite number of freeholders and proceed as a capital court.[28]

The assembly believed that some masters might "be tempted" to conceal even the most serious crimes because they preferred to dispense their own brand of justice rather than lose the services of their slaves for the length of time it took for the official judicial procedure to run its course.[29] Other masters might fail to report capital offenses involving property rather than risk the execution and thereby the permanent loss not only of a worker but also of a valuable capital asset. To circumvent this problem the slave code provided for compensation of up to £50 to be paid to owners of executed slaves. The stick was that anyone who concealed a capital crime would be liable to a fine of £50. Those who failed to report a noncapital offense could be fined up to £20.[30]

The final section of the slave code was concerned with the employment of slaves, a subject that had prompted exhaustive discussion during the Trusteeship. The Trustees and the malcontents had agreed that some occupations would present slaves with excellent opportunities of offering violent resistance and, moreover, that because of the low wages they commanded blacks ought to be restricted in their occupations so as not to discourage white migration to Georgia. Although the second of these points was debated in the late 1750s, it was not referred to explicitly in the slave code. Neither was any mention made of the dangers that might attend the employment of slaves as domestic servants. The assembly's main concern was not to restrict slave employment but to try to tighten up controls on those slaves who were permitted by their owners "to go and work where they please upon Condition of paying to their [master] certain Sums of money." Like Bolzius before them, Georgia's legislators believed that this was a highly undesirable practice because it encouraged blacks to "pilfer and Steal to raise money for their Owners as well to Maintain themselves in Drunkenness and evil Courses."[31] The assembly tried to remedy matters by introducing a ticket system for slaves who worked out and eventually drafted an ordinance that established clearly defined rates of pay and conditions of employment for those slaves who worked as porters and carters in Savannah.

Although the slave code of 1755 laid the basis and established the legal superstructure of slavery and race relations in late colonial Georgia, it was supplemented by additional legislation that elaborated the theme that precautions must be taken by all whites to guard against the misbehavior of the colony's slaves. In large measure this legislation, such as the act of 1770 which required that all white males who attended "any Church" must be armed with "a gun, or a pair of pistols . . . with at least six charges of gunpowder and ball," paralleled procedures in force in South Carolina.[32] This was certainly true of the two acts passed in 1757 which created a watch in Savannah and slave patrols elsewhere in Georgia.

By 1757 the assembly had formed the opinion that Georgia required a more formal system of slave surveillance than that provided by the slave code and militia act of 1755. It also recognized that an urban setting presented opportunities for misconduct of a type usually denied rural slaves, and it was with a view to diminishing these opportunities that a ten o'clock curfew was imposed on Savannah's blacks. The slave code required that justices of the peace and constables assume the main responsibility for policing the town's slaves; the new act not only established a more regular system of surveillance but also spread the responsibility for the same. Thus the curfew would be enforced by a watch of between five and ten men, which would patrol the streets "on every night throughout the year." All white men aged between sixteen and sixty, with the exception of ministers of religion, would be "oblig'd & made liable to do Watch duty."[33] A second act extended this system of public policing to the countryside. The rural patrols created by this legislation were instructed to "visit every Plantation within their respective Districts once in every Month" and, whenever they thought it necessary, "to search and examine all Negro-Houses for offensive Weapons and Ammunition." They were also authorized to enter any "disorderly tipling-House, or other Houses suspected of harbouring, trafficking or dealing with Negroes" and, like the Savannah watch, could inflict corporal punishment on any slave found to have left his owner's property without permission.[34]

It is important to emphasize that all white males, including nonslaveholders, were being called upon to police Georgia's slaves and that nonslaveholders were being required to fulfill the additional function of safeguarding the property interests of the rapidly emerging planter elite. But most were willing to comply with this requirement. At a time when Georgia society was becoming characterized by great inequalities in the distribution of wealth, race, particularly racial fears, united the members of that society in a common cause.

The slave code of 1755 continued in force for a decade. Early in 1765 the assembly, with the approval of Governor Wright, enacted a fresh code which, although based on that of 1755, was noticeably harsher than that which it replaced.[35] In many respects 1765 marked the final break with the ideals and practices advocated in Georgia's first slave code. The persistence of these ideals and practices after 1765 reflected the choice of individual owners rather than the consequence of a course of action legally demanded of them.

There were three major and several minor points of difference between the slave codes of 1755 and 1765. Thus the latter made some adjustments to the judicial procedures applicable in cases involving slaves, including a provision that allowed capital courts to take cognizance of "any favourable Circumstances" and delay execution "until the Matter can be laid before the Governor . . . and his Pleasure known therein."[36] The fine for the concealment of slave crimes was increased to £200, and there were other, but generally less severe, amendments to the penalties imposed on whites for such offenses as abusing the ticket system. The removal of the Spanish threat after 1763 explains why greater rewards were no longer offered for runaways taken in the south of the colony.

The three main points of difference between the two codes were the absence in the new code of any directives concerning the maintenance of slaves; the attention paid to the possible use of poison by bondsmen; and the attempt to encourage free blacks to settle in Georgia. Although the new legislation was concerned to ensure that masters were not unduly harsh in the punishments they meted out—the list of unacceptable punishments was unchanged—no mention was made of the hours of work, material comforts, or spiritual condition of Georgia's slaves. Only the regulation concerning Sunday work remained in force.

The only reference to poison in the code of 1755 was in the list of crimes deemed to be "Felony without the Benefit of Clergy," which scarcely suggests that poison constituted one of the most important weapons available to Georgia's slaves. The new code more than compensated for the neglect, or oversight, of the earlier legislation: no fewer than five clauses were devoted to the subject. Why poison should have assumed such a significance in 1765 is unclear. Although the code drawn up in that year noted that "The detestable Crime of poisoning hath frequently been committed by Slaves," there is no evidence that Georgia's bondsmen indulged in an orgy of poisoning, or attempting to poison, their masters during the decade after 1755. It seems that the Georgians, who modeled this section of their legislation on the South Carolinian slave code of 1740 and the additional ordinance drawn up by that colony in 1751, were responding as much to the anticipated as to the actual behavior of their slaves. No doubt a report in the *South Carolina Gazette* early in 1761 that the colony's slaves had "again begun the hellish practice of poisoning" had not escaped their attention.[37]

Begining in April 1763 with the publication of the *Georgia Gazette,* the Georgians received regular reports of slave misconduct and often violence elsewhere in the Americas. The *Gazette,* in keeping with most colonial newspapers, made no attempt to suppress or play down reports of black misbehavior but, on the contrary, published accounts that can have served only to heighten white anxieties. Two examples drawn from 1763 demonstrate this point. On 7 July the *Gazette* included reports of slave resistance in Surinam and Jamaica. In Surinam twenty-two plantations had been "cut off by the Negroes who, in the most cruel manner, murdered all the white people they could come at.

The inhabitants are in the most miserable condition . . . and it is generally thought that the colony will be intirely ruined." Of importance were the reference to the indiscriminate violence indulged in by the black rebels and the inference that slaves had it in their power to effect the complete overthrow of white society. If anything, the bulletin from Jamaica was even more gruesome. Apparently, "a number of Negroes" had rebelled and, in the process, visited "one house, and butchered the master by cutting off his hands, then his arms, his feet, and legs, and then broke his thighs. They afterwards killed three of his children." These accounts provided awesome reminders, if the Georgians needed any reminder, of what might happen if the white community ignored the precautions set out in the slave code.

From the outset the *Gazette* published accounts of slave misbehavior closer to home. The first edition of the newspaper, for example, reported the murder of Alexander Crawford, an overseer on John Milledge's plantation, by the slave Scipio and "A most shocking murder" which had been committed "near Orangeburg, by a negro fellow belonging to one John Meyer." Meyer's slave was said to have "murdered Mrs. Meyer, her daughter about 16 years of age, and her suckling infant." This "cruel wretch" then "dressed himself in his masters best clothes, and set fire to the house, which was burnt to the ground."[38] Other, less violent misconduct, and most notably running away, was also reported in the *Gazette* during the 1760s and early 1770s.

No doubt white anxieties were also reinforced by the rapid growth of Georgia's black element after the mid-1750s. Between 1750 and 1766 the colony's black population increased from around five hundred to approximately seventy-eight hundred. But from the white standpoint the growth of the black component relative to that of the white element was probably more important than the absolute increase. In the early 1750s blacks accounted for around 20 percent of Georgia's population; within fifteen years that percentage had doubled.[39]

Although fears of slave misbehavior had found an important expression in the slave code of 1755, they took on a much sharper focus in the legislation enacted in 1765 and, as mentioned above, nowhere was this more evident than in those clauses concerned with poison. By 1765 the mere enumeration of poisoning as a "Felony without the Benefit of Clergy" was deemed to be insufficient defense against "one of the most logical and lethal methods [of] black resistance."[40] The new code, in language similar to that employed by the South Carolinians in 1740 and 1751, stipulated death for any black found guilty of poisoning "any Person or Persons, (whether free or bond)" or who was "privy (and not reveal the same) to the furnishing, procuring or conveying any Poison to be administered by any Person or Persons." Obviously, the assembly was hoping that blacks might inform on their compatriots because although it did not promise freedom to informers it did guarantee a reward of £1 per annum and exemption from labor on every anniversary of "the Day that such discovery was made." But blacks were cautioned against giving false evidence: any black who misinformed the colonial authorities was likely to suffer the same fate as the person he had testified against. In two other clauses the assembly attempted to prevent the dissemination of knowledge concerning the art of poisoning. Any slave who taught "another Slave in the Knowledge of any Poisonous Root, Plant, Herb or other sort of poison" would be sentenced to death, and the slave so instructed would suffer corporal punishment. Slaves who administered "Medicine or pretended Medicine" to other blacks without first having obtained the permission of a white person could also expect a whipping.[41]

Without doubt the most surprising section of the slave code of 1765 was that pertaining to free blacks. Of course, Georgia was not the first colony to legislate for its free blacks, and neither was this the first time in its history that free blacks had been the subject of attention. But why the assembly should have resurrected the idea of attracting free blacks to the colony, albeit not as a substitute for slaves, is a matter for speculation. A partial explanation was provided in its declaration that Georgia had made "no Provision" for the "further Protection Priviledge and Encouragement or for the Trial and Punishment of Persons born of free parents being Mulattoes or Mestizoes." Free mulattoes and free blacks were in an anomalous position and, although they numbered fewer than one hundred, it is not surprising that the assembly should have wished to clarify their legal situation. More puzzling is the fact that the slave code talked of ways whereby free blacks might be encouraged to settle in Georgia. If they were willing to "give good Testimony of their humble duty and loyalty to his Majesty and their Obedience to the Laws and their Affection to the Inhabitants," they would not only be allowed to enter the colony but also to apply for naturalization. Once naturalized, they would enjoy "all the Rights, Priviledges, Powers and Immunities whatsoever which any Person born of British parents within this Province may, can, might, could or of Right ought to have." The one significant exception was that they would not be permitted to "vote for or be Elected a Member" of the assembly.[42]

Had the Georgians been confronted by an aggressive Spanish presence in Florida this section of their slave code might have been explained by military need. After all, they had intimated that if necessary they would arm certain of their slaves, and free blacks would have proved an attractive proposition as front line troops. But there was not such a critical need for military manpower in the mid-1760s, and it is probable that the assembly was concerned with Georgia's economic advancement rather than its military security. In 1758 it had made a half-hearted attempt to encourage white migrants by forbidding slaves to occupy various skilled and semiskilled positions in the urban economy, and it is possible that this was another attempt to attract free labor.[43] No doubt the assembly's thinking was similar to that of the Trustees: free blacks would have no reason to resist the white community. But the attempt to attract free blacks proved very short-lived.

In 1767, much to the Georgians' surprise and anguish, their slave code was disallowed by the British authorities.[44] It was not immediately apparent to them why this should have been the case, but eventually Governor Wright's frantic inquiries elicited the reply that the problem centered on the definition of slaves as chattels rather than as real estate. In the meantime the Georgians were left without a valid slave code, and they considered their situation to be absolutely desperate. As Wright explained to the Board of Trade, "The Negro Law is so absolutely Essential to our Local Circumstances, that without a Law to keep our Slaves in Order, no Man's life or Property would be safe a Moment. In Short our very existence depends upon it." In order to "Prevent the Province from being thrown into the utmost Confusion & distress," Wright contravened his instructions and approved a slave code that would remain in force for a year. He hoped that by the end of that time the situation regarding the disallowed legislation would be clarified. After further consultations with the Board of Trade, which resulted in the Georgians being allowed to define their slaves as chattels, a new slave code was drawn up in 1770.[45]

The code of 1770, which remained on the statute books for the rest of the colonial period, was similar to that of 1765, but with two main differences. First, the rape or attempted rape of a white woman and the breaking into or destruction "of any dwelling house or other building" were added to the list of capital crimes.[46] Second, the clause pertaining to free blacks was omitted. Why this was done is unclear, but one very plausible explanation lends itself for consideration. Although few in number, Savannah's free blacks not only presented an example of black freedom to their enslaved compatriots but also encouraged the misbehavior of the town's slaves. In 1773, for example, the Grand Jury complained that "free Negroes are allowed to rent houses, whereby many notorious offenders are encouraged and screened from publick Justice."[47] But this is not to say that relations between free blacks and slaves were always amicable. Thus in 1768 the slave Dickson was sentenced to death for "the Murder of a free Negroe" and, although the court recommended mercy, it appears that he was executed.[48] But obviously the assembly, probably reacting to pressure brought to bear by constituents who were uneasy about the relationship between slaves and free blacks, had second thoughts about the desirability of augmenting the colony's black element with a significant number of free blacks.

The sum total of the increasingly rigorous legislation enacted between 1755 and 1770 was to impose, at least in theory, a clearly defined and closely supervised code of behavior on Georgia's slaves. But for the majority of slaves the private law operative on their owner's estate was much more significant than the public laws of slavery. In fact, public laws designed to contain black misbehavior made as many, if not more, demands of whites. All whites were expected to involve themselves in the attempt to secure a docile and submissive black work force. But the practical experience of the years after 1750, which was instrumental in persuading the assembly of the need to tighten the public laws of slavery, was to demonstrate that the Georgians were only partially successful in both endeavors.

CHAPTER EIGHT

THE PUBLIC LIVES OF

GEORGIA BLACKS

lthough the mode of slave employment which characterized late colonial Georgia reflected the persistence of the economic needs that had been expressed clearly during the course of the slavery debate, it did not conform precisely to the pattern envisaged in the colony's first slave code. The malcontents had insisted that Africans would constitute a much cheaper and more productive agricultural work force than white servants, and this proposition was not called into question after 1750. On the contrary, it was precisely this belief which underpinned the development of Georgia's plantation economy. But the lower maintenance costs associated with slaves largely explains why the Georgians came to disagree about the desirability, rather than the advisability, of employing bondsmen as skilled and semiskilled workers.

Before 1750 the Trustees and some of their supporters had argued that the low wages commanded by slaves would discourage white migration to the colony; thereafter a similar argument was used by Georgia's white artisans and craftsmen who, although not objecting to the employment of Africans in the agricultural sector, believed that their own economic well-being would be severely jeopardized were they forced to compete with cheaper black workers. These fears found limited expression in legislation enacted by the Georgia Assembly in 1758. In that year the assembly, reacting to pressure exerted by local artisans, declared its intent "to encourage white Tradesmen to Settle in the several Towns within this Province" and, in the process, to safeguard the interests of those craftsmen already in Georgia, "by preventing the employing Negroes & other Slaves being handicraft Tradesmen in the said Towns." The only slave artisans whom the residents of Savannah, Augusta, Frederica, and Ebenezer would be allowed to employ were those who worked as "Ship-wrights, calkers, Sawyers, [and] Coopers." All other trades and crafts would be reserved to whites. The act did permit some exceptions. The assembly recognized that some artisans owned slaves who had "been brought up to" their "Trade" and, provided that their slaves had followed this "Trade" for at least a year, they would not be "debarred the privilege & benefit of such negro or other slaves Work." Georgia's legislators feared that in the absence of black competition white artisans might be tempted to "make Exorbitant Demands for their respective Work," and to prevent this they appointed commissioners who would meet annually "to Limit rate and appoint the Price of the work of all Carpenters Joiners Bricklayers and Plaisterers either by the day week or Month." If any white tradesman held out for a higher rate than that fixed by the commissioners it would be lawful for his customers "to engage and employ in that particular work any negroe or other slave Artificers without Limitation."[1]

From the artisans' standpoint the legislation drafted in 1758 by an assembly dominated by planters, who had a vested interest in retaining the maximum flexibility in the employment of their slaves, left much to be desired. First, those tradesmen cited in the act could not be expected to enthuse over the external regulation of their fees. Moreover, the legislation offered them no formal means of redress should those fees be fixed at an unacceptably low level. Their choice was simple: they could accept the sum stipulated by the commissioners or see their work taken by slaves. Second, the assembly confined its attention to the urban economy. No limitations were placed on the employment of skilled and semiskilled slaves on the colony's farms and plantations. Finally, no mention was made of the hiring out of skilled and semiskilled slaves. Those planters who sat in the assembly were keenly aware that skilled slaves had an economic value over and above that which accrued from the work they performed on their owner's estate, and they were unwilling to forego the income that might derive from their hire. By the same token, they had no wish to deny themselves the possibility of engaging cheaper black labor as and when the need arose. Their view did not change over the course of the next twenty years and, because of the political influence they continued to exert, the Georgia Assembly never restricted the hiring out of skilled and semiskilled bondsmen. The only legal obligation under which masters were placed was that of providing slaves who worked "out of their respective Houses" with "a Tickett in Writing." Similarly, it was forbidden to employ a slave who was not in possession of such a document.[2] Depending upon the precise nature of their skills, white artisans could expect to meet the full force of black competition, and by the end of the 1750s the element of protection promised by Georgia's first slave code had virtually disappeared.

The objective of Georgia's farmers and planters was economic self-sufficiency, and this often meant that slaves were required to undertake most of the skilled and semiskilled tasks associated with the day-to-day operation of their owner's estate. These tasks covered a broad spectrum: slaves worked as sawyers, coopers, carpenters, bricklayers, blacksmiths, cordwainers, tailors, and seamstresses.[3]

Obviously, the occupational structure of a slaveholding depended upon the nature of the master's economic operation and the number of slaves at his disposal. The manner in which John Graham deployed his 262 slaves points to the range of skills and the high proportion of skilled and semiskilled bondsmen typical of Georgia's largest slaveholdings. Of Graham's slaves, 190 were described as "Field Slaves" and presumably lacked any specialized occupational skills, and four were employed as drivers. The remainder of his work force included fourteen sawyers, fourteen seamstresses and washerwomen, twelve squarers and carters, eight house carpenters, five coopers, four gardeners, three boatmen, two blacksmiths, two cooks, a tailor, a bricklayer, a coachman, and a hairdresser.[4] Just over a quarter of his slaves filled skilled or semiskilled positions, apparently on a full-time basis. But in the size of their slaveholdings and the options thereby open to them, owners such as Graham, Wright, and Habersham were the exceptions. As we have seen, far more typical were those masters who held less than ten slaves.[5] Yet although occupational structures varied somewhat from estate to estate, there was one major difference and one very important point of similarity between the employment patterns found on these smaller properties and those that characterized Georgia's largest plantations.

On most farms and plantations, regardless of their size, the majority of slaves worked as unskilled laborers. For obvious reasons, the smaller estates did not contain the range of specialized skills available to such planters as John Graham and, predictably, the skills that were most in evidence on these properties were those connected with the productive side of the master's economic operation. So far as most farmers and planters were concerned, skills like sawing and squaring, coopering, and carpentry assumed a top priority; hairdressers and coachmen were nonproductive hands who, depending upon the success of the owner's economic endeavor and his social pretensions, might be added to the estate at some future date. In this context, it is not without interest that the fears expressed during the Trustee period concerning the potential threat to white life and limb posed by black domestics persisted after 1750. But it is not entirely clear just how important the fear of physical assault was in determining employment patterns; economic and social considerations were probably more significant. Many owners could not afford to employ black domestics, at least not on a full-time basis; others wanted to employ them for purely social reasons. Masters were aware of the prestige that attached to the ownership of black servants and, as Alexander Hewatt observed, it was often "out of mere ostentation" that they ran the risks involved in having blacks "about their families."[6]

The employment patterns that characterized Georgia's towns suggest that in practice the Act of 1758 counted for little. Indeed, planters were so opposed to any restrictions being placed on the ways in which they could employ their slaves that when the act expired in 1765 it was not renewed.[7] During the 1760s and 1770s urban slaves worked as brickmakers, bricklayers, chimney sweeps, blacksmiths, blockmakers, carpenters, and tailors. Generally speaking, the only trades closed to them were those such as silversmithing and cabinetmaking which called for a high degree of technical expertise.[8] But in the towns, as in the countryside, the skilled slave was the exception. Most blacks were employed as unskilled workers and, given the growing importance of the port of Savannah, this often meant that they worked as porters and carters.

The avilable evidence suggests that no more than about 10 percent of Georgia's slaves occupied skilled or semiskilled positions on a full-time basis. In the absence of detailed work schedules it is impossible to say how many slaves divided their time between skilled, semiskilled, and unskilled activities. It is evident, however, that on many properties, both urban and rural, and especially on those employing relatively few hands, a slave might be required to undertake several different types of work. For example, Samuel Douglass employed a West Indian–born slave named Jack who "understands a little of the house carpenter's business; [and is] also a good waiting man." Sambo, a country-born slave owned by Philip Dell, was even more versatile: he was "a good hand to plow, to cut with an axe . . . work with a hoe, saw with a whip saw, . . . or to do any plantation work [and] pretends to be a kind of taylor."[9] Obviously, it made a great deal of economic sense to employ slaves who could turn their hands to different types of work, and it may be safely assumed that Jack and Sambo were by no means atypical.

Little is known of Georgia's skilled and semiskilled slaves other than their names, occupations, market values, and, occasionally, their ages and places of birth. All that can be said with certainty is that they were not recruited exclusively from any one section of the colony's black element. Slave women occupied various skilled and semiskilled positions and not just those of a domestic nature. Some did work as cooks and seamstresses, but others were employed alongside their menfolk as sawyers and squarers. Neither were skilled and semiskilled jobs reserved to country-born slaves; African-born bondsmen worked as sawyers, coopers, and brickmakers and were also used to man Georgia's trading boats.[10] Unfortunately, the records that have survived shed no light on the relationship between skilled and unskilled slaves or between domestic servants and field hands. For example, it is by no means clear whether valuable and often highly valued skilled workers received preferential treatment such as was likely to cause resentment in the slave quarters. It is equally impossible to say whether, because of their skills and regardless of any favored treatment, they were held in especially high regard by their unskilled compatriots. These, like so many other aspects of slave life in late colonial Georgia, are shrouded in mystery.

The annual and daily work regimes experienced by Georgia's slaves depended, first, upon their occupation, which in turn reflected their owner's place of residence and the nature of his economic operation, and, second, upon the amount of work their owner or overseer expected them to complete on any given day. Although the assembly addressed itself to the question of how much work ought to be demanded of slaves, the regulations it drafted imposed no serious constraints on owners. Of course, it is hardly surprising that the planters who dominated the assembly should have sanctioned a six-day working week and up to a sixteen-hour working day for slaves. But masters were able to exact even more work than this: they could employ their slaves in "Works of absolute necessity" on the sabbath and were left to decide for themselves what "Works" fitted such a description.[11]

Although Georgia's planters were concerned to produce such cash crops as rice, indigo, and tobacco, they did not ignore their own food requirements and few, if any, estates were single-crop operations. Most planters set aside some land for the cultivation of foodstuffs, which usually included Indian corn, beans, peas, potatoes, and garden crops, and many satisfied their meat requirements by raising livestock and poultry. Needless to say, crop and livestock mixes varied and reflected the economic possibilities presented by the local environment, the size of the plantation, and the size of the slave work force. Generally, however, in determining how many acres would be allocated to particular crops, masters worked on the assumption that a slave could "plant and cultivate" between three and five acres of rice and up to "10 acres of corn and potatoes" a year.[12] Bearing in mind that crop and livestock mixes varied, but that it would have been a most unusual estate which did not combine the production of at least one staple crop with the cultivation of the foodstuffs mentioned above, it is possible to reconstruct an annual work regime that would have been familiar to most of Georgia's planters and their slaves.

Although there was an essential continuity about the plantation year, agricultural operations usually got under way at the end of March, when "all the Negroes" were set to work planting potatoes and Indian corn. According to Bolzius, masters expected "a good Negro man or woman" to plant at least half an acre of corn a day. The two main staple crops, rice and indigo, were also planted in late March or early April, the latter on lands that had been plowed, or more commonly hoed, during the preceding winter. Indigo required little further attention before being harvested some four months later; it was then that the most arduous and unpleasant part of indigo production began.[13] Once they had planted the indigo crop, field hands could give their undivided attention to other commodities. Rice production, on the other hand, involved a complex sequence of hoeings and floodings, and the cultivation of other crops had to be fitted into the periods between these essential operations.

The six weeks or so between the planting and the first hoeing of the rice crop were devoted to the weeding of cornfields and, for men and women alike, "a day's work [was] half an acre" and the planting of beans among the corn. The corn and beans were weeded for a second time during the three- to four-week interval before the first flooding of the rice fields. The rice was flooded and hoed in mid-May, when each hand was expected to "complete $\frac{1}{4}$ acre daily." This part of rice cultivation, and that which followed, involved grueling and unpleasant labor.[14]

The corn and bean fields were tended during the weeks immediately before and after the hoeing and flooding of the rice crop in early July. After being hoed for a fourth time, the rice was harvested "at the end of August or in September." It was then threshed, winnowed, and stamped before being packed, often in barrels produced by the plantations's slave sawyers, and shipped to market. The beans were picked at the same time as the rice was being harvested, and the corn was harvested last.[15]

It was very much in every master's interest to ensure that his slaves were gainfully employed throughout the year, and on most estates this meant that the winter months were given over to land clearance, which provided timber for domestic use or for sale off the plantation, effecting repairs, and preparing lands for cultivation. Garden crops might be planted "During the 12 days after Christmas."[16] One way and another, owners ensured that their slaves were kept fully occupied until the end of March when the planting season began anew.

The public laws of slavery stipulated that every slaveholding must be supervised by "a White person" and, moreover, that the ratio between "Working" slaves and white men must not exceed twenty, and in some cases twenty-five, to one.[17] This ratio accorded with the contemporary belief that "thirty slaves is a proper number . . . to be tended with one overseer."[18] Most masters, and the majority held less than twenty slaves, complied with these requirements, and in all but a very few cases, plantation slaves performed their work under the close supervision of a white person.[19] On small and medium-sized estates, which meant on most estates, it was likely that they would be supervised by their owner; on larger plantations, or if their masters did not live in Georgia or farmed at more than one location, they were supervised by an overseer who had been engaged specifically for that purpose. Some slaves saw little, if anything, of their owner. William Knox, for example, who by the mid-1770s owned more than one hundred slaves in Georgia, did not visit the colony after 1761 and was content to leave the management of his Knoxborough estate to an overseer.[20] James Habersham, although not an absentee owner, managed his slaves from a distance after the mid-1760s. In 1765 he remarked that since his wife's death he had "almost wholly resided" in Savannah. His Silk Hope plantation, only seven miles away, had become "disagreeable" to him, and he did not "sleep there more than once in 14 Days." Habersham found "the rice Fields pernicious to [his] health" and visited them only "once a Season," but he claimed that his "Business is as well executed, as any Planters in the Province."[21] He took a keen interest in every facet of his agricultural operations but delegated the responsibility for the daily deployment of his slaves to his three overseers.

There is a dearth of evidence concerning the backgrounds and qualifications of those employed as overseers. John Lynn, for example, who was hired by John Gibbons, had arrived in Georgia as an indentured servant and, it must be assumed, had limited experience with plantation agriculture. Other overseers were more experienced than Lynn and, as Bolzius and the Trustees had predicted, included men who had been displaced by slave workers.[22]

During the 1760s and 1770s Georgia planters usually secured the services of an overseer by word of mouth, by advertising in the *Georgia Gazette,* or by replying to an advertisement placed in the *Gazette* by a would-be overseer. The duration of an overseer's appointment, the duties required of him, and the payment he would receive were usually set down in a formal contract of employment. The length of service depended upon the requirements of the planter and the applicant, but usually overseers were engaged on an annual basis. In some cases, and especially if they were dubious about the suitability of the man they were hiring, owners required the applicant to work for a trial period.[23] Overseers were paid in one of two ways: some received a salary of between £25 and £40 per annum and usually their board and keep; others contracted for a sum of money plus an agreed proportion of certain commodities produced on the estate.[24] If the overseer was married, his wife might help out around the plantation. Her duties could include cooking, making clothes, and nursing sick slaves. Most planters did not pay their overseer's wife a fixed salary but, according to Bolzius, allowed her "her food, half the fowl, and half of the third part of the butter [produced on the plantation]."[25]

Planters had definite views about the qualities that a good overseer should have and about the productivity of their slaves. Obviously, familiarity with the techniques of rice and indigo production counted for a lot, as did experience in slave management. Otherwise the words mentioned most frequently in advertisements were "Sobriety" and "Honesty." The question is, did Georgia's overseers measure up to these requirements? Some, such as

Joseph Weatherly, who worked for Governor Wright, were highly proficient; others proved less satisfactory and, as might be expected, these are the overseers who figure most prominently in the records. The most common complaints made by planters concerned the inefficiency and dishonesty of overseers. James Habersham, for example, was placed in a highly embarrassing situation by one of William Knox's overseers. Habersham had agreed to sell some shingles for Knox and was appalled to discover that the overseer in question had given him "an account of 60 or 70,000 shingles more, than he had to deliver." Apparently, this "very plausible" individual had "taken the Negroes Account of their daily work without further examination." Habersham thought that he had been made to "look very foolish," and he told Knox that he was so angry with the overseer that had there been "somebody proper to take his Place" he would have "turned him away."[26]

As Henry Laurens's dealings with Mark Noble, the overseer of his Altamaha plantation, reveal clearly, dishonesty, as well as inefficiency, could prove problematical for absentee planters. It was while on a visit to Georgia in 1769 that Laurens first became aware of "several parts of Mr. Noble's behaviour . . . which had been hid from me before" and realized that "he is not competent for the charge that he has taken." Laurens's criticisms were twofold: first, Noble "wants diligence & he wants sincerity." The consensus among those whom Laurens consulted was that his overseer was idle, vain, and obstinate. The South Carolinian needed little persuading that Noble's inefficiency had resulted in the "loss of my Canoe, Horses, Cattle, tools, etc. etc." But this was not all. Noble had employed slaves from Laurens's Broughton Island plantation on lands of his own. For Laurens, who had no hesitation in dismissing Noble, the problem was how to replace his overseer. He decided to place his Broughton Island and New Hope plantations under the overall management of John McCullough, presently his overseer at New Hope, and to leave the day-to-day running of Broughton Island to Conrad Fabre, an indentured servant. Until he could find a suitable replacement for Noble, Laurens's New Hope plantation would be in the charge of Matthias Zophi, "the Carpenter who seems to be a careful Fellow," and Old Cuffy, a trusted slave who had probably worked as a driver.[27]

Laurens was convinced of McCullough's ability to manage two plantations. Indeed, all went well until October 1770, when Laurens discovered that McCullough was "keeping a Wench in the House in open Adultery." This was behavior which Laurens found "extremely offensive . . . & very hurtful to my Interest, as it must tend to make a good deal of jealousy & disquiet amongst the Negroes." McCullough took exception to his employer's "kind and friendly Admonition" and threatened "to Withdraw as soon as I can supply his place with another Overseer." But apparently he had a change of heart because within days Laurens had received "a very penitential Letter full of Contrition and grateful Sentiments."[28] Although this incident points to another problem faced by absentee planters, it is of enormous interest because it is one of only a handful of reported cases involving sexual relations between an overseer and slave women. If Laurens's remarks are any indication, such liaisons were actively discouraged by planters.

The question remains as to whether those slaves who were superintended by an overseer were worked harder and in other ways treated more severely than those who labored under the direction of their owner. Alexander Hewatt was firmly of the opinion that they were, especially when the owner had "several settlements at considerable distance" from his main residence which he visited perhaps "only three or four times a year." He believed that "many" overseers were "ignorant and Cruel" and that "all" were "totally disinterested in the welfare of their charge." By implication, even those owners "whose humanity, . . . and sense of interest will not permit them to treat their negroes in a harsh manner" bore heavy responsibility for the behavior of "such monsters." But although the evidence is scanty, it is reasonable to suppose that the picture was more complex than that painted by Hewatt. It is by no means certain that all, or even the majority, of overseers behaved in the sadistic fashion he depicted as being characteristic of the Lower South. Much must have depended upon the instructions given by the owner, the conduct he condoned, and the vigor with which he checked up on his overseer's behavior. Henry Laurens was a case in point. He gave his overseers explicit instructions about the punishment of slaves. He insisted that "With the well ones" overseers were to "use gentle means mixed with easy authority. If that does not succeed make choice of the most stubborn one or two chastise them severely but properly & with mercy that they may be convinced the end of correction is to be amendment."[29] In none of his letters to his overseers or to his Georgia friends who kept an eye on his estates did Laurens suggest that his instructions were being contravened.

There was no intrinsic reason why overseers should have been any more brutal than the owners who supervised their slaves themselves. An overseer's job, and sometimes part of his salary, might depend upon how hard he worked the slaves in his charge but so did the livelihood of those masters who could not afford or who did not need an overseer. Brutality was not the sole preserve of any one section of white society.

By the early 1760s the hiring out of slaves was a well-established practice in the agricultural sector of Georgia's economy, and it was entirely possible that at some point in their lives plantation hands would find themselves working for someone other than their owner. Usually the leasing of plantation slaves proceeded on a very formal basis and, in this respect, differed from the system commonly employed in the towns. If slaves were being hired for lengthy periods, and it was not unknown for them to be leased for up to five years at a time, the term and conditions of their hire would be set out in a contract. Although these contracts varied in detail, they were broadly similar in their essentials: they listed the names and values of the slaves being leased, the term for which their labor had been contracted, the arrangements made for their upkeep during that time, and the payment due to their owner.[30]

Plantation hands might also be hired out by the day, week, or month and return to their owner's estate for the night or the weekend. This was the case with the five slaves leased by William Gibbons to Noble Jones in 1769. For five months the slaves divided their time between the two estates: they worked for Jones only as and when required and not on a full-time basis. Jones and Gibbons did not sign a formal contract but Gibbons, and presumably Jones also, kept a record of the work completed.[31]

Finally, plantation slaves might be hired out or loaned for very short periods during particularly busy times in the agricultural year. In July 1773, for example, Habersham arranged for "20 good Hands" to be sent "for a complete Week" to work on one of Governor Wright's plantations. The slaves were not enthused by the prospect of being made to work or travel on their one free day of the week, and "to make them cheerfully go" Habersham promised them "half a Crown a Piece for the two Sundays." He told Wright that the offer of money and the "Dram Each" they were given upon their arrival at his plantation had achieved the desired result. The fifty shillings had been "prudently bestowed, as it will make the People happy, and probably save you a great many barrels of Rice."[32] How many other hands were able to negotiate in this manner must be a matter for speculation.

The working life of urban slaves lacked the seasonal rhythm and generally close supervision which characterized that of plantation hands. Most urban slaves lacked specialized occupational skills and, more often than not, they worked about the town rather than within the confines of their owner's property. The majority of Savannah's slaves fetched and carried, loaded and unloaded trading vessels for their owners or for other people. Usually unskilled slaves were hired out for short periods, and it was most unlikely that the terms of their employment would be written down in a formal contract. Indeed, most owners had few, if any, direct dealings with those who engaged their slaves. The latter would be required to earn a certain amount of money each day or each week and left to hire out their own labor. Although such an arrangement had certain practical advantages, it was widely recognized that this system posed something of a threat to the white community. It was with a view to minimizing this threat that the casual employment of slaves in Savannah was made subject to clearly defined rules and regulations.

To prevent slaves from charging excessive fees, which rather than going to their owners might be spent on alcohol and other "evil Courses," the assembly drew up a list of payments for particular tasks. Unskilled slaves could be hired for the whole or part of a day or for specific jobs, and the rate of pay for each type of work was fixed by law. For example, it cost one shilling and six pence to hire a slave from dawn "until Dark" (the slave was allowed half an hour off for breakfast and an hour off in the middle of the day), one shilling for half a day's work, and six pence for "the fourth part of a day." If the slave was required for work "on Board any Ship or Vessel" the daily charge was increased to two shillings and the "Owner . . . to furnish necessary Provisions." Specific chores were priced according to the time they took and the amount of labor they involved. Thus the charges that might be levied for moving commodities from the Savannah waterfront ranged from nine pence per "Hogshead of Rum, Pipe of Wine or Hogshead of Sugar" taken from "the Top of the Bluff" to "the Strand or any place between that and Saint Julien Street" to one shilling and six pence for delivering the same items "to any part of the Town on the North line of the Common." Any slave who refused to work for these rates was liable to receive thirty lashes "on the Bare Back."[33]

The second area of legislative concern centered on the identification and movement of slaves who were available for hire. Any slave not under the direct supervision of a white person was a potential threat, and elaborate precautions were devised to ensure the good behavior of those slaves whose work took them off their owner's property. First, and in an attempt to ensure that they returned to their owners after each day's work, it was forbidden to rent out rooms or houses to slaves. But that this regulation was not strictly enforced may be inferred from the fact that in 1771 the Grand Jury complained that "slaves are permitted to Rent houses in the lands and Invirons of Savannah." The reason for this concern was clear enough: in these houses "meetings of slaves are very frequent, Spirits and other liquors are sold, and stolen goods often concealed."[34] Second, any slave who worked out had to have a special ticket. Owners who wished to hire out their slaves as porters or laborers for "less than Six days at any one time" or employ them "to sell fruit, fish, garden stuff or any other Commodities" had to obtain a license from commissioners appointed by the assembly. The slaves concerned, whose names had to be registered with the commissioners, had "to wear a Public Badge or Ticket," and it was strictly forbidden to employ a slave who was not wearing a badge. Finally, to control the movement and thereby the behavior of unsupervised slaves and to ensure that would-be employers had no difficulty in securing their services, the Market House was made into a central clearing house for hired hands. Licensed slaves had to make their way there by daybreak, stay on the spot "until employed," and return there after every job.[35] But although these procedures were designed to minimize the risk involved in the casual employment of slaves, urban slaves were provided with perfectly legal opportunities to fraternize with slaves belonging to other owners. Such opportunities were usually denied to the majority of plantation slaves.[36]

Although the slave code of 1755 stipulated that masters must provide their slaves with "Sufficient" food and clothing, it did not elaborate on the word "Sufficient" and, to all intents and purposes, owners were left to their own devices.[37] In practice, the material conditions of life enjoyed by Georgia's slaves reflected what their owners could afford and what they considered to be an appropriate standard of living for their bondsmen. But not everything depended upon the owner's ability and willingness to provide for his slaves. By their resourcefulness both on and off the plantation many slaves secured material comforts over and above those supplied by their masters.

The provision of slave housing was part and parcel of the farm-building operation, and the cost to the owner in labor and materials was modest. Indeed, it was so modest that neither Bolzius nor De Brahm included it in their estimates. Land clearance provided the timber for huts, and all that had to be bought were "a few nails." Given the extent to which the slaves' life revolved around the slave quarters, it is unfortunate that there is virtually no evidence concerning the housing provided for Georgia's bondsmen. Bolzius's brief comments suggest that masters usually quartered their slaves at some distance from their own residence. The requisite number of huts would be arranged around a barn "built about 600 feet" from the main plantation house and, to avoid the danger of the entire slave quarters being destroyed by fire, they were set "at a little distance from one another." If Bolzius is to be believed, and there is no reason to doubt his report, each hut housed one family or "two persons."[38]

More information exists about the food and clothing allocated to slaves. The cost of feeding his slaves was an essential item in every owner's budget and, predictably, most masters hoped to spend as little as possible. This does not mean, however, that slaves were forced to survive on the rudimentary and scarcely adequate diet envisaged by the malcontents.[39] As in the other plantation colonies, slaves subsisted partly on foods provided by their owners, although usually grown by themselves, and partly on foodstuffs which they grew, hunted, or otherwise managed to forage in their spare time.[40] Planters looked to their estates to provide the bulk of their basic food requirements: the corn, cabbages, beans, peas, and potatoes grown on most estates, and rice, which was produced for export rather than for domestic consumption, all figured in slave diets. But although most farms and plantations contained poultry and livestock, meat, or at least meat provided by owners, some farms and plantations did not. Bolzius commented that meat, but presumably offal rather than the choicest joints, might be given "a few times a year" to "loyal" slaves, and other reports suggest that it might also be fed to slaves when they were ill.[41] These meager meat rations were supplemented by trapping and fishing. Some slaves were trusted sufficiently to be issued guns, which they no doubt used to shoot game as well as to "scare off birds" from the rice fields. Hunting and fishing were spare-time activities and, obviously, much depended upon the slave's skill.[42]

Unfortunately, there are not detailed accounts of the precise amounts and cost of the foodstuffs distributed by masters. Bolzius reckoned that an adult slave consumed about twenty bushels of grain, usually Indian corn, a year and that the cost of this, together with the other items supplied by owners, amounted to just under thirty shillings per slave per annum.[43] But the exact sum depended upon how much the master chose to spend, what he raised on his estate, and how much his slaves managed to grow in their off-duty hours. The malcontents had argued that maintenance costs could be reduced by forcing slaves to grow foodstuffs in their own time, and this became the standard practice in Georgia. Most masters gave their slaves a plot of land for their own use, and contemporary reports suggest that a wide range of crops, including "corn, potatoes, tobacco, peanuts, water [and] sugar melons, and pumpkins," were grown in these gardens.[44] Although most of these vegetables, which apart from their food value added a certain variety to the rations issued by the owner, were consumed by the slaves who grew them, some were sold or bartered off the plantation. Little is known about these transactions other than that through them, and often with their master's blessing, slaves managed to secure "trifles" and "some necessary things." The latter probably included utensils and furniture for slave huts, clothing, and foodstuffs not available on the plantation.[45]

Writing in the early 1750s, Bolzius suggested that in clothing their slaves Georgia masters, like their counterparts in South Carolina, adopted minimal standards. He noted that in the summer some owners issued their male slaves with "a pair of pants of coarse linen and a cap or bad hat for the head" but that many others permitted their bondsmen "to go naked, except [they] cover their shame with a cloth rag." Black women wore "a short skirt of coarse linen" or "a petticoat," which left their "upper body . . . bare." They, too, might be given "a handkerchief to cover the head." In the winter slaves would be issued a pair of shoes and garbed in "a woolen blue or white camisole, a pair of long pants of cloth down to the shoes, no shirt, and a woolen cap."[46]

The picture painted by Bolzius of a slave population dressed in a simple, cheap, and uniform fashion is confirmed by other evidence, including the published advertisements for fugitive slaves. If they thought it would help to identify their slaves, and if they knew, masters described the clothes worn or taken by their runaways. Even the most cursory examination of this evidence confirms Bolzius's report that male slaves were usually attired in trousers and a jacket or shirt made of negro cloth, "the coarsest, thickest cloth," or oznabrig and that most women wore a wrapper, a petticoat, or a coat and jacket made from the same materials. There were some variations in the style and the quality of the clothes worn by runaways. Three fugitives, for example, wore "leather" breeches, and two were kitted out in kilts rather than in trousers. Jack, an Angolan-born slave owned by John Gruber, "had on when he went away an old hat sewed all round the brim with white thread, a pair of old leather breeches, a cheque shirt, a pair of white boots, [and] a blue and white jacket with flat enamel buttons." Charles, who ran away from David Murray in 1767, "carried with him a green coatee, a snuff coloured broad cloth coat broke under the arm, black knit stocking breeches, duck breeches with negro cloth boots, and an old beaver hat with a black satin or silver lace hatband with a silver buckle." Some slaves possessed more clothes than those they were wearing when they ran away. Thus Richard Donovan Murray reported that his slave woman Jenny, who could "dress herself very well if she thinks proper," had taken "a small box or chest in which she has her cloaths," and Robert Reid believed that because one of his female runaways had "plenty of other clothes in town" it was likely that she had changed out of the "blue negro cloth wrapper and petticoat" she was wearing when she took flight.[47] There is no suggestion that any of these slaves were skilled workers or domestic servants who might have received preferential treatment.

Masters obtained clothes for their slaves from two main, but by no means mutually exclusive, sources: either locally or from England. A few planters, including Habersham and Wright, imported some made-up garments from England, not because they believed them to be cheaper than those manufactured locally but because they were of a better quality. As Habersham explained, a pair of trousers and a jacket made from "Plains" cost "about 10s" in Georgia, but the same sum spent in London would purchase a "stronger . . . more durable and consequently warmer and more comfortable" outfit. Of course, in the long term savings could be effected by buying such well-made clothes as those ordered by Habersham in March 1764.[48] But it was an exceptional owner who sent to England for slave clothing and an even more exceptional master who expressed concern for the physical comfort of his slaves. Most did not go to the trouble and expense of ordering clothes from London but purchased cloth, much of which was imported from England, and, whenever possible supplementing this with fibers and hides produced on their own estates, had the requisite number of garments made up by their own employees. Bolzius reported that it was usual for slave clothing to be made by the overseer's wife, but on some estates, and especially on the larger plantations, slaves were employed as tailors, seamstresses, and cordwainers. Masters could expect to pay around two shillings a yard for the five or so yards of negro cloth it took to make a pair of trousers and a jacket or a "woman's gown," and Bolzius estimated that the material required for a summer outfit of linen pants or a linen skirt cost about two shillings. The cost of having these garments made up locally worked out to about one shilling and six pence per set of clothes. Masters who provided their slaves with shoes could find themselves paying between two shillings and six pence and three shillings for a pair of leather "negroe shoes."[49]

Although contemporaries, including Bolzius and De Brahm, produced fairly precise estimates of the cost of outfitting a slave, the actual cost depended upon how well and how often a master chose to clothe his slaves. Whether by choice or out of necessity, owners could economize by dressing their slaves in their own castoffs, by not providing them with shoes, by forcing their male slaves to wear loin clothes, and so on. But on the other hand, slave clothing could be, and was, used as a means of impressing one's neighbors. As Bolzius remarked, when some masters "drive or ride to town with Negroes, they give them better clothes."[50]

The malcontents had argued vigorously that Africans were better able than whites to undertake arduous labor in the Georgia environment, but even they were forced to concede that from time to time blacks would fall ill and that unless they were prepared to run the risk of losing their highly prized workers masters would have to spend money on medical care. But whereas an owner could make a reasonably accurate forecast of the annual cost of feeding and clothing his slaves, the medical costs that might be incurred during the year were entirely unpredictable. De Brahm suggested that masters must expect to pay at least ten shillings per slave per annum for "Medicines & Doctors fees," but this was only a rough estimate.[51]

Unfortunately, it is extremely difficult to ascertain the precise incidence of ill health in the slave community or the comparative resistance of blacks and whites to the diseases encountered in the Georgia environment. These questions are further complicated by the vagueness of diagnosis that characterized the medicine practiced in the colony.[52] Given our knowledge of the environmental conditions under which most plantation slaves lived and worked, the symptoms mentioned, and the remedies prescribed by Georgia's doctors, it is possible to identify a number of the ailments that were lumped together under such headings as "pestilential fevers" and "malignant diseases."

A malady said by contemporaries to be common in Georgia and South Carolina was the "intermittent fever" and, as Peter Wood has suggested, there is every reason to suppose that this was the name given to malaria. The coastal and river swamps in which the Georgians established their rice plantations were a fertile breeding ground for the mosquito and, although they might be given for other illnesses than malarial fevers, the febrifuges, anodynes, and tonics frequently prescribed by Georgia's physicians point to the widespread incidence of the symptoms associated with malaria. No doubt drawing heavily from the South Carolina experience, the Georgians consumed large quantities of "Peruvian" or "Jesuits" bark in an attempt to ward off the "intermittent fever." On the larger plantations bark was bought on a fairly regular basis from local suppliers and, although it is impossible to be definite on this point, it is likely that the more prudent masters did not restrict its use to their own families but issued it to at least some of their slaves. Contemporary reports also suggest that "diarrheas and dysenteries," probably protozoal or amoebic dysentery, and various pulmonary ailments were just as common local diseases as malaria. Like their neighbors in Carolina, the Georgians believed that most of these afflictions, together with the "intermittent fever," could be ascribed to "the local very unsettled weather" and the colony's miasmic swamps.[53]

Although whites and blacks alike suffered from the maladies mentioned above, contemporaries believed, and probably correctly, that blacks were particularly prone to pleurisy and pneumonia, which they ascribed to the work conditions associated with rice production. As Anthony Stokes recorded, on many plantations it was the usual practice during the winter months for field hands to get up before dawn and begin their long day's work "in a close building, warmed with fire." Once they had completed their chores inside, they were "turned out to work in the Rice Swamps, half leg deep in water, which brings on pleurisies and peripneumonies." Conditions were scarcely any better in the summer when, according to Stokes, "the quantity of water let into the Rice-fields make it very sickly."[54]

The two diseases feared, with good reason, by the Georgians above all others were the highly contagious smallpox and yellow fever, two "Distempers" which they associated with Africa and the African. The quarantine regulations set down in the colony's first slave code, which were added to during the next twenty years, were based on the assumption that unless adequate precautions were taken both diseases would be introduced into the colony as an automatic, and so far as contemporary medicine was concerned virtually irremediable, consequence of the African slave trade. Possibly because of the Georgians' strict observance of their quarantine laws, the colony did not experience a major outbreak of yellow fever. The most serious outbreak of smallpox, which occurred in 1764, claimed the lives of two hundred whites and an unknown number of blacks.[55]

The inadequacy of the medical data for the years between 1750 and 1776 makes it difficult to arrive at any hard and fast conclusions concerning the comparative health records of blacks and whites. Given the similar West African origins of the slaves imported into South Carolina and Georgia, however, Peter Wood's comments regarding malaria and yellow fever cannot be allowed to pass unnoticed. He has argued that the "high incidence" of the sickle-cell trait, and thereby some protection against malaria, to be expected among slaves imported from West Africa would have persisted for "as long as it served a function in a highly malarious region." Yellow fever was also endemic in West Africa, and Wood suggests that for reasons of "acquired rather than inherited resistance" Carolina's blacks were "more likely to resist the disease than were those European newcomers who had no previous exposure." His overall conclusion is that the sickle-cell trait, together with a greater immunity to yellow fever, gave Carolina's blacks "an obvious if highly dubious advantage in the cultivation of rice."[56] It may be safely assumed that Wood's argument is equally valid for Georgia.

The plantation records that have survived suggest that although they might have scrimped and saved on food and clothing for their slaves, most masters were willing to spend more than the sum mentioned by De Brahm in an attempt to restore their bondsmen to good health. On the larger estates it was usual for medicines to be bought and dispensed by the owner or overseer. A typical medicine chest would have contained emetics, of which the most favored was inpecacuanha, cathartics, which included calomel and glauber salts, and sweating agents such as saline julep. Opium compounds were employed as pain killers and sedatives or to relieve respiratory infections, and it was an unusual medicine chest that did not contain at least one tonic. Most masters also kept a supply of ointments and tinctures for the treatment of minor injuries.[57] Some idea of the number, type, and cost of the medicines bought by one leading planter may be gathered from the fact that between April and December 1765, Doctors James Cuthbert and David Brydie supplied William Gibbons with thirty-nine different items, including febrifuges, tonics, anodynes, and worm powders valued at £12.6.6. But Gibbons was by no means atypical. In 1775, for example, Basil Cowper paid Brydie just under £8 for twenty-five different potions, which ranged from "Eye Water" to laxatives and "vomits."[58]

If an owner's attempts to treat a member of his family or one of his slaves proved unsuccessful, or if he considered the condition to be sufficiently serious, he was likely to call upon the services of a doctor.[59] For the patient, be he black or white, this meant additional exposure to the somewhat dubious benefits of "such drastic remedies" as "Bleeding to the point of exsanguination, purging to the state of depletion, vomiting and sweating to the line of exhaustion, and blistering to a painful degree."[60] For the master it meant an additional outlay: he could expect to pay at least seven shillings and six pence for a house call and more if the doctor was called out after dark. Usually this fee did not include the cost of medication. Medical treatment could prove costly. Between May and July 1765, for example, William Gibbons paid Henry Lewis Bourquin £1.15.4 for treating his slave Peter, and in December 1765 Doctors Brydie and James Irvine charged him fifteen shillings and six pence for "sundry dressings . . . of a negro fellows finger." In 1773 Basil Cowper spent £1.14.6 in just two weeks on treatment for four of his slaves.[61] But masters such as Gibbons and Cowper could easily afford the charges levied by Georgia's doctors. Although not always successful—Bourquin charged Gibbons three shillings for "Burrying" Peter—such expenditure made sound economic sense. But not all owners were motivated simply and solely by considerations of profit and loss. A few acted out of genuine concern for the well-being of their slaves and were visibly distressed when one of their bondsmen died. James Habersham, for example, remarked that the death of one of his slave women, who had been "a favourite of my dear deceased wife and nursed two of my Daughters," had "affected me more than all the Negroes I have ever lost." But even Habersham's concern could be tinged with a degree of economic self-interest. In the same letter in which he mourned the loss of "Oronoko's wife" he commented that he had "lost by Death 6 fine able Negroes besides a lusty girl and also a man . . . and I suppose, I cannot replace them for Four Hundred Pounds Sterling."[62]

Although there is a fair amount of evidence relating to the medicine practiced by Georgia's physicians and planters, there is a dearth of information concerning that practiced in the slave quarters. But that owners were appreciative of the Africans' "awareness of plants and their powers" and the uses to which that knowledge might be put may be evinced from the relevant sections of the slave codes of 1765 and 1770, which prescribed death for any slave who instructed another "in the knowledge of any Poisonous Root, Plant, Herb or other sort of poison" and corporal punishment for the slave so instructed. Although no Georgia slave was described as a "doctor" and none was rewarded for making herbal cures available to the white community, it seems safe to assume that the colony's black element, like their West African compatriots in South Carolina, were accomplished "with the [medicinal] uses of wild plants . . . [and] . . .

regularly gathered berries and herbs for their own use and sale."[63]

Although leaving much to be desired, the records that have survived from the two decades before the War for Independence do offer some insights into the ways in which Georgia masters housed, fed, clothed, and otherwise maintained their slaves. Unfortunately, they shed little light on that part of the bondsman's life which was focused on the slave quarters and those interpersonal relationships which, it may be safely asserted, were of fundamental psychological and social significance for Georgia's slaves.

CHAPTER NINE

THE PRIVATE LIVES OF

GEORGIA BLACKS

*G*eorgia, like the other plantation colonies, made no legal provision for slave marriage, and masters were free to separate black couples and split black families as and when they saw fit. To a considerable extent the formation and subsequent fate of slave unions depended upon the moral and religious inclinations and economic interest of the owner or owners of the slaves concerned.

Writing in the early 1750s, Bolzius asserted that Georgia's slaves, like those of South Carolina, lived "in whoredom." By this he did not mean that slavery in Georgia was characterized by the absence of permanent and loving relationships between slaves but that most masters did not share his concern for the spiritual welfare of the African and, for that reason, refused to grant their slaves a Christian wedding.[1] Although Bolzius was correct in supposing that most owners were indifferent to the spiritual condition of their bondsmen and that many were positively opposed to the attempted conversion of their slaves, some may have been unwilling or felt themselves unable to permit black couples the permanence implied by the Christian marriage ceremony. But the fact that most owners, for whatever reason, did not favor Christian marriage for their slaves should not be taken to mean that they frowned on or actively discouraged monogamous relationships. Far from it. Such relationships, especially the sexual order and stability they conferred on the slave quarters, were very much to the masters' advantage. This did not mean, however, that there might not come a time when they found it necessary or convenient to break these partnerships.

In most cases wedlock appears to have involved slaves who resided on the same estate. But what is not so clear is the degree of choice enjoyed by slaves in the selection of a marriage partner. Bolzius states categorically that they had no choice but were forced "to take as their wives or husbands whomever the master gives them."[2] The evidence is so sparse as to preclude a detailed assessment of this statement. Although the lists of slaves included in inventories of estates often indicate the familial relationships that existed in the slave quarters, they do not reveal when and why particular partnerships were formed, and it is therefore impossible to say whether masters acted in the arbitrary manner described by Bolzius. But of course his comment can be interpreted in two ways. There is no evidence to support the first of these interpretations—that owners, with a view to securing slave children, obliged particular slaves to cohabit. The second interpretation—that an owner required slaves to select partners from among those resident on his own estate—is more plausible. Such a policy would do away with the need for visiting and with the danger of slaves running away in order to be reunited with their families. Indeed, owners had every incentive to encourage unions of the slaves' own choosing.

Although the precise manner in which slave unions originated must remain open to question, there can be no doubting the depth of the affection and the strength of the bonds that united the black family. In fact, this was one aspect of black life which contemporaries thought worthy of comment. James Habersham, for example, recorded a slave husband's love for his spouse when he noted that "Oronoko's wife dyed last Night, and the poor fellow is inconsolable." An incident that occurred during the course of his visit to Pastor Christian Rabenhorst's plantation in 1775 left Henry Melchior Muhlenberg in no doubt as to the strength of a black father's attachment to his child. Rabenhorst wanted to give him the "half-grown daughter . . . [of] . . . An old, stooped, worn-out Negro," but when Muhlenberg "asked the father whether he was willing to let her go with me, promising I would treat her as my own child . . . he showed by his fearful countenance and gestures that he would rather lose his own life than be separated from his daughter." Muhlenberg remarked, with some embarrassment, that he "was only too glad to desist, for I had not been in earnest." Bolzius believed that the sentiments alluded to by Habersham and Muhlenberg were not atypical but, on the contrary, characteristic of the deep affection felt by Africans for their kin. There could be no doubting that slaves "love their families dearly, and none runs away from the other."[3] He might have strengthened his argument by adding that slaves ran away for precisely the opposite reason: to be reunited with their loved ones.

The slave's fear of being separated from family and friends is impossible to quantify. An owner did not have to split many families to remind his slaves, if they needed any reminder, that the fate of every black couple and every black family on his estate rested squarely in his hands. The splitting of just one family or the separation of just one couple must have made a deep and lasting impression on those who remained in the slave quarters. Even those slaves who belonged to the most benevolent and well-intentioned owners could not be certain that they would be allowed to live out their lives near their loved ones. Economic necessity might force an owner to sell some of his slaves, and his death might result in the dispersal of his slave-holding. These eventualities could not be predicted and might not happen during a slave's lifetime. But they were possibilities that could not be entirely discounted, and at one time or another they must have preyed on the mind of every slave. The fear of separation, with all that it implied, might wax and wane according to a slave's temperament and circumstances, but it never disappeared. At no point in his life could a slave be absolutely certain that he would not be forcibly separated from those closest to him.

Bolzius asserted that in Georgia the splitting of slave families was regarded as "somthing unnatural and barbaric."[4] It is odd and not a little perplexing that while castigating the colony's masters for forcing their slaves to "live in whoredom" with partners not of their own choosing, Bolzius should have considered them capable of such high-mindedness when disposing of their slaves. No other contemporary made such a sweeping claim, and there is little evidence to suggest that colonial Georgia was characterized by a universal concern for the welfare of the black family. Indeed, the very fact that some runaways were said to be seeking their relations testifies not only to the strength of the bonds that united slave families but also to the willingness of the masters concerned to split those families. Not all owners, of course, displayed a callous disregard for the black family, and a change of owner did not necessarily result in separation from family and friends. Some owners did their best to preserve the integrity of the slave family, and a few, when contemplating the sale or purchase of slaves, even consulted the bondsmen concerned. In 1772, for example, John Bowman asked John Houstoun to buy "six prime thoroughly seasoned negroes" on his behalf. He requested Houstoun not to "buy negroes of unruly character or bred under a master too indulgent" and was adamant that he "would not have families desirous of being together separated." James Habersham insisted that the Georgians did "not treat [their] Negroes as some people imagine" and assured the Countess of Huntingdon that he "would not keep" any slave "that wou'd prefer any Persons service to mine." On at least one occasion he allayed a slave's fears by promising that he would not "sell him *Softly,* that is without his Consent and Knowledge."[5]

Masters such as Bowman and Habersham might have been prompted by the moral and religious considerations hinted at by Bolzius, but another, and in Bowman's case a more plausible, explanation seems probable. Owners knew that their slaves were likely to take flight in search of their relatives, and it is likely that some black families were kept intact simply because the owners wished to diminish the risk of losing their labor and capital. Thus it is unlikely that Bowman, who branded his slaves in the same way and for the same reason as he branded his cattle, was motivated by anything other than a crass desire to protect his investment.[6] It was the sheer strength of the affection that united slave families and the economic value of black bondsmen, rather than a genuine moral or religious concern on the part of Georgia's slaveholders, which ensured the survival of many black families.

Although the work loads imposed upon bondsmen varied from estate to estate, and in the countryside from season to season, the time most slaves had to themselves was limited to Sundays and a few hours after each day's work. But to say that slaves had some free time is not to say that they were left to their own devices in organizing their off-duty hours. To a considerable extent, their leisure time reflected the demands that might be made and the pursuits that might be denied by their owners and overseers. But in addition, the ways slaves might elect to use their spare time did not escape the notice of Georgia's legislators, and the slave codes were based on the assumption that this was precisely the time when bondsmen were likely to concoct, if not actually engage in, "wicked Designs."[7] Devices such as the ticket system, the prohibitions placed on the sale of alcohol to slaves, the renting out of houses to bondsmen, and, perhaps above all, the slave patrols were all introduced with a view to ensuring the good behavior of blacks and, although not always strictly enforced, they played a vital part in shaping the nonworking life of Georgia's slaves.

The Trustees and their officials had intended that slaves would spend much of their spare time receiving religious instruction or attending divine worship. In fact, one of the most marked points of divergence between the system of slavery envisaged by the Trustees and that which evolved in Georgia centered on the importance attached to the spiritual welfare of the colony's slaves. One of the earliest indications that the religious life of Georgia's slaves was likely to differ significantly from that advocated in the colony's first slave code came in 1755 when the assembly rewrote the public laws of slavery. The code drawn up at the end of the 1740s required owners to attend to the spiritual needs of their slaves; that of 1755 did not mention religion and left owners to decide for themselves whether or not their slaves were exposed to Christian teaching.

The Trustees were not the only group in England to take a keen interest in the religious welfare of Georgia's blacks. At the same time they were drawing up their slave code, the Associates of the Late Reverend Dr. Bray approached the Society for the Propagation of the Gospel with a view to arranging the joint sponsorship of a catechist for the colony's slaves. This proposal received the wholehearted support of the Trustees, and in 1750 they approved the appointment of Joseph Ottolenghe to the post. Ottolenghe, a Piedmontese who had converted from Judaism to Anglicanism, began his mission in Georgia a year later.[8] The mission was to achieve considerably less than its proponents had hoped because during the quarter century before the War for Independence most of Georgia's slaves received little formal religious instruction.

The neglect of their slaves' religious welfare and in many cases an outright refusal to sanction the conversion of their bondsmen cannot be ascribed to a widespread belief among Georgia masters that Africans were incapable of learning. Even William Knox, who was of the opinion that newly imported Africans were "a complete definition of indolent stupidity," thought that country-born blacks were "undoubtedly capable of receiving instruction." Those who advocated the instruction of Africans found themselves confronted by two major difficulties. The first had to do with language. As Ottolenghe pointed out in 1754, "Our Negroes are so ignorant of ye English Language, and none can be found to talk in their own, yt it is a great while before you can get them to understand what ye Meaning of Words is." The problem was clear: "How can a Proposition be believed, without first being understood? & how can it be understood if ye Person to whom it is offer'd has no Idea even of ye Sound of those Words which expresses ye Proposition?" Knox believed that "in order to make himself understood" the missionary had no alternative but to learn the "dialect peculiar to those Negroes who had been born in our colonies, or have been long there."[9] But sometimes it was the inability of the missionary rather than of the African to speak English that posed the problem. In 1775, for example, Knox "sent over two Moravian Brethren, both German, to instruct his Black People." One of them had been to college and, in Habersham's opinion, was "a man of considerable Erudition," but the other, a tailor by trade, could not "speak English well enough to be understood, altho' he reads it Tolerably." Habersham reported that the man in question had settled at his plantation and "begun a school with about 30 children and young People." Habersham hoped that "he will soon be able to speak to the Grown People."[10]

The difficulties posed by language were irksome but in the long term did not constitute an insuperable barrier to the conversion of the African. The same could not be said of the second problem: the attitude of Georgia's slaveowners. Some were indifferent to the religious condition of their bondsmen; many were violently opposed to any and all attempts to convert their slaves. Some resisted instruction because they felt that time given over to religious pursuits was time that should be put to more practical uses: they preferred their slaves to spend their off-duty hours working on their own behalf. Others did not relish the thought of their slaves leaving the plantation. Missionaries might find it convenient to instruct slaves in groups, but many owners felt that such gatherings, especially if they involved slaves from several different estates, provided every opportunity for those concerned "to teach each other mischief." Knox and Ottolenghe thought that the obvious solution would be for slaves to be instructed on their own plantations by "Itinerant missionaries," but they were soon to discover that most owners were less than enthusiastic about the prospect of such visitations.

Although important, the desire to reduce maintenance costs by obliging slaves to grow and hunt their own food during their off-duty hours and the fear of facilitating organized resistance by permitting slaves to leave the plantation were not the only considerations important to masters. There is some suggestion that slaves were denied religious instruction because their owners were concerned about how they would interpret what they had been taught—that conversion to Christianity might give them ideas above their station and encourage them to question, if not to actively resist, their status and condition.

None of those who pressed for the religious instruction of Georgia's slaves suggested that the scriptures provided compelling arguments against the continuance of chattel slavery or that conversion to Christianity necessarily altered the relationship between a slave and his master. On the contrary, they tried to win over owners by reassuring them that far from weakening their authority, religious instruction would serve the highly desirable purpose of securing the loyalty and good behavior of their slaves. As Ottolenghe explained, an owner "would be a great Gainer if his Servant should become a true follower of ye Blessed Jesus, for in such a case he would have instead of an immoral dishonest Domestic a faithful servant."[11] Although not referring specifically to Georgia, William Knox endorsed this view. He suggested that "very few" owners "would be so brutal or ignorant as not to perceive, that were their Negroes instructed in religion, and taught to serve their masters for conscience sake, that they would be much better served by them." Knox believed that the desired end result could be achieved by giving slaves "a very short summary of religion" that emphasized the loyalty and obedience required of the slave in this world and the bountiful rewards that awaited the dutiful servant in the next. He thought that slaves should be told that

> there is one God in heaven who never dies, and who sees and knows every thing. . . . That he punishes all roguery, mischief, and lying, either before death or after it. That he punishes them for it before they die, by putting it into their masters hearts to correct them, and after death by giving them to the Devil to burn in his own place. That he will put it into their masters hearts to be kind to those who do their work without knavery or murmuring. To take care of them in old age and sickness, and not to plague them with too much work, or to chastise them if they are not able to do it. That in the other world, after they die, he will give all good Negroes, rest from all labour, and plenty of all good things.[12]

It would be difficult to find a more explicit statement of the value of Christianity as a device to secure racial control. But the argument that they had a good deal to gain and little to lose by permitting their slaves to convert to Christianity cut little ice with Georgia masters. Indeed, contemporary reports suggest that most of them took precisely the opposite view.

Ottolenghe reported that many owners, and "especially those who resort to us from ye West Indies," opposed the conversion of their slaves because they believed that "a slave is ten times worse when a Xn, yn in his State of Paganism." Although Ottolenghe thought that such an argument was "invidious, and of ye Devil's framing," many owners believed that, far from serving to

control the slave's behavior, a knowledge of the scriptures, especially if it included learning to read, would provide him with
grounds upon which to challenge his status. As Knox put it,
"Our planters objection to their Negroes being instructed is simply this, that instruction renders them less fit or less willing to
labour."[13] This was certainly the impression gathered by Muhlenberg during the course of his visit to Georgia. Muhlenberg,
who likened the attempt to instruct "young Negroes" to "writing Hebrew Text with points and accents on coarse blotting
paper," made much of an episode involving a black boy at Ebenezer who had been "baptized and instructed so that he was able
to read and write well." The boy wanted to emulate his master
and "spend half the day in the shade with his devotions," but
when the latter remonstrated with him and told "him from
God's Word that one must work if one would eat, he made a wry
mouth and declared that kind of Christianity was not becoming
or suitable to him." Muhlenberg believed that this incident,
which of course indicated that some blacks were fully aware of
the inconsistency implicit in the stance adopted by their Christian masters, demonstrated that despite the instruction they received "Most [Africans] retain their savage spite and cunning
trickiness."[14]

The reluctance of masters to have their slaves instructed if this
meant teaching them to read was perfectly understandable. As
Knox observed, if a slave was taught "to read one book, he will
of himself read another, and such has been the imprudence of
some ill informed writers, that books are not wanting to exhort
the Negroes to rebel against their masters." He believed that
"Were the Negroes universally taught to read . . . there would be
little doubt that the next ships informed us of a general insurrection." Muhlenberg's report suggested that "the knowledge of
letters even in the lowest degree, is too often supposed to carry
with it a sort of qualification for an easy life, and an exemption
from a laborious one and the latter being the Negroes lot, they
might perhaps bear it with more unwillingness, or seek some
desperate means of ridding themselves of it" were they taught to
read. Knox thought that, although desirable, the ability to read
was not a prerequisite for religious instruction, and he con-

sidered that the liturgy he had devised for slaves was not only "better adapted to their capacities and condition" but could be learned by rote.[15] But even this argument did not diminish the staunch resistance of many masters.

Knox, who was writing at a time when chattel slavery was coming under increasingly fierce attack on economic, moral, religious, and ideological grounds (although not in Georgia), appreciated that it was "the height of folly to expect any owners of Negroes to permit them to be told, that he violates all divine and human laws by retaining them in his service, or to allow them to have any notions of a religion, whose sanctions he must appear to them to contemn, by making them slaves."[16] But there is no evidence of the existence in late colonial Georgia of a body of opinion which subscribed to or was greatly influenced by Knox's proposition that the fundamental tenets of Christianity could constitute a compelling argument in favor of the immediate and unconditional ending of chattel slavery. As we have seen, Georgia masters received nothing but reassurance on this point from local ministers of religion of all denominations who, in many cases, were themselves slaveowners.[17] If some owners did have any doubts or misgivings about the propriety of one Christian holding another Christian in bondage—and there is no suggestion that any of them did—those sentiments were expressed in a negative fashion: in the withholding of Christianity rather than in manumission. Although the public laws of slavery did not prohibit manumission, fewer than fifty slaves received their freedom between 1751 and 1776. Manumission, which might be by deed of gift or by the last will and testament of the owner, tended to be the reward for "faithful service" rather than a reflection of any religious, moral, or ideological qualms on the part of the master.[18]

So far as most masters were concerned, the second of Knox's propositions, that slaves might interpret and act upon what they had been taught in such a way as might threaten the very foundations of white society, was more important than the first. Despite the assurances of ministers of religion, the majority of owners believed that the religious instruction of their slaves would be fraught with danger. They rejected Christianity as a likely means of securing racial control and instead attempted to impose their will by more practical means.

It will be evident from the foregoing that Christianity played little or no part in the lives of most slaves.[19] Obviously, those slaves whose owners turned away, often in no uncertain fashion, the missionaries who sought to instruct them had little chance of assessing for themselves the merits of the religious doctrines thought suitable for their consumption. The reverse was true of those slaves who belonged to the minority of masters, including James Habersham, William Knox, and Jonathan Bryan, who insisted upon providing religious instruction for their slaves as a matter of course. These slaves were forced to receive instruction and attend divine service, whether they wanted to or not. But although some owners attempted to foist a distorted version of Christianity on their slaves, it must be assumed that some bondsmen did not simply pay lip service to Christian teaching in an attempt to please their masters but were genuine converts. This was certainly true of those slaves who formed the nucleus of the black Baptist church that began to evolve in Georgia on the eve of the War for Independence but did not flower and gain a degree of white acceptance until the 1780s. Mainly through the acquiescence of Jonathan Bryan and other like-minded planters, the Virginian-born black preacher George Liele was permitted to minister to at least some of Georgia's slaves.[20] Although there is no record of his sermons or of the exact number of slaves who listened to them, there is nothing to suggest that he gave his audience any cause to question or resist their condition. Indeed, it may be safely assumed that had this been the case his missionary work would have been ruthlessly suppressed. The interpretation placed by slaves on what they had been taught, whether by Liele or by white preachers, must remain open to question. There is no firm evidence, however, to support the view that the worst fears of Georgia masters were realized and that Christian doctrines provided an additional stimulus to and were used in justification of black resistance.

Like so many other aspects of slave life in colonial Georgia, the activities which, in the absence of the formal religious instruction envisaged by the Trustees, filled the bondsmans' off-duty hours are very badly documented. Georgia masters and the colonial authorities interested themselves only in pursuits that were, or seemed to be, threatening their own security. Slaves who got drunk or who met "together in alarming crowds for the purpose of dancing, feasting, and merriment" were a matter for comment; slaves who whiled away their spare time tending their garden plots were not.[21]

As might be expected, patterns of leisure varied according to the slave's place of residence. Most rural slaves spent their spare time, as well as their working day, within the confines of their owner's estate. Often they had no choice but to spend their off-duty hours growing or hunting food to supplement the provisions supplied by their owners. From the owner's standpoint this requirement made sound economic sense. But it also served another purpose: it was an excellent way of keeping slaves out of mischief.[22]

The other ways in which plantation hands occupied the time available to them must remain a matter for speculation. No doubt black women spent much of their nonworking life preparing food and taking care of their children while their menfolk hunted and trapped. Probably the entertainment rural slaves made for themselves included music and the telling of folk tales.[23] There is no firm evidence concerning the extent to which, with or without the consent of their owners, bondsmen socialized with slaves from other plantations. But given the often dispersed nature of settlement in Georgia, and what must have been the sheer physical exhaustion of field hands after a working day of as long as sixteen hours, it is probable that this happened infrequently. Certainly it was a practice which few masters condoned. Their slaves might wish to meet with those from neighboring plantations for purely innocent reasons, but then again they might take such an opportunity to plot mischief.

The situation in the towns, and particularly in Savannah, was very different. As we have seen, the working life of most urban slaves took them off their owner's property and into direct daily contact with slaves who belonged to other masters. Precisely the same was true of their nonworking life. Although some slaves might have observed the ten o'clock curfew for the simple reason that they did not wish to incur the wrath of their owners or run the risk of being caught and punished by the Savannah watch, it is clear that many others were not constrained by these considerations. Thus at fairly regular intervals the Grand Jury complained about "the frequent meetings of slaves in the streets on Sundays and other holidays" and "in the night" and expressed its concern that some slaves were allowed to lease houses where "Spirits and other liquors" were "sold" and "corn, wood and other commodities" disposed of without the permission of owners.[24] Although it may be safely assumed that most of these activities were confined to black participants, it appears that some urban slaves spent part of their leisure time in the company of whites. Indeed, one or two of Savannah's innkeepers were notorious for their willingness to serve black customers. Luke Dean was censured by the Grand Jury "for keeping a disorderly house" in which he entertained not only slaves but also "horse-stealers, and other persons of ill-fame," and Peter Johnson, said by the Grand Jurors to be a man of "infamous character and conduct," kept "a most disorderly and riotous house" which was frequented by "Negroes and loose people at all hours of the day and night."[25] Clearly, these two men were perfectly happy to cater for a racially mixed clientele. Unfortunately, these are the only references to the interaction, on a purely social level, between urban blacks and, it may be safely inferred from the Grand Jury's comments, those who occupied the lowest ranks of white society. Obviously, it would be foolish to generalize from these examples, but they do suggest that in certain leisure-time pursuits the relations between the two groups were amicable, that in this twilight world race and status did not count for a great deal.

By the early 1760s the problem of securing an acceptable degree of racial control in an urban environment that offered slaves innumerable opportunities to fraternize and, if they so inclined, to hatch mischief was causing grave concern to many in the white community. For the Grand Jury, which was representative of this opinion, the line between innocuous spare-time activities and what might develop into serious misconduct was very narrow indeed. This is not to say that plantation slaves lacked, or were believed by the white community to lack, opportunities to resist, but simply that the comparative freedom enjoyed by urban slaves, the fact that their spare time could not be filled by such devices as requiring them to grow their own food, and the many possibilities Savannah offered for fraternization were seen as posing a particularly potent threat to white society. As we shall see in the next two chapters, these fears were amply justified.

CHAPTER TEN

BLACK RUNAWAYS

*A*lthough the militia act of 1755 acknowledged the possibility that some blacks might prove faithful and trustworthy, Georgia's slave codes were based on the premise that far more typical would be slaves who responded in an essentially aggressive manner to their situation. The assembly anticipated that, as had happened elsewhere in the Americas, these responses would be of three main, but in practice sometimes interrelated, forms: organized resistance such as was tasted in 1739 by South Carolina; acts of violence perpetrated by individual slaves or small groups of slaves against white persons and their property; and attempts to evade slavery by running away. The public laws of slavery did not take cognizance of day-to-day resistance—malingering, careless use of tools, feigning illness, and the like.

Georgia's slaves never engaged in organized resistance on the scale of Stono, but in other respects their behavior confirmed white anxieties. One of the most pervasive modes of black misconduct and, not least because of the ingenuity and determination displayed by slaves, that which proved virtually impossible to prevent, was running away. Georgia's runaways, like those of the other American colonies, may be subdivided into two broad but not always distinct categories: those who, for whatever the reason, left their master's property with no intention of returning and those who absented themselves for a few hours or days and then returned of their own accord. As Peter Wood has observed, and his comment is applicable to both types of runaway, "No single act of self-assertion was more significant among slaves or more disconcerting among whites, than that of running away."[1]

By the mid-eighteenth century the practice of advertising slave runaways in the colonial press was well established. Not until April 1763, with the publication of the *Georgia Gazette*, however, were Georgia owners presented with the opportunity of advertising their runaways and thereby reaching a much larger audience than had been possible hitherto. Similarly, it was only after 1763 that the colony's white community received regular reports about those black fugitives who had been taken up in Georgia but whose owners could not be readily identified. There is virtually no evidence about those slaves who ran away from or who were apprehended in Georgia before 1763; therefore, any detailed study of the colony's runaways must be based on information culled from the last twelve years of the colonial experience.

Between 7 April 1763 and the end of 1775, advertisements for 453 fugitives were placed in the *Gazette* by more than 160 different owners.[2] Given the size of Georgia's black element, fewer than 500 runaways distributed over a twelve-year period might not appear very significant. An average of fewer than 40 runaways a year scarcely suggests a slave population that was seething with discontent or a white community that had much to fear from this mode of black behavior. There are, however, three main reasons for believing that, as in Virginia and South Carolina, the number of fugitives was considerably in excess of that suggested by the published advertisements. First, there was the problem of the periodic unavailability of colonial Georgia's only newspaper. At times, for example during the Stamp Act crisis, the nonpublication of the *Gazette* meant that masters were unable to advertise. Accurate statistics cannot be obtained because some copies of the newspaper have not survived the passage of time.[3]

Although large slaveowners figured prominently among the owners who advertised, there is no evidence that those beneath them on the economic ladder refrained or were debarred from advertising for financial reasons. The cost involved was modest and, it may be assumed, well within the reach of all masters.[4] As Harold E. Davis has suggested, it is much more likely that some owners, and especially those who lived in the more remote parts of Georgia, found it inconvenient or unnecessary to send details of their runaways to James Johnston, the publisher of the *Georgia Gazette,* in Savannah. If runaways from these areas were thought to be visiting or hiding out locally, nothing would be gained by advertising outside the immediate neighborhood.[5] Of course, owners who lived in or close to Savannah might not have advertised for precisely the same reason. In addition, it is unclear whether owners followed a consistent policy and advertised for all their runaways or whether they sometimes, or even usually, relied on less formal means of communicating information about their slaves.

Finally, it appears that some owners expected their slaves to return or be apprehended after a short spell of freedom and that for either of these reasons an advertisement was not placed, or not placed immediately, in the *Gazette.* Unfortunately, not all of the advertisements mentioned the date on which the slave or slaves concerned had run away. Of the 60 percent of runaways for whom this information is available, 16 percent were sought within a week of their disappearance, which suggests that the owners did not anticipate the early return or speedy capture of their slaves. Just over 42 percent of the runaways for whom there is information were sought between one and four weeks after they had absconded; the remainder were absent for at least a month and sometimes for well over a year before their owners advertised. No doubt masters such as Hugh Burn, who in 1768 advertised for "a Negro fellow named Yamow" who had run away in 1765, and William Gibbons, who sought "a short well set black Ebo fellow named Nero" who had taken flight "about twenty months ago," regarded an advertisement as something to try when all other attempts to retrieve their slaves had failed. These advertisements, placed so long after Yamow and Nero had run away, might have been prompted by a sighting of the slaves, indicating that there might be some prospect of their recapture.[6]

Although the evidence is fragmentary, it is evident that the advertised runaways represented what Peter Wood has described as "little more than the top of an ill-defined iceberg."[7] It is impossible to ascertain the precise dimensions of that "iceberg," and any estimate is pure conjecture. We simply do not know how many slaves ran away, how many returned voluntarily, and how many were apprehended without any mention of the fact appearing in the *Georgia Gazette* or elsewhere.

As in Virginia and South Carolina, men predominated among Georgia's advertised runaways. Only sixty-one, or fractionally over 13 percent, of the fugitives were women, a sex ratio among runaways very similar to that which obtained in South Carolina. But such an imbalance is not to be explained by an equivalent imbalance in the sex ratio of the black population as a whole. Peter Wood has suggested that significant numbers of women did absent themselves but "they were more likely than men to visit other slaves and then return of their own accord in a pattern less likely to prompt public advertising."[8] It is impossible to say whether the behavior of Georgia's slave women conformed to this pattern. The few records that have survived do not allude to the propensity of slave women to visit and "return of their own accord," nor does a survey of the published advertisements shed much light because in only twenty-two cases was the woman's motive mentioned by her owner or overseer. Seven of these women were said to be visiting. In May 1769, for example, William Gibbons advertised for "a Negro Wench named Darque or Darchus" who had run away with her "child about 8 or 9 months old." Gibbons believed that Darque might "be harboured in or near Savannah, as she has many acquaintances in and about that town."[9] Six women, including Darque, took at least one child with them, and perhaps the fear of being separated from their offspring or actual separation from the child's father had prompted them to run away.

The owners and overseers, who are the only available source of information, believed that at least eleven of the female runaways were determined to secure their permanent escape from bondage. Thus in the spring of 1764 Thomas Cater of Sunbury advertised for an unnamed girl "about 16 years old, Guiney born," who had been captured at Ogeechee Ferry but who had "made her escape again with handcuffs on." This girl's determination was matched by that of Flora, a black woman owned by

Elizabeth Deveaux. In mid-1774 Mrs. Deveaux reported that Flora, who obviously had proved troublesome in the past because she bore "marks with a whip on her right arm," had absconded and was "supposed to be harboured under the Bluff by Sailors." Flora was recaptured but within a short time had run away again. The second advertisement placed by Mrs. Deveaux suggests why Flora sought the company of sailors: her owners believed she had been "carried off in Capt. Lewelling's vessel or concealed in the Georgia Packet."¹⁰ Nine of the female runaways joined with men in an attempt to secure their freedom. Two such were Minda and Esther, aged twenty and twenty-one respectively, who together with four men ran away from Governor Wright's Ogeechee plantation. The group managed to cross the Ogeechee River and was believed to have joined up with "a parcel of Mr. [William] Elliott's Negroes who have been run away some time."¹¹

If men predominated among Georgia's advertised runaways, so did African-born slaves. Although masters did not always mention the origin of their runaways, this information is available or may be deduced for half the fugitives. Among these, 25 percent were country-born, 30 percent were African-born slaves who had spent some time in the mainland colonies or the West Indies, and around 45 percent were newly enslaved Africans. In view of the heavy slave imports into Georgia during the 1760s and early 1770s, however, it is probable that most of those runaways whose origins were not mentioned were African-born and that the ratio between African-born and country-born runaways was somewhat in excess of three to one.

More often than not, masters did not mention the age of their runaways, and when they did they tended to give an approximate date of birth. Why their ages were uncertain, especially those of African-born slaves, is patently obvious. If the young children, infants, and babes in arms taken away by adults are excluded from the reckoning, the lower end of the age scale was represented by a newly imported boy named Edinburgh, "though he sometimes calls himself Tom." Edinburgh, or Tom, who spoke "little or no English," was "about 10 or 12 years" old when he ran away in 1765. Among the more "elderly" slaves to take flight was

Pompey who, according to his owner, was "aged about 50."[12] Just over 4 percent of the runaways were said to be over forty, "middle aged," "elderly," or "old." But although the ages of runaways covered a broad spectrum, fractionally over 60 percent of those for whom there is information were aged twenty-five or under.

There is every reason for supposing that owners would be diligent in advertising any skills possessed by their slaves and, moreover, that they would advertise quickly for the return of these highly prized bondsmen. Nine percent of the runaways were said to be skilled or semiskilled, and they included ten sawyers, ten coopers, six carpenters, nine sailors, a tailor, and a blacksmith. Ten of them were sought within a week of their disappearance although six, all sawyers, belonged to the same owner.[13] Eight were sought between one and four weeks after they had run away, and the rest were at large for over a month before their masters advertised. Boson, a cooper who belonged to Hugh Burn, was absent for about ten months before a notice appeared in the *Gazette,* and another cooper, Leith, or Leaf as he liked to call himself, was not sought for six months. Leith had been owned by James Herriott, who had sold him "some years ago" to George Delegall. Delegall, in his turn, sold Leith to a Mr. Gamble. Herriott heard that Leith had "often . . . expressed an inclination to live with me again" and arranged to buy him back from Gamble. But in the meantime Leith ran away. Herriott was convinced that if he "is alive and knows I have bought him he will return."[14] There is no evidence that the slave lived up to Herriott's expectation.

Georgia's advertised runaways, like those of Virginia and South Carolina, were predominantly male, African-born, young, and unskilled and, in these respects, constituted a fair cross-section of the colony's black population. But what prompted them to run away? What were their objectives? How much cooperation was there among runaways, and how much help did they receive from the black community at large? Gerald W. Mullin has suggested that in the case of Virginia the answers to the first two of these questions were highly dependent upon the slave's birthplace and occupation. Thus he argues that African-born and what he terms unacculturated plantation hands responded in an essentially "inward" way to their situation whereas country-born and assimilated slaves had the means, opportunity, and inclination to react in an "outward" fashion. The former did not have the requisite linguistic skills or a sufficient familiarity with the realities of life outside their immediate environment "to pass as free men" and "most often directed their limited, sometimes self-defeating acts against the plantation itself." The linguistic ability and knowledge of the white man's world possessed by acculturated and particularly by skilled slaves enabled them to resist "outwardly in the sense of setting and goals: they were determined to get as far as possible from their masters and the plantation. Their flight from and repulsion of the plantation, moreover, were a fitting corollary to the psychological consequences of their training and work routine." Mullins would suggest, therefore, that the acculturated slave was likely to run away in the hope of securing his freedom; the unacculturated slave was more likely to stay with the restricted and restrictive confines of the plantation world he knew. Newly imported slaves conformed to a different pattern. They were slaves "without a job," who "reacted to slavery on the basis of the communal lives which they had been living when enslaved." It was only as the African began to work on the plantation and to learn a little English that his job began to "replace aspects of his heritage as a basic reference point for his reaction to slavery."[15]

The behavior of Georgia's "New Negroes" was very similar to that predicated by Mullin in that group action, which often owed much to the common African origins of those concerned, was a marked characteristic of their initial response to slavery. But, of course, whether a slave, newly imported or not, ran away alone or with others depended upon several considerations. Was he or she a member of a large or a small slaveholding? Could other potential runaways be easily contacted and persuaded to abscond? Did the slave believe that his or her purpose in running away could be more easily achieved by individual, as opposed to organized, endeavor?

The first major difficulty that is encountered when trying to answer these questions is that masters did not always indicate whether their slaves had run away alone. Sometimes they waited until several of their slaves had absconded before advertising, and then their notice might be ambiguous as to whether those concerned had run away together. It may be inferred from the advertisements that at least two hundred slaves ran away alone and that they included a minimum of thirty-three "New Negroes," forty-eight unskilled African- and country-born slaves, and twenty skilled workers. At least eighty-four runaways were accompanied by one other slave. Just over one-fifth of these couples were married, and it is likely that the fear of separation had prompted them to take flight. Common African origins appear to have been the bond between thirteen pairs of runaways. For example, Cork and Mingo, who ran away from Joseph Gibbons in 1767, were said to be "Two Lusty New Ebo Fellows"; Toby and Job, who belonged to John Bare, were "both of the Angola Country"; and Sancho and Drummond, who ran away together in 1769, were "New Negroe Men, of the Gambia Country." In only a handful of cases did country-born and skilled slaves run away with an unskilled slave or a "New Negro." Hector, the African-born slave who took flight with the Jamaican-born Palm, and Jack, a country-born bondsman who took with him "a new Negro named Joshua," were the great exceptions.[16] No doubt linguistic difficulties constituted an often formidable barrier to the formation of such pairings but, as will be suggested below, the objectives of many country-born and skilled slaves demanded independent action. They did not necessitate and would have been severely jeopardized by the presence of a partner who spoke little or no English.

Georgia's slaves not only ran away alone and in pairs but also in groups ranging in size from three to eleven slaves. In some cases occupation was the all-important bond. In 1765, for example, "Six Negroe Fellows . . . all Sawyers" ran away from Mark Carr; Lisbon, Prince, and Brutus, three coopers owned by James Deveaux, "were sent to cut hoops but never returned." But the most striking characteristic of this group endeavor was the extent to which it involved "New Negroes." Thus a quarter of the slaves who ran away with two or more companions were newly imported. Usually these groups owed much, if not everything, to the common African origins of those concerned. In

1769 Pitt, Pompey, and Carlos, "three new Negro men of the Gambia Country," ran away together, as did Lempster, James, Peter, Silvia, and Fanny, "new Negroes of the Gola Country."[17] Obviously, the owners of these runaways did not apply the principle of buying slaves from different parts of Africa in the hope of diminishing the potential for organized resistance.

The destinations of newly imported African runaways were in striking contrast to those of Georgia's other slave fugitives. Any assessment of the motives of runaways, however, must of necessity be based on the information supplied by owners and overseers, and only rarely is it possible to test the accuracy of their assumptions against the actual behavior of the slave. Masters seldom recorded a slave's voluntary return or apprehension in a particular place on a particular day, and the published reports of slaves taken up in Georgia are too imprecise to permit any significant comparisons with the advertised runaways. Owners and overseers did not always speculate about the motives of their slaves, and it must be assumed that often this was simply because they had no idea why their bondsmen had taken flight or in which direction they might be heading. Sometimes a slave's previous behavior permitted a well-informed guess. Thus in 1769 David Douglass advertised for two country-born slaves, Cyrus and Coffee, and an Angolan-born slave named Caesar. The three slaves had run away before, and Douglass believed that Cyrus and Coffee might have "gone toward Augusta, as Cyrus was seen and in custody near that place, and the other was taken up there last year." Caesar, on the other hand, was "supposed to be lurking near Savannah, as he has been taken near that place several times before."[18]

Despite Harold E. Davis's assertion to the contrary, there were significant patterns of escape and marked differences in the behavior of newly imported Africans, unskilled African- and country-born slaves, and artisans. A quarter of those runaways for whom there is information were believed to be in or heading toward Savannah and another forty-one were said to be "well known" in the town (see Table 1). Savannah offered a number of possibilities to the fugitive slave, not least of which was the chance to blend into the black urban crowd. If their owners and

TABLE 1. *The Motives and Destinations of*
Slave Runaways, 1763–1775

Motive or Destination	Men	Women	Country-born	African-born	New Negro	Unknown
In, near, or heading for Savannah	31	5	13***	3	3	17
To friends, family, former plantation	11	1	5	–	1	6
Around plantation, hiding out locally	3	2	–	4	–	5
Master uncertain, assumes still in Georgia	24	2	3	10	5	8
Will try to pass as free black	10	–	3**	1	–	6**
Will try to escape by sea; heading for coast	16	4	1*	2*	10	7
To backcountry; Indian Nation, going upriver	15	1	2	–	–	14
To the salts or to backcountry (master uncertain)	3	3	–	–	6	–
To join other runaways	5	2	–	–	6	1
Other						
Gone Southerly	1	–	–	–	–	1*
To Savannah or to South Carolina	1	–	–	–	–	1*
To South Carolina	1	–	1*	–	–	–
Killed slave	1	–	–	–	–	1
Killed overseer	1	–	–	–	–	1
Gone North	3	1	–	–	–	4***
Harbored by white person	–	1	–	–	–	1
Total	126	22	28	20	31	73

Key: One asterisk = one skilled slave; two asterisks = two skilled slaves; three asterisks = three skilled slaves.

overseers are to be believed, some slaves headed there in the hope of finding employment and passing as free blacks. This was the objective of Will, a Virginian-born slave who ran away from Philip Dell in 1769. Will, who was aged "about 35" and said to speak "very good English," took with him "tools . . . for making wooden bowls etc," and Dell believed he would "probably endeavor to pass as a free man." As Mullin has observed, the linguistic and occupational skills of slaves such as Will "enhanced their ability to cope resourcefully when they became fugitives." It is also apparent that slaves without a ticket, be they residents of Savannah or runaways from the countryside, could expect to receive significant support from the town's black community. In addition, some white employers did not ask too many questions of those they hired as casual laborers. In 1774, for example, James Bulloch advertised for "Polydore, Morris, and July, well known in town as labourers and porters." He knew that Morris and July "keep commonly about town cutting and selling grass and jobbing sometimes by land and sometimes by water" but was having great difficulty in retrieving his bondsmen. A similar problem confronted Alexander Wylly, who complained that one of his slaves, a carpenter named Ishmael, was "daily employed by Masters of vessels . . . [although] he has no ticket or licence to work out." Not only that, but "in the evenings he has been often seen playing the fiddle at tippling houses."[19]

Yet as Mullin has noted, the position of slaves such as Will, Ishmael, Morris, and July "was often tenuous; they were still productive and only partially free in a slave society."[20] They faced the ever-present threat of discovery and, however articulate and familiar with the white man's ways, the fugitive could not always count on being able to talk his way out of trouble. The situation was infinitely more problematical for those plantation hands and "New Negroes" who spoke little or no English. Even if they knew of the opportunities presented in Savannah, few of them possessed the language, the occupational skills, or a sufficient familiarity with the world outside the immediate environs of their plantations to stand any realistic chance of passing as a free black. But not all of the slaves who made for Savannah intended to remain there. If Savannah offered some of them the prospect of a semiautonomous existence, albeit an existence fraught with the possibility of discovery, it also offered a possible escape route from Georgia. The owners of nine runaways believed that their slaves would try to secure passages on boats leaving the port of Savannah; either they would try to stow away, perhaps after having enlisted the help of some of the crew, or try to persuade the ship's captain that they were free blacks.

If Savannah was a magnet for acculturated slaves, the coast and the backcountry seem to have been particularly attractive to "New Negroes." Among runaways for whom there is information, 15 percent were believed to be heading in one or other of these directions, but half the newly enslaved runaways whose destination was mentioned, but less than 10 percent of the unskilled African- and country-born fugitives for whom there is information, fell into this category. Whether out of a sense of shock and bewilderment at the fate that had befallen them or a more aggressive intent to escape from bondage, the prime object of many "New Negroes" was to put as many miles as they could between themselves and their owners and, in the process, to avoid contact with whites. Obviously, the inhospitable environment of the coastal and river swamps and the sparsely settled backcountry offered the best prospects for those slaves who, for whatever reason, did not wish to encounter whites. But, of course, the direction in which "New Negroes" headed owed little, if anything, to a detailed knowledge of the Georgia environment. Such knowledge and the range of options thereby presented came only with time. Nevertheless it is apparent that some rudimentary geographical knowledge combined with a clearly defined objective to determine the route taken by at least one group of "New Negroes." In January 1775, four men and a woman owned by Governor Wright set off "in a small paddling boat . . . to look for their own country." The party was known to have gone downstream, but their overseer did not think it would head out to sea. Rather, he believed it "probable" that the group would "keep along shore and be taken up either to the southward or northward of Savannah."²¹ The fate of these runaways, like that of so many others, is unrecorded. How many other "New Negroes" took flight in the hope of finding their way back to Africa must be a matter for conjecture.

Only four of the advertised runaways said to be making for the backcountry were believed to have the "Indian Nation" as their objective; evidently they hoped to be given sanctuary by the Creeks. A survey of the advertisements placed in the *Gazette* for runaways captured in Georgia suggests that fugitives could not be certain of receiving aid and succor from the Creeks, at least not on a permanent basis. From the 1730s the British had been careful to include in their treaties with the Creeks clauses that promised they would return to bondage any black runaways who made their escape to the "Indian Nation," and generally these clauses were honored. It was not unknown for the Creeks to return blacks, including some who had spent several years in their midst, to the colonial authorities and, as Peter Wood has commented, "the prospect of total absorption into a compatible culture had to be balanced against the risk of betrayal, captivity, or death."²² Yet during the colonial period some of Georgia's slaves were willing to take this risk.

During and after the mid-1750s Georgia's white residents were alarmed by the activities of bands of fugitive slaves who operated along the southern frontier and in the river swamps to the north and northeast of Savannah. Not infrequently, and despite the efforts of the slave patrols, these groups obtained many of their essential supplies by raiding outlying plantations. Little is known about the number, size, and structure of these groups. They must have included some runaways from Georgia, although only seven of the advertised runaways were said to have joined up with or been "decoyed away" by one of these bands.²³ There is no readily apparent reason why owners and overseers should have suppressed the fact that their slaves hoped to join forces with a band of fugitives. Of course, some of them might have been unaware that this was the case.

Down to the early 1760s, Florida and Spanish offers of freedom had attracted black runaways from Britain's plantation colonies, but after the Seven Years' War those slaves who were determined to secure their escape from bondage were more likely to head for Savannah, the more remote parts of the coast, or the backcountry than they were to head south. After 1763 only one runaway was said to be heading "in a southerly direction," and even in this case it is not certain that the slave concerned was heading for Florida.[24] During the 1760s and 1770s Florida held little attraction for Georgia's slaves; they may have been aware of the outcome and implications for themselves of the Seven Years' War and adjusted their escape routes accordingly.

Among the runaways for whom there is information, 8 percent were believed to be attempting to rejoin friends and relations from whom they had been separated, and another 9 percent were thought to be harbored by other blacks, not referred to as their family or friends, in the countryside. The endeavor to be reunited with their loved ones involved many destinations, both within and outside Georgia, and often great distances, which testify to the strength and significance of family ties. In 1769, for example, Harry, "a mustee fellow," and his wife Cassandra were said to be making for Mobile "where the wench's parents and other relations live."[25] Other masters thought their slaves would head for Carolina, Virginia, and even the West Indies in search of their kin. Although it is not always evident when their transfers had occurred, at least 10 percent of the advertised runaways had belonged to more than one master, suggesting that the attempt to maintain links with family and friends might have motivated more slaves than the relatively small number said by their owners to have this as their objective. It is also possible that some of the slaves who ran away together did so because they thought they were about to be separated, although no advertisements cited this as a motive.

Two slaves ran away in order to avoid severe physical punishment. The first issue of the *Gazette* included an advertisement for Scipio, a slave who had "stabbed and murdered" his overseer, one Alexander Crawford. According to the *Gazette,* which did not elaborate on his motive, Scipio had "made his escape," and although "Rangers were . . . sent in search of him [he] has not yet been heard of." The colonial authorities believed that it was of "publick utility" that Scipio "be brought to justice" and offered a reward of £10 sterling for his recapture and £5 sterling for his body. But despite this inducement, Scipio managed to remain at large at least until the end of 1765. Two years later, in May 1765, the *Gazette* recorded that "a Tall Fellow named Bon" had run away from Peter Nephew's plantation, "having that morning killed a negro fellow . . . by stabbing him with a knife."[26] As with Scipio, there is no information about Bon's reason for killing the other slave. Only one advertisement was placed for him, so it is likely that he was taken up almost immediately.

Although no mention was made of the motive or destination of over three hundred runaways, it may be assumed that many of them, and indeed many of the fugitives who were not advertised in the *Gazette,* ran away for reasons and to destinations similar to those of the slaves whose masters were able to supply this information. No doubt some slaves took flight for reasons that were not revealed in advertisements, either because their owners were unaware of them or because they preferred not to say why their bondsmen had absconded. These reasons might have included physical punishment, the fear of punishment, such abuses as overwork and short rations, and a preference for the regime of a former owner.

Whip marks and brands could provide an important aid to the identification of a runaway, and Georgia masters were not reluctant to include graphic details of both in their advertisements. Just under 6 percent of the runaways had been branded and 1 percent scarred by the whip, and in some cases the master's brand was deemed to be a sufficient description of the fugitive. Whip marks, like tribal markings, were usually included as part of a detailed description. For example, Carolina, who ran away from John Mullryne in 1768, was said to be "of the Guiney Country," about forty years old, five feet six inches tall, "of a strong make, with filed teeth," and "upon his breech [he] bears the marks of an old offender."[27] Although there is no evidence to indicate the time lag between the branding or whipping of a slave and that slave absconding, it is probable that in some cases running away was a direct response to brutal treatment. It is also likely that some slaves ran away to avoid being whipped or branded.

Overwork or work assignments the slave found onerous or unacceptable for other reasons might have prompted some running away, but neither possibility was cited by any of the owners who advertised in the *Gazette*. Neither does an analysis of the months in which slaves ran away reveal any decisive peaks at particularly busy times in the plantation year. Probably many of those who wished to express their discontent at the type or amount of work demanded of them but who did not wish to abandon their family and friends did so by leaving the plantation temporarily. In other cases the slaves' anger and resentment might have been reflected in work slowdowns, careless work, or the feigning of illness. Only two masters suggested that their slaves had absconded because they preferred the regime of a former owner.[28] Other owners might have known or suspected that this was the case with their own slaves but, understandably perhaps, they might have been reluctant to broadcast the fact in the pages of the *Gazette*.

Four kinds of information provided by owners—whether the slave had run away before, the items taken by fugitives, their mode of transport, and their behavior while at large—testify to the often grim determination of Georgia's slave runaways. Because they believed that previous attempts to escape might offer a vital clue as to the slave's present whereabouts, masters usually included this information in their advertisements. Just under 5 percent had run away before, and four of them, all men, wore the neck or leg irons which denoted a persistent offender. Some owners were familiar with the ploys resorted to by their slaves to avoid recapture. Henry Parker, for example, reported that his slave Peter would "probably assume the name Boson, as he generally does when out," and David Murray knew that one of his bondsmen, Charles, "sometimes goes by the name of Charles Time, and at other times Charles Walker." Previously, Charles had "attempted to get off for the West Indies," and Murray assumed that on this occasion he would do likewise.[29]

As Peter Wood has suggested, the items taken by runaways shed a good deal of light on their intentions and assume a particular significance in those cases where the slave's motive or destination was not mentioned by his owner.[30] A survey of the items carried by Georgia's runaways reveals, first, that very often the decision to abscond had been carefully considered, and, second, that whatever their reason for taking flight many slaves had no intention of returning to their owner. It is evident from the information supplied by masters that several runaways took with them most if not all of their clothes. The contents of slave wardrobes varied, however, and it is likely that some fugitives, especially "New Negroes," owned no more clothes than those they were wearing when they ran away. Nevertheless, 6 percent of the runaways were said to have taken at least one item of extra clothing. Obviously, these slaves had given some thought to their escape, and the fact that they carried extra clothing suggests that they did not intend to return, at least not in the foreseeable future. Almost certainly the same was true of those slaves, especially skilled ones, who carried off their tools. If their owners are to be believed, only a handful of runaways were in possession of lethal weapons. Although plantation practice did not always conform precisely to the public laws of slavery, it seems that most owners took seriously those regulations governing the use of firearms by their slaves. Thus only four fugitives were said to have taken guns. Another slave, owned by Henry Parker, had armed himself with "a felling axe."[31] Of course, these weapons would enhance the chances of survival in the more remote parts of Georgia, but they might also testify to a grim determination not to be retaken without a struggle.

Although some slaves managed to obtain canoes and, less frequently, horses, the majority made their escape on foot. Given the fact that most Tidewater estates had their own boats and canoes, it is surprising that less than 6 percent of the runaways were said to have escaped by water. But no doubt several considerations over and above the availability of vessels helped to determine the slave's mode of transport. Was his or her destination more easily accessible by land or by water? Did slaves believe that unaccompanied blacks journeying along the colony's waterways would be more likely to attract attention than those traveling overland? There are no ready answers to these questions because masters did not often suggest why their slaves had stolen boats or canoes rather than escaping on foot. Most of the runaways who escaped by water were "New Negroes." Georgia's rivers and creeks held an obvious appeal for those whose main objective was to put as much distance as they could between themselves and their owners.

Not surprisingly, few of the published advertisements included details of the runaway's actual, as opposed to anticipated, behavior while at large. Some masters knew that their slaves were living and working in Savannah; others believed that their bondsmen were heading out of Georgia. But occasionally they received and included in their advertisements explicit reports of the steps taken by their slaves in an attempt to avoid recapture. Usually these were reports about runaways who had been apprehended but who had managed to escape. Some slaves were sufficiently fluent in English and sufficiently persuasive to be able to convince their captors that they were free blacks. Thus Cato, "an artful and cunning" slave owned by John Hume, was recaptured "soon after he went away at Mr. Rae's plantation [but] passed with the Overseer as a free man." Obviously, it is impossible to know how many runaways did likewise without arousing the suspicions of those whom they had duped. But not all runaways who were challenged tried to pass as free blacks. This might have been because they had no knowledge of black freedom, because they had been positively identified as a fugitive and realized that such a ploy would be pointless, or because they appreciated that their English was not good enough to carry the part. Sometimes they managed to secure their freedom by more aggressive means. One such was Dick, "a cooper by trade," who was captured in St. John Parish but who "in his way home made his escape from the person who had him in charge upon a stout dun coloured horse."[32]

While it is obvious that many runaways were both determined and inventive, the question remains as to their success in securing their objectives. It is difficult to ascertain how long Georgia's runaways remained at large and whether their actual destinations tallied with those predicted by their owners and overseers. The latter did not always report the date on which their slaves had absconded, their voluntary return, or their apprehension in a particular place on a particular day. Moreover, there is no way of knowing why owners stopped advertising for any particular runaway. The slave concerned might have returned or been recaptured, or the owner might have given up all hope of ever retrieving his human property. Just under half the advertised runaways were at large for over a month and some were missing for well over a year. Mahomet, who belonged to John Graham, was absent for more than three years; Somerset, Mark, and Limus, unskilled African-born slaves owned by John Laurens, ran away in 1772 and were still being sought in 1774.[33] At the other end of the spectrum, 10 percent of the fugitives were the subject of only one advertisement, which did not mention the date the slave or slaves concerned had run away, suggesting that these slaves were caught or returned voluntarily after a relatively short time at large.

Linguistic and occupational skills and the length of time spent in Georgia do not appear to have had a direct bearing on the period of freedom enjoyed by runaways. Other considerations and contingencies, which could not be predicted or planned for, were more important. As has been suggested, the inventiveness and resolution displayed by the slave as well as by those blacks who harbored and in other ways assisted fugitives could be of decisive importance. Similarly, the route taken by the escaper might be of the utmost significance. Slaves who made for the more remote parts of Georgia were not likely to encounter many whites; those who remained in or headed for Savannah could expect to meet whites daily. Finally, of course, luck was important—the luck not to be stopped by a white person and not to be taken up and interrogated by the Savannah watch or one of the rural slave patrols.

CHAPTER ELEVEN

SLAVERY AND THE LAW

Georgia masters, like their counterparts elsewhere in British America, countenanced a degree of slave mobility. In theory, the movement of slaves was subject to rigid controls; in practice, slave mobility diverged sharply from that envisaged by those who drafted the public laws of slavery. The very different circumstances of plantation and urban life provided slaves with many opportunities to absent themselves from their owner's property, and even the most conscientious owners and overseers must have found it virtually impossible to supervise their bondsmen on a round-the-clock basis. On most properties, both urban and rural, it was relatively easy for slaves to slip away for a few hours after the day's work or, alternatively, to take flight.

From the owners' standpoint, any absentee represented the loss, albeit not always permanent, of both labor and capital. For large slaveowners the absence of half a dozen slaves at any one time might be irksome and something to be discouraged insofar as the rest of his work force was concerned, but it would not jeopardize the success of their economic operations in either the short or the longer term. But for those who were lower on the economic ladder, who owned one or two slaves, the loss of a single slave, especially during a particularly busy time in the farming year, might prove disastrous. Insofar as the white community at large was concerned, slave fugitives, be they in search of their freedom or enjoying a few illicit hours away from their owner's estate, were viewed less as lost labor and capital than as slaves outside the immediate jurisdiction of a white person. Predictably, the view of most whites toward absentees was intimately related to the anticipated as well as to the actual behavior of blacks while at large.

As Peter Wood has pointed out, "Although no single runaway posed a threat to the slave system, scores of absentees constituted not simply a minor nuisance . . . but the potential nucleus for more concerted acts of rebellion."[1] Reports from the 1760s and early 1770s certainly point to the nuisance value of Georgia's slave fugitives, particularly those who remained in or close to Savannah. A steady stream of complaints from private individuals as well as from the Grand Jury focused on two interrelated problems: the misdemeanors that had or might be committed by absentees and the casual attitude, if not the downright irresponsibility, of many whites, which allegedly facilitated black misbehavior. Such was the gist of one of the first published complaints, a notice placed in the *Georgia Gazette* by Patrick Mackay in October 1763.

Mackay was incensed because his plantation was "grievously and insufferably annoyed and disturbed by negroes who come there by land and water in the night time." Specifically, these blacks "not only rob, steal, and carry off his hogs, poultry, sheep, corn and his potatoes, but create great disorders among his slaves by debauching his slave wenches who have husbands, the property of the subscriber." Mackay was determined to stamp out these depredations and warned "all proprietors of slaves" that he had hired "a properly armed" white man to guard his property. This employee had been instructed to shoot on sight "all negroes" who infiltrated Mackay's plantation "after sun-sett, and before sun-rise." Another owner who was prepared to take drastic action was John Stevens of Josephs Town. Stevens claimed that it was "a common practice for trading boats and others to land their people, and remain whole nights on his plantation." The incident that prompted his notice in the *Gazette* was the theft of "a quantity of rum and madera wine." Stevens warned that any blacks "found landing, or within the fences" of his property would be "whipped according to law," and he added that "for the better securing [his] property by night" he intended to install "two spring-man-traps" near his landing and keep "fire-arms ready in case of the least attempt."[2]

Implicit in these complaints was the charge that certain owners and overseers were failing in their duty to supervise their slaves, especially during the hours of darkness. The same charge was made more explicitly on several occasions by the Grand Jury. In December 1766, for example, the jurors recorded their displeasure and unease at the fact that "the Negro Act is not put in force." They were particularly worried by reports they had received to the effect that slaves were meeting "in large bodies in the night," that they frequented "tipling houses," and that they were disposing of various commodities "without tickets from their masters." Similar sentiments were expressed in a statement published in 1767 by some of Georgia's leading planters. They, too, recorded their concern at the "cabals and riotous meetings of negroes in . . . Savannah, which of late have abounded, particularly on Sundays," and insisted that they would do their best to "suppress and prevent" such illicit gatherings. But they were not successful because eighteen months later the Grand Jury was again presenting "as a very great grievance" the fact that "many negroes in . . . Savannah are allowed to live so much at large, and from under the immediate supervisions of their masters or owners, or any other white person."[3]

If they deemed it to be in the public interest, and probably in the hope that public censure would deter others from offending in a similar manner, the Grand Jury named those whites who were believed to be acting in a particularly irresponsible manner. Some owners were willing to report on those of their neighbors whom they knew to be in serious breach of the slave laws and who, by their negligence, were exposing the white community to potential danger. In 1773, for example, Archibald Bulloch and John Bowman informed the Grand Jury that Samuel Douglass, a Savannah merchant, not only failed to employ an overseer on his Skidaway plantation but also allowed "his Negroes to keep fire-arms."[4] Obviously, Douglass believed that his slaves were totally trustworthy; Bulloch and Bowman were horrified at the thought of unsupervised slaves possessing arms and ammunition.

Most of the offenses committed by slave absentees in and close to Savannah involved individual blacks or very small groups of slaves who apparently did not liaise. That is, there is no suggestion that these misdemeanors constituted a coordinated or systematic assault on white society. Indeed, had they been pressed on this point most Georgians no doubt would have conceded that the behavior of which they complained was hardly likely to result in the imminent collapse of the colony's slave system. Henry Preston, however, who aired his views before the Grand Jury in 1768, hinted at a fear that undoubtedly haunted many whites when he suggested that if owners and overseers failed to execute the public laws of slavery and if the white community as a whole relaxed its guard and became willing to tolerate an ever-increasing degree of absenteeism, the scene would be set not only for "robberies" but also for "other bad practices."[5] The Georgians must not allow themselves to be lulled into a false sense of security because if that happened those slaves who presently met "in large bodies in the night, rioting and frequenting tipling houses" might seize the initiative and organize themselves with a view to launching a bloody assault on white society.

This fear of organized resistance stemmed partly from an acute awareness of the experiences of the other plantation colonies; but closer to home, the activities of the fugitive bands who operated along the southern frontier and in the river swamps close to Savannah raised the spectre of black rebellion. These fears were reinforced by the violent acts perpetrated by individual slaves and small groups of slaves against white Georgians and their property.

At first glance the incidence of serious slave crime in colonial Georgia—those acts deemed to be capital offenses—was not sufficient to warrant the grave concern of whites. Despite the worst fears and forebodings of many Georgians, the colony did not experience organized resistance comparable to Stono or the New York City Rebellion of 1712. The most serious outbreak of black violence, which occurred in 1774, involved less than a dozen slaves. These bondsmen, who belonged to a Captain Morris of St. Andrew Parish, killed their overseer and his wife and "dangerously wounded a carpenter named Wright, also a boy who die'd the next day." Then they seriously wounded Angus M'Intosh, the owner of a neighboring plantation. One of M'Intosh's slaves, "a sensible fellow," joined them, and the group made its way to the "house of Roderick M'Leod, wounded him very much and killed his son." Apparently, M'Leod's son had seen the slaves coming, went out to challenge them, and "broke the arm" of M'Intosh's slave before he was killed. The group was apprehended on the same day that all of this happened, but where and by whom is uncertain. What is certain is that two of the participants, M'Intosh's slave and the black thought to be the ringleader of the others, were condemned to be burned alive.[6] As we shall see, the St. Andrew Parish Revolt was significant in another respect: it provides a partial explanation for the timing if not the actual content of the Darien antislavery petition of 1775.

Virtually nothing is known about the blacks involved in the St. Andrew Parish Revolt other than that with the exception of M'Intosh's slave they were all "New Negroes." The stark report published in the *Georgia Gazette* did not mention how long they had been in the colony and, therefore, what they might have known about Georgia. We do not know whether they killed their overseer in the heat of the moment or whether they had given careful thought to the form their resistance would take. It is equally unclear whether they set out from Morris's plantation in the hope and expectation of enlisting the support of other slaves and, if so, to what end they intended to use that support. It is apparent, however, that they were not afraid of encountering whites and did not differentiate among them. All the whites they came across were subjected to the same violent treatment. This lack of discrimination between slaveholders and nonslaveholders was at the root of many white fears and served to confirm impressions derived from published reports of black rebellion elsewhere in the Americas. It is impossible to say whether the "New Negroes" involved in this episode were aware of the punishment meted out to blacks who offended in this manner; M'Intosh's slave must have known the fate that awaited him should he be apprehended.

Although Georgia's slave laws established procedures for the trial and punishment of black offenders, there are no extant records of the courts that were convened during the 1760s and early 1770s. The implementation of another provision of the slave codes—the payment of compensation to the owners of executed slaves—offers some insights into the type and frequency of serious offenses. The records of these payments are fragmentary, but they suggest that between 1766 and 1773 at least seventeen slaves were executed for such offenses as robbery, arson, and murder. Although there are no relevant legislative records for 1774 and 1775, other sources indicate that a minimum of three slaves were condemned to death.[7] Between 1766 and 1775 fewer than two dozen slaves were executed and no more than a dozen whites met their deaths at the hands of the colony's bondsmen. These bare statistics give rise to two vitally important and highly controversial questions: first, why was there not a greater number of serious slave crimes and, second, how did the white community perceive and respond to those acts of violence that did occur?

There are several possible explanations as to why Georgia's slave system was not characterized by more overt acts of violence against white persons and their property. The least plausible is that the colony's slaves had been broken and demoralized to the point where they offered little more than token resistance. But, as Georgia masters appreciated, slaves were individuals and, as such, were not bound to respond in a uniform manner to lives which, although broadly similar in many essentials, could and did vary enormously. Not all slaves were totally docile and submissive beings who were prepared to endure any treatment, however arbitrary, without striking back. But neither were they all rebels who, regardless of the personal cost, were determined to offer continuous and uncompromising violent resistance to any and all members of the white community. The situation was infinitely complex. Undoubtedly, many slaves did spend their lives conforming to one or other of these extreme behavioral patterns. Some slaves were sufficiently trustworthy to be considered for enlistment into the militia; others seized every opportunity that presented itself of resisting their owners. The public laws of slavery operated on the principal that *all* slaves had to be guarded against; the militia act acknowledged the possibility that the good behavior of some slaves could be guaranteed.

In practice, the behavior of most slaves varied according to the situation that confronted them at any given moment. Separation from family and friends, workloads that were considered excessive, severe punishments, or punishments that were believed to be undeserved could trigger an aggressive response on the part of a usually placid and uncomplaining slave. This response, which might be spontaneous or carefully considered, could assume various forms: verbal abuse, running away, assaulting the owner or overseer, work slowdowns, or the destruction of property. Most masters could not be entirely certain of their slaves' breaking point or predict the form their discontent would take. For example, some slaves were trusted sufficiently to work out on the understanding that they would return voluntarily after a specified time. Many slaves lived up to their owner's expectation; others, for reasons known only to themselves, took flight. Two such were Cato, "a cooper by trade," and his wife Judy, "a washer-woman." Cato and Judy had been given a "written licence" to work in Savannah for a month, and their master, James Bulloch, expected them to reappear at the end of that time. It was only when they failed to return on the date stipulated on their ticket that he realized they had run away. He then wasted no time in placing an advertisement in the *Gazette*.[8]

No slave who had spent any length of time in Georgia could have been ignorant of the modes of physical punishment resorted to by many owners or those indulged in by the colonial authorities. The stance adopted by their owners and overseers provided slaves with their closest and most important point of contact with the motifs of white authority. From the slave's standpoint the private law operative on his owner's estate had much more immediate relevance than the public laws of slavery. Although the slave codes provided some guidelines and made certain demands of owners, in practice the day-to-day management and disciplining of slaves were left almost entirely to the discretion of owners and, predictably, they differed in their approaches to the problem common to them all: how to secure the good behavior of their bondsmen.

It is difficult to assess just how often owners and overseers resorted to the lash, perhaps the most visible symbol of the authority to which they laid claim. Many owners probably appreciated that it was not necessarily in their best interest to try to impose that authority by constant use of the whip. Slaves not only provided essential labor but were often extremely valuable capital assets. Masters stood to lose, in some cases considerable sums, by an undiscriminating use of the lash. One option was that favored by Henry Laurens: to chastise severely those deemed to be the worst offenders and, if necessary, send them to the workhouse in Savannah for additional punishment.[9] Not every slave had to be whipped half to death for the owner's point to be made; the threat of the lash was significant. Owners must have assumed, and probably correctly, that slaves who had witnessed a whipping would think twice before committing a similar offense. Many slaves must have determined precisely what their owners and overseers would tolerate, just how far they could be pushed, before they reached for the lash and adjusted their behavior accordingly. This does not mean that all slaves were cowed into total submission but simply that their disgruntlement and frustration might have found an outlet not in acts of overt violence but in stratagems that were less obvious and less likely to result in a whipping. But it is obvious that the lash held no terror for some slaves, that there were bondsmen who, regardless of the price to be paid, were unwilling to accept or adjust to the fact of their enslavement. Among them must be numbered those runaways who, despite the whippings they received and the neck and leg irons they were forced to wear, refused to be broken. For these slaves there could be no compromise, no accommodation, with the physical and psychological demands made of them by white society.

If some owners tried to impose their authority with the whip, others, including James Habersham, adopted a different approach. Habersham, who expressed a genuine concern for the physical and spiritual welfare of his slaves and who referred to them as his "Family," did not defend or advocate paternalism on the grounds that such kindly treatment would secure the good behavior of his work force. Rather, he adhered to the view expressed by Bolzius: it was the duty of the Christian master to treat his slaves in this manner.[10] But as we have seen, owners who adopted this stance were the exceptions rather than the rule. Moreover, as Benjamin Martyn and Pastor Bolzius had opined and as the attempted murder of Pastor Rabenhorst and his wife demonstrated, "gentle" treatment did not necessarily secure the continuing good behavior of slaves.

Most slaves, no doubt by an often difficult process of trial and error, became reasonably certain of the kinds of behavior their owners and overseers would tolerate and, at the same time, formed their own ideas as to what was acceptable behavior on their part. They knew full well that the Georgians were willing to countenance, and in a sense had no alternative but to countenance, a certain amount of absenteeism and, up to a point, would turn a blind eye to such illicit activities as visits to Savannah's taverns. But some whites argued forcefully that Georgia's slaves were overstepping the mark; that by permitting too many "riotous meetings" of slaves, by not reacting more sternly to "the daring insolence of the negroes,"[11] and by not stamping out misbehavior such as was complained of by Patrick Mackay and John Stevens, the white community was exposing itself to an unacceptable degree of risk. These anxieties found an important expression in the public laws of slavery, but specific incidents could prompt a more immediate and practical response from the colonial authorities, which can have left Georgia's slaves in little doubt as to the firepower at the white community's disposal. In 1763, for example, the *Gazette* recorded that "several attempts have lately been made by negroes to commit robberies on the road to Ogechee Ferry." A sailor had been beaten up and robbed, and a "gentleman" had barely managed to fight off the five blacks who "endeavored to lay hold of his horse's bridle." Governor Wright decided that the situation was so serious as to warrant immediate attention, and he announced that in the future the road in question would be patrolled by "some of the rangers" as well as by "the first regiment of foot militia."[12] But of course, if necessary all white Georgians could be called upon to take up arms against the colony's slaves.

The acts of violence perpetrated by Georgia's slaves and the penalties exacted by the white community had a significance out of all proportion to their number. As Eugene Genovese has written of a later period of southern history, "Murder did not have to occur often: one nearby, perhaps no closer than a neighboring county and perhaps only once in a decade, made a deep impression on masters as well as slaves."[13] The same was true of colonial Georgia. Such incidents as the St. Andrew Parish Revolt, the murder of Alexander Crawford, and the attempted murder of

Pastor Rabenhorst and his wife served to reinforce white fears and to remind the Georgians of the arbitrary and often unpredictable violence that might be indulged in by any of their slaves.

Georgia's slaves, with the possible exception of the most recent arrivals from West Africa, must have been familiar with the harsh and bloody punishments inflicted on those of their number convicted of capital offenses. "New Negroes," who had experienced and who remembered freedom, were soon taught that lesson. The penalties exacted by the white community, like the punishments inflicted on the plantation, had the twin objectives of punishment and prevention. Capital courts were instructed to select punishments that would deter other slaves, and they always opted for death by hanging or death by fire. The latter was a punishment reserved exclusively for blacks; no white malefactor, however serious the crime, was burned at the stake. If the form of death selected for black offenders was designated to act as a deterrent, so was the fact that, as in the other mainland colonies, slaves were executed publicly and often in the most hideous manner. It is difficult to imagine the feelings of a slave who had witnessed or heard about one of his compatriots being burned alive or who had seen the head of an executed slave "fixed upon a post near the place where he committed the murder."[14]

The virtual absence of organized black resistance and the relatively small number of violent crimes committed by individual slaves do not signify that Georgia's blacks were totally demoralized. That some were shocked and bewildered by the fate that had befallen them cannot be denied. But it is abundantly clear that many others were not and that they appreciated that they could assert themselves and their individuality in ways that did not involve the offering of violent resistance and thereby invite harsh retribution. Any slave who contemplated the murder or assault of a white person or the destruction of his property could have been in little doubt as to his fate if apprehended. Similarly, even the most determined black rebel must have appreciated the many practical difficulties that stood in the way of organizing and coordinating resistance throughout a colony or even a county. Georgia's slaves were shrewd enough to recognize that violent resistance was tantamount to committing suicide and, understandably, this was a path few of them chose to follow. But such acts of violence as were committed meant that Georgia's masters and the white community at large could never be entirely certain that this would invariably be the case.

The attempt to exclude slavery from Georgia occurred at a time when few voices were raised against the institution. The formative period of the colony's plantation economy, however, spanned the years when slavery was coming under increasingly heavy attack on both sides of the Atlantic but, significantly, not in the Lower South. The often bitter debate on the Trustees' labor policy came to an abrupt end in 1750. The arguments that had been expressed with such conviction by the Trustees and their supporters did not constitute the basis of an antislavery movement which persisted and gathered strength in the Georgia of the 1760s and 1770s. Indeed, slavery was not a significant political, economic, religious, or social issue in late colonial Georgia.

That there were important divisions and disagreements in Georgia during the years of royal government is indisputable; the gulf between rich and poor was becoming more evident as was the extent to which a rapidly emerging planter elite was strengthening its grip on the economic, political, and social life of the colony. Georgia had never been a politically passive society, but after 1750 the major source of strife focused not on a power struggle betweeen the early settlers and the South Carolinian newcomers or between slaveholders and nonslaveholders but between two elites: the planters of St. John's Parish and the coalition of Christ Church Parish planters and merchants that, according to Harvey H. Jackson, gained control of the lower house of assembly soon after the coming of royal government.[15] The rivalry between these groups exerted a profound influence on the timing and course of the Revolution in Georgia but, in the present context, the important point is that neither would have disputed the economic significance of slavery. In this respect and regardless of their other differences, Georgia's premier planters spoke with one voice.

Slavery provoked little discussion or dissension lower down in the social order. Although artisans complained bitterly that the use of blacks as skilled and semiskilled workers threatened their livelihood, they never employed this argument against the continuing enslavement of the African. They would have been perfectly satisfied had blacks been limited to unskilled plantation work, but, as we have seen, this was a concession the planter elite was unwilling to make. Although this refusal to accede to the wishes of white artisans constituted an important source of dissatisfaction, it never sparked off demands for the abolition of slavery. Similarly, there is no evidence that landholders who found themselves unable to afford slaves or agricultural workers who had been displaced by blacks expressed these resentments by calling into question the legitimacy of slaveholding. In fact, Georgia's leading planters were objects of envy and emulation. Prestige depended not upon such considerations as the length of time spent in the colony but upon the ownership of wealth, which meant the ownership of land and slaves.

Although the Tidewater elite was becoming increasingly well defined and closed to outsiders, an abundance of land and a generous land policy meant that Georgia continued to hold out the prospect of upward mobility. The rise to prominence of such men as William Ewen, who had gone as a servant to Georgia, Edward Barnard, a former apprentice, James Habersham, Francis Harris, and Noble Jones was recent enough to suggest to the ambitious that it was still possible to climb to the top rungs of the social and economic ladder in this essentially frontier society.[16] This belief and the aspirations it encouraged were as important as the fact that in practice the ease of access to the financial capital necessary to acquire or expand a slave-manned plantation could make all the difference to an individual's prospects.

Whatever the extent of their ambition and regardless of whether they held slaves, all whites were called upon to police Georgia's black element and thereby to safeguard the interests of those who laid claim to human property. Although it is tempting to assume that the planter elite that drew up the public laws of slavery deliberately played upon or even manufactured the racial fears that permeated Georgia's slave codes, the truth is much simpler: it might have been in the elite's interest to portray the African as a potential rebel but in fact the continuing good behavior and the docility of slaves could not be guaranteed. It was by no means certain to the Georgians that those blacks who were bent on offering violent resistance would distinguish between slaveholders and nonslaveholders or between cruel and kind masters. All whites were exposed to a degree of risk and all had, or were made to believe that they had, a great deal to fear from Georgia's rapidly growing black element.

In practice, slavery in Georgia did not always conform to the theory elaborated in the slave codes. White infringements, however, were not symptomatic of an antagonism toward the property interests or the wealth and prestige of slaveowners or of a degree of sympathy for the African but indicative of the appreciation of many settlers that black behavior did not invariably coincide with the pattern predicated in the public laws of slavery. Yet as some Georgians were at pains to point out, slaveowners, and indeed white society at large, must not be deluded by the good behavior of the majority of blacks but must work on the assumption that every slave posed a threat. The complacency of some settlers was compensated for by another and in the longer term a more important sentiment: a nagging fear of organized black resistance on a scale that might topple white society. But at no point was it suggested that this might be a good reason for dispensing with slave labor. The South Carolinian and West Indian migrants were firmly committed to slavery both as an economic regime and as a means of securing racial control; those settlers who had experienced the hardships of the Trustee period needed little persuading that the increasing prosperity of Georgia was directly linked to the introduction of black workers. In fact, the Georgians, like the other southern colonists, exaggerated the threat to their collective security posed by their black element. Even when conspiracies did occur, they involved only a handful of slaves and were hardly likely to bring about the downfall of Georgia's white society. But although exaggerated, these white fears were significant. They were conducive to a mode of racial discipline and control, both on and off the plantation, which helped to ensure that the envisaged revolt would never be remotely possible.

Between 1750 and the War for Independence Georgia's slave system was not subjected to any serious criticism from within, and on only one occasion, in 1775, did a group of settlers declare, in unequivocal language, their outright opposition to chattel slavery and their desire to rid Georgia of the institution.

On 12 January 1775 the residents of St. Andrew Parish, headed by Lachlan McIntosh, drew up a set of resolutions in which they not only declared their support for "the decent, but firm and manly conduct of the loyal and brave people of Boston and Massachusetts Bay, to preserve their liberty" but also asserted that

> To show the world that we are not influenced by any contracted or interested motives, but a general philanthropy for all mankind, of whatever climate, language, or complexion, we hereby declare our disapprobation and abhorrence of the unnatural practice of Slavery in America (however, the uncultivated state of our country, or other specious argument may plead for it,) a practice founded in injustice and cruelty, and highly dangerous to our liberties (as well as lives,) debasing part of our fellow creatures below men, and corrupting the virtue and morals of the rest, and is laying the basis of that liberty we contend for (and which we pray the Almighty to continue to the latest posterity) upon a very wrong foundation. We therefore resolve, at all times to use our utmost endeavours for the manumission of our Slaves in this Colony, for the most safe and equitable footing for the masters and themselves.[17]

Here was an antislavery sentiment which closely resembled that expressed by the Highland Scots in 1739 and, moreover, one which tacitly acknowledged the force of the religious, moral, economic, and ideological arguments currently being employed by both British and colonial opponents of chattel slavery. But the ringing phrases of this declaration were not indicative of an enduring opposition to slavery on the part of the Highland Scots who, despite their comments in 1739, had found it possible to hold slaves once the Trustees' prohibition was relaxed. Nor did the resolution prompt its author, Lachlan McIntosh, to free his own slaves or result in a spate of manumissions in St. Andrew Parish.[18] Finally, it did not provoke a second slavery debate in Georgia. The question is, why was this declaration drawn up and what did it signify?

It is important to emphasize that the resolution condemning slavery was but one of six which together were concerned to express and rally support for the Patriot cause in a Georgia which, as late as 1775, was by no means wedded to the prospect of American independence.[19] The inclusion of such a stinging indictment of slavery, and especially the admission that the institution was at odds with the fundamental tenets of American Whig ideology, might well have been a deliberate attempt to win over support for the Patriots by seeking to silence those who alleged hypocrisy on the part of those who were demanding their own liberty while adamantly refusing to free their slaves. But as Harvey H. Jackson has pointed out, it is also likely that this same resolution was aimed at a black as well as a white audience.[20] In this interpretation the St. Andrew Parish Revolt assumes a crucial significance.

Regardless of its precise objectives and despite the small number of blacks involved, the St. Andrew Parish Revolt, which occurred two months before the Darien "congress" drafted its resolutions, demonstrated vividly to the local inhabitants the potent threat to white lives posed by Georgia's blacks. But it is entirely possible that McIntosh and his group perceived another danger: blacks might well take advantage of the political divisions and crisis within Georgia's white society. It was also conceivable, as Dunmore's Proclamation later in 1775 confirmed, that if necessary the British would not hesitate to foment black unrest and in the process threaten the property rights and essential labor claimed by southern slaveowners in an attempt to bring the Patriots to heel.[21] From the Patriot standpoint it was essential that Georgia's blacks remain passive and, if at all possible, firmly committed to the American cause. There is a sense in which the Darien resolution sought to achieve both ends by suggesting to the colony's blacks that "their freedom . . . was conditional on the success of the Whig cause, which they could best support . . . by remaining slaves."[22]

In view of Lachlan McIntosh's reluctance to free his own slaves and his position by the mid-1780s as an ardent defender of the southern view on slavery, it might reasonably be argued that the Darien resolution was merely a calculating, and in its appeal to Georgia's slaves cynical, attempt to muster support for the Patriot cause. Even if, for one brief moment in 1775, McIntosh was swayed by a sense of guilt or even an idealism that "envisioned a new system under which slaves could be freed on a 'safe and equitable footing for the masters and themselves,' " he was also enough of a pragmatist to appreciate that his own standing in Georgia society depended upon the continuing employment of slaves on his own estates and not alienating a local planter elite that was firmly committed to the continuation of chattel slavery.²³ The loss of wealth and social standing, the isolation and ostracism that would have resulted from the manumission of his slaves and would have been the inevitable consequence of continuing to lambast slavery in the uncompromising language of the Darien resolution was a price McIntosh was not prepared to pay. His guilt, idealism, or both simply did not extend that far.

Lachlan McIntosh had only to look around him to appreciate that at least one of the arguments he employed in 1775—that which cast doubt on the economic value of slavery—would have been considered specious by the majority of Georgians. It was abundantly clear to everyone in the colony, regardless of political affiliation, that the prosperity which was coming to characterize the lowcountry stemmed from the employment of slaves. Georgia's economy was expanding and hungered for as many slaves as could be brought to the colony. The Georgians saw no need to apologize for or defend that fact. If they drew any lesson from the earlier slavery debate and the years of royal government, it was a simple one: their economic well-being depended upon slavery.

By the mid-1770s Georgia's slaves represented a capital investment of around £1 million and, even had some form of compensation been offered, the colony's slaveowners would not have willingly divested themselves of their human property.²⁴ The capital tied up in slaves was of vital importance, but so was the fact that were slavery brought to an end, either immediately or gradually, the Georgians would be denied the undoubted economic advantages of a labor system that, for rice and indigo culture, was far more profitable than any that depended on free or indentured white workers. There was no guarantee that free blacks would work for the low wages commanded by slaves, and even if they would, it was entirely possible that former slaves might seek to revenge themselves on their former owners. For the majority of white Georgians the racial and social dislocations, as well as the economic disadvantages, which they associated with emancipation, with a postslavery society, were unthinkable. Indeed, such was their commitment to slavery that it would be more accurate to say that on one level the possibility of a postslavery society was not seriously contemplated. By the 1770s the Georgians refused even to consider the manumission of around eighteen thousand slaves. As the events and arguments of the years between 1775 and 1789 were to demonstrate, the Georgia Patriots' participation in the War for American Independence and the new nation was to be conditional upon the tacit recognition of their slave system.

Although distinctly probable, it was not inevitable that black slavery would be introduced into Georgia by the early 1750s and that thereafter the history of slavery and race relations in that colony would closely parallel the South Carolinian model. In theory, the early settlers of Georgia had two opportunities, in the 1730s and 1740s and again after 1750, to forge a society quite unlike any found elsewhere in British North America. Both opportunities were spurned. It was not by chance or accident that black slaves were brought to the colony.

The Trustees' design for Georgia reflected not only the proposed military role and requirements of the new colony but also, and far more important to them, a clearly defined impression of the adverse effects of chattel slavery on white manners and morals. To them, the unfettered agricultural capitalism of the southern and West Indian colonies demonstrated only too vividly the moral and social as well as the physical and psychological cost to white society of a heavy dependence upon slave labor. Only rarely did they contemplate the cost to the African of the slave systems that had evolved in the American colonies.

The malcontents accepted at least a part of the Trustees' anti-slavery argument. Although they virtually ignored the Georgia Board's comments about the moral and social cost of slavery, they acknowledged that to permit the unlimited importation of slaves would pose a potent threat to their physical and psychological well-being. But against this possibility had to be set the undoubted economic advantages of slave labor and, from first to last, their pro-slavery argument hinged on the economic necessity of employing slaves. They claimed that even the modest economic aspirations of the Trustees, the "comfortable subsistence" they envisaged for the settlers, could not be attained without black labor. That this line of argument was shaped primarily by their knowledge of South Carolina is indisputable. But the malcontents did not regard the South Carolina model as one to be emulated in its entirety. They conceded that the Carolinians had erred in permitting the unrestricted importation of blacks, but they confidently asserted that they could avoid making the same mistake in Georgia.

The collapse of the Trustees' prohibitory policy, which in large measure reflected their defeat at the hands of arguably one of the most effective of all colonial pressure groups, provided the Georgia settlers with the opportunity to introduce a modified version of South Carolina's slave system into their colony. But as the Trustees and their supporters had predicted, this attempt was almost certain to fail—not necessarily because of any insincerity on the part of those who helped to draft Georgia's first slave code but because of the aspirations and the influence of those slaveowning South Carolinians and West Indians who, by the late 1740s, were already moving to Georgia. These newcomers were attracted not by a slave code that promised to eliminate the mistakes made in South Carolina and the Caribbean but by the prospect of being able to recreate the agricultural capitalism of those societies in the southern borderlands. The South Carolinians especially had never made any secret of their intentions regarding the potentially rich rice lands of Georgia and, throughout the Trusteeship, they posed a serious and ultimately irresistible threat to the integrity of the Trustees' design. The initial advantage they enjoyed with respect to labor and capital enabled them fully to exploit the possibilities presented by the Georgia environment during the years of royal government. Not surprisingly, the slave-based plantation economy that evolved in low-country Georgia during the 1750s and 1760s closely resembled that of neighboring South Carolina.

The great tragedy of Georgia's early history, influencing the subsequent history of the state, was twofold: the rejection of the Trustees' attempt to impose a total ban on slavery and the optimistic belief that the mistakes made by the South Carolinians could be avoided. It is indisputable that at the end of the 1740s the early settlers of Georgia and the South Carolinian and West Indian newcomers were presented with an alternative path to follow. Had they seized the opportunity to forge the pattern of race relations envisaged in Georgia's first slave code, the consequences for that state and possibly also for the rest of the South might have been truly profound. But in fact, and as some of the early settlers appreciated only too well, the second Georgia plan was as unrealistic and as fragile as the first. By the 1740s the South Carolinian commitment to black slavery was such as to make that plan little more than a pipe dream.

Within a decade Georgia's first slave code, together with all the hopes and possibilities it represented for subsequent generations of whites and blacks alike, had been swept away and replaced by a slave system that in its essentials was an extension of that which had already taken firm root in Tidewater, South Carolina. It was not by chance or by accident that those who settled Georgia rejected the alternative patterns of social, racial, and economic development offered to them during the first two decades of their colony's history.

NOTES

CHAPTER ONE

1. For the definitive study of these schemes see Verner W. Crane, *The Southern Frontier* (1928; reprint, Ann Arbor, 1956). See also Trevor R. Reese, *Colonial Georgia: A Study in British Imperial Policy in the Eighteenth Century* (Athens, 1963).

2. A Rhode Island law of 1652 forbade slavery but was never systematically enforced. See Winthrop D. Jordan, *White Over Black: American Attitudes towards the Negro, 1550–1812* (1968; reprint, Pelican Books, 1969), 70–71.

3. For a sample of this literature see Oscar and Mary Handlin, "Origins of the Southern Labor System," *William and Mary Quarterly,* 3d ser., 7 (1950): 199–222 (hereafter *WMQ*); Carl N. Degler, "Slavery and the Genesis of American Race Prejudice," *Comparative Studies in Society and History* 2 (1959): 49–66; Jordan, *White Over Black;* and Edmund S. Morgan, *American Slavery— American Freedom: The Ordeal of Colonial Virginia* (New York, 1975).

4. For a list and brief biographical sketches of all the Trustees see William B. Stevens, *History of Georgia,* 2 vols. (1847, 1859: reprint, Savannah, 1972), 463–75.

5. The personalities and agencies involved in this process have been examined in considerable detail elsewhere and are mentioned here only insofar as they impinge upon the decision to exclude slavery. Studies of particular importance include Richard A. Roberts, "The Birth of an American State: Georgia," *Transactions of the Royal Historical Society,* 4th ser., 6 (1922): 22–50; Leslie F. Church, *Oglethorpe: A Study of Philanthropy in England and Georgia* (London, 1932): H. F. B. Compston, *Thomas Coram: Churchman, Empire Builder, and Philanthropist* (London, 1918); Amos E. Ettinger, *James Edward Oglethorpe: Imperial Idealist* (Oxford, 1936): Reese, *Colonial Georgia;* Albert B. Saye, *New Viewpoints in Georgia History* (Athens, 1943); Paul S. Taylor, *Georgia Plan, 1732–1752* (Berkeley, 1972); B. Phinizy Spalding, *Oglethorpe in America* (Chicago, 1977); Verner W. Crane, "Dr. Thomas Bray

and the Charitable Colony Project," *WMQ*, 3d ser., 19 (1962): 49–63; Geraldine Meroney, "The London Entrepot Merchants and the Georgia Colony," *WMQ*, 3d ser., 25 (1968): 230–44; and Albert B. Saye, "The Genesis of Georgia Reviewed," *Georgia Historical Quarterly* 50 (1966): 153–61 (hereafter *GHQ*). For an invaluable contemporary account see Richard A. Roberts, ed., *Diary of Viscount Percival, afterwards First Earl of Egmont*, 3 vols. (London, 1920–22). Somewhat surprisingly there is no full-length study of Egmont. For two short sketches see Benjamin Rand's introduction to *Berkeley and Percival: The Correspondence of George Berkeley, afterwards Bishop of Cloyne, and Sir John Percival, afterwards Earl of Egmont* (Cambridge, 1914), and Robert G. McPherson's introduction to *The Journal of the Earl of Egmont, 1732–1738* (Athens, 1962). See also Ruth and Albert Saye, "John Percival, First Earl of Egmont," in Horace Montgomery, ed., *Georgians in Profile: Historical Essays in Honor of Ellis Merton Coulter* (Athens, 1958), and Betty Wood, "The Earl of Egmont and the Georgia Colony," paper presented to a conference held in Savannah in February 1983 to commemorate the 250th anniversary of the founding of Georgia.

6. Roberts, ed., *Diary of Egmont*, 1:44–46.
7. Ibid., 98, 99; Rand, ed., *Berkeley and Percival*, 277; Wood, "Egmont and the Georgia Colony."
8. Ruth Scarborough, *The Opposition to Slavery in Georgia prior to 1861* (Nashville, 1933), 62. The notion of Oglethorpe as a prototype abolitionist has appealed to certain of his biographers. Ettinger described him as "a forerunner of Abraham Lincoln," and Henry Bruce wrote that "in later life he used language which would almost make us hail him as the first prominent abolitionist" (Ettinger, *Oglethorpe*, 150–51; Bruce, *Life of General Oglethorpe* [New York, 1890], 99). For a more sober account see Spalding, *Oglethorpe in America*.
9. Ettinger, *Oglethorpe*, 147–48. Through his involvement with the Royal African Company Oglethorpe met Francis Moore, an employee at the Joar Factory in Gambia. Moore settled in Georgia and wrote an account of the colony's early years entitled *A Voyage to Georgia Begun in the Year 1735* (London, 1744). Another of the original Trustees, John Laroche, also served as a deputy-governor of the Royal African Company. See Meroney, "The London Entrepot Merchants and the Georgia Colony," 230–34.
10. Ettinger, *Oglethorpe*, 147–48.

11. Allen D. Candler and Lucian L. Knight, eds., *The Colonial Records of the State of Georgia*, 26 vols. (Atlanta, 1904–16), 1:11–26, 50–52 (hereafter *Col. Recs.*). The legislation was entitled "AN ACT for rendering the Colony of Georgia more Defencible by Prohibiting the Importation and use of Black Slaves or Negroes into the same."

12. Benjamin Martyn to Governor Johnson, London, 18 October 1732, ibid., 29:1–2 (unpublished volume on microfilm in the University of Georgia Library). Martyn requested that "twenty Negro Labourers and Four Pair of Sawyers be hired to assist in clearing the grounds for this new settlement." The implication is that they would be required for only a limited period. Colonel Bull and Jonathan Bryan of South Carolina supplied "20 Slaves whose Labour they gave as a free Gift to the Colony" (Oglethorpe to the Trustees, Savannah, ca. December 1733, Egmont Papers, 14200, pt. 1, 51–52, University of Georgia Library). For the relevant portion of Bishop Gibson's statement see Lorenzo J. Greene, *The Negro in Colonial New England, 1620–1776* (New York, 1942), 261.

13. Rand, ed., *Berkeley and Percival*, 276–77; Benjamin Martyn, *Reasons for Establishing the Colony of Georgia* (London, 1733), in *Collections of the Georgia Historical Society*, 15 vols. (Savannah, 1840–), 1:204, 216–22 (hereafter *Colls., GHS*). In fact, debtors and former prisoners were numerically insignificant in the Georgia project. See Albert B. Saye, "Was Georgia a Debtor Colony?" *Georgia Historical Quarterly* 24 (1940): 323–43 (hereafter *GHQ*).

14. John E. Crowley, *This Sheba Self: The Conceptualization of Economic Life in Eighteenth-Century America* (London, 1974), 30.

15. Ibid., 32; Martyn, *Reasons for Establishing*, 216; Handy B. Fant, "The Labor Policy of the Trustees," *GHQ* 16 (1932): 1–16.

16. Jordan, *White Over Black*, 269ff.; David Brion Davis, *The Problem of Slavery in Western Culture* (Ithaca, N.Y., 1966); and Duncan J. Macleod, *Slavery, Race, and the American Revolution* (Cambridge, 1974).

17. Masters of slave runaways apprehended in Georgia had to reclaim their property "within three months." The slaves would be returned as soon as the owner had paid "all such Costs and Charges as shall have been expended in apprehending or taking" them and made restitution for "such Damages or Mischiefs . . . Committed . . . within the said Province of Georgia" (*Col. Recs.*, 1:51–52).

18. Crane, *Southern Frontier;* Lewis C. Gray, *History of Agriculture in the Southern United States to 1860,* 2 vols. (Washington, D.C., 1933), 1:378–80; James C. Bonner, *The History of Georgia Agriculture* (Athens, 1964), chaps. 1 and 2; Robert G. Lipscomb, "Land Granting in Colonial Georgia" (M.A. thesis, University of Georgia, 1970).

19. Similar fears were hinted at by Montgomery. He suggested that the climate of the borderlands was such that the settlers would "be under no necessity to use the *Dangerous* Help of Blackamoores" (Sir Robert Montgomery, *A Discourse Concerning the design'd Establishment of a New Colony to the South of Carolina, in the Most delightful Country of the Universe* [London, 1717], edited by J. Max Patrick and reprinted in Emory University Publications, Sources and Reprints, ser. 4, no. 3 [Atlanta, 1948], 22; emphasis added).

20. *Col. Recs.,* 1:50.

21. For a discussion of Spanish policy see John J. TePaske, "The Fugitive Slave: Intercolonial Rivalry and Spanish Slave Policy, 1687–1764," in Samuel Proctor, ed., *Eighteenth-Century Florida and Its Borderlands* (Gainesville, 1975), 1–12. For an account of the free black settlement at Moosa or Mosé see "Dispatches of Spanish Officials Bearing on the Free Negro Settlement of Gracia Real de Santa Teresa de Mosé, Florida," *Journal of Negro History* 9 (1924). In 1742 the Spanish forces at St. Augustine included "One Regiment of Negroes, regularly officered by Negroes and One Regiment of Mullattas" (Egmont Papers, 14206, 128).

22. Benjamin Martyn, *An Impartial Inquiry into the State and Utility of the Province of Georgia* (London, 1741), reprinted in *Colls., GHS* 1:169.

23. They were particularly influenced by Montgomery, *Discourse;* Jean Pierre Purry, *Memorial Presented to His Grace My Lord the Duke of Newcastle . . . Upon the present condition of Carolina, and the Means of its Amelioration* (London, 1724); and Purry, *A Description of South Carolina Drawn up at Charles Town, in September 1731* (1731). See also Crane, *Southern Frontier,* 210–14, 283–87.

24. Martyn, *Reasons for Establishing;* James Oglethorpe, *A New and Accurate Account of the Provinces of South Carolina and Georgia* (London, 1733), in *Colls., GHS,* vol. 1; Martyn was the Trustees' most important propagandist and, later, apologist. In addition to *Reasons for Establishing* and *An Impartial Inquiry* (1741) he

wrote *An Account Showing the Progress of the Colony of Georgia* (London, 1743). For a brief biographical sketch see Trevor Reese, "Benjamin Martyn, Secretary to the Trustees for Georgia," *GHQ* 38 (1954): 142–48. For the Trustees' most important promotional literature see Reese, *The Most Delightful Country in the Universe: Promotional Literature of the Colony of Georgia, 1717–1734* (Savannah, 1972). See also Verner W. Crane, "The Promotion Literature of Georgia," in *Bibliographical Essays: A Tribute to Wilberforce Eames* (Freeport, N.Y., 1967). As B. Phinizy Spalding has argued, the sermons preached before the Trustees and the Associates of the Late Rev. Dr. Bray comprised an important element in the Trustees' propaganda campaign. Later on they served to defend unpopular policies. For a list of the sermons see Spalding, "Georgia and South Carolina during the Oglethorpe Period, 1732–1742" (Ph.D. dissertation, University of North Carolina at Chapel Hill, 1963), 419, 421. See also his "Some Sermon Preached before the Trustees of Colonial Georgia," *GHQ* 57 (1973): 332–46.

25. Oglethorpe, *New and Accurate Account,* 49–53; Oglethorpe to Samuel Wesley, London, 19 November 1734, in George Fenwick Jones, ed., *Henry Newman's Salzburger Letterbook* (Athens, 1966), 514; Oglethorpe to the Trustees, 12 August 1733, Egmont Papers, 14200, pt. 1, 37–39. Purry had argued that "if People are sick, 'tis generally an Effect of their bad Conduct, and not knowing how to regulate themselves suitably to the Country where they live" (*Description of South Carolina,* 10).

26. Roberts, ed., *Diary of Egmont,* 1:46; Martyn, *Reasons for Establishing,* 210–12; Martyn to Sir Thomas Lombe, 24 January 1734/5, *Col. Recs.,* 29:9; Oglethorpe, *New and Accurate Account,* 68–69.

27. A rare mention of slavery was in the Anniversary Sermon preached by Dr. Thomas Rundle, prebendary of Durham, in 1734. Rundle thought black slavery "the misfortune, if not the dishonour, of other plantations . . . let avarice defend it as it will, there is an honest reluctance in humanity against buying and selling, and regarding those of our own species as our wealth and possessions" (*A Sermon Preached at St. George's Church Hanover Square . . . To Recommend the Charity for Establishing the New Colony of Georgia* [London, 1734], 15). Geraldine Meroney has argued that the Trustees' emphasis on "the commercial and colonial advantages" of Georgia was of decisive importance in securing govern-

ment backing for the colony in 1733 ("London Entrepot Merchants," 243–44).

28. Richard S. Dunn, "The Trustees of Georgia and the House of Commons, 1732–1752," *WMQ*, 3d ser., 11 (1954): 551; Handy B. Fant, "Financing the Colonization of Georgia," *GHQ* 20 (1936): 1–29.

29. Martyn, *Reasons for Establishing*, 220; Roberts, ed., *Diary of Egmont*, 1:370, 298, 376.

30. Martyn, *Reasons for Establishing*, 216.

31. This occupational structure was as follows: agriculturalists, three men; traders, five men; silk and wine experts, two men; carpenters, sawyers, etc., ten men; textile workers/experts, six men; peruke makers, two men; potash maker, one man; miller and baker, one man; cordwainer, one man; vintner, one man; military officer, one man; writer, one man; surgeon, one man; apothecary, one man; tailor, one man; basketmaker, one man; upholsterer, one man; and servants, six men, four women (E. Merton Coulter and Albert B. Saye, eds., *A List of the Early Settlers of Georgia* [Athens, 1949], 105–11).

32. Ibid., x–xii.

33. The sex ratio and age structure of the first embarkation are given in ibid., 105–11. See also Milton L. Ready, "An Economic History of Colonial Georgia, 1732–1754" (Ph.D. dissertation, University of Georgia, 1970), 41–42, published as *The Castle Builders* (New York, 1978).

34. Francis Moore, *A Voyage to Georgia* (London, 1744), in *Colls.*, *GHS*, 1:84; Martyn, *Reasons for Establishing*, 220–21.

35. Governor Johnson to Oglethorpe, Charles Town, 28 September 1732, Egmont Papers, 14200, pt. 1, 1–3; Martyn to Johnson, London, 24 January 1732/3, *Col. Recs.*, 29:3–4.

36. For recent studies of race and racial attitudes in seventeenth- and eighteenth-century Britain see Jordan, *White Over Black;* James Walvin, *The Black Presence* (London, 1971); and Walvin, *Black and White: The Negro and English Society, 1555–1945* (London, 1973).

37. Robert G. McPherson, ed., "The Voyage of the *Anne*—A Daily Record," *GHQ* 44 (1960): 222.

38. Thomas Causton to Mrs. Causton, Savannah, 12 March 1733, Egmont Papers, 14200, pt. 1, 23; McPherson, ed., "Voyage of the *Anne*," 227–29.

39. The *South Carolina Gazette*, 22 March 1733, reported that the settlers referred to Oglethorpe as "FATHER."

40. Oglethorpe to the Trustees, Savannah, 12 August 1733, Egmont Papers, 14200, pt. 1, 37–39; Oglethorpe to Samuel Wesley, London, 19 November 1734, in Jones, ed., *Henry Newman's Salzburger Letterbook,* 514; Martyn to Oglethorpe, London, 22 November 1733, Egmont Papers, 14207, 57.

41. Oglethorpe to the Trustees, Charles Town, 9 August 1733, Egmont Papers, 14200, pt. 1, 32–34.

42. Oglethorpe to the Trustees, 12 August 1733, 39.

43. Roberts, ed., *Diary of Egmont,* 1:451.

44. Eveleigh to the Trustees, South Carolina, 6 April 1733; to Oglethorpe, South Carolina, 5 August 1734; to Oglethorpe, Charles Town, 19 October 1734; to Martyn, South Carolina, 20 January 1734/5, Egmont Papers, 14200, pt. 1, 25–27, 93–95, 114; pt. 2, 193–95.

45. Martyn to Eveleigh, London, 1 May 1735, Egmont Papers, 14207, 138–45.

46. Eveleigh to Martyn, South Carolina, 10 September 1735, *Col. Recs.,* 20:302.

47. Eveleigh to Oglethorpe, Charles Town, 19 October 1734. West, who had worked as a smith in England, went to Georgia on the *Anne* (Coulter and Saye, eds., *List of Early Settlers,* 111).

48. Gordon and his wife were among the first embarkation of settlers. William Waterland, the original second bailiff, was removed from office in August 1733 and replaced by Richard Hodges, who died in October 1734; Causton was promoted in his place. Oglethorpe assigned Causton to look after the stores when the *Anne* stopped off at Port Royal en route for Georgia (Coulter and Saye, eds., *List of Early Settlers,* 19, 107, 108, 111; E. Merton Coulter, ed., *The Journal of Peter Gordon, 1732–1735* [Athens, 1963]; Causton to Mrs. Causton, Savannah, 12 March 1733, 20; Anne O'Quinn, "Thomas Causton's Career in Georgia" [M.A. thesis, University of Georgia, 1961]; [Unsigned] to Oglethorpe, Savannah, 5 June 1735, *Col. Recs.,* 20:368–71; Paul Amatis to the Trustees, Savannah, 30 June 1735, ibid., 414).

49. Causton claimed that Watson "gave himself to drinking, and was so seldom Sober That it was hard to Guess if he was not Mad" (Causton to the Trustees, Savannah, 24 March 1734, *Col. Recs.,* 20:546–48).

50. McPherson, ed., *Journal of Egmont,* 242; Egmont Papers, 14207, 68–71.

51. Taylor, *Georgia Plan,* 81–83.

52. Thomas Christie alleged that many settlers had been unable to fence and clear their lands because the boundaries of their grants had not been properly surveyed. He argued that this uncertainty had caused the diversion of manpower, which might have been more profitably employed on outlying acreages, into the improvement of town lots (Christie to Oglethorpe, Savannah, 14 December 1734, *Col. Recs.*, 20:81–83). Christie was the author of *A Description of Georgia by a Gentleman who has Resided there Upwards of Seven Years, and was One of the First Settlers* (London, 1741).

53. Dobree to the Trustees, Savannah, 6 February 1735, *Col. Recs.*, 20:613; Martyn to Dobree, London, 15 May 1735, Egmont Papers, 14207, 178–80.

54. Dobree to the Trustees, Savannah, 17 October 1734, 29 January 1735, *Col. Recs.*, 20:25–26.

55. Gordon held out "great hopes that the cultivation of Madera grapes would bring employment & profit to the Inhabitants . . . and that the growing of Silk would do the same" (McPherson, ed., *Journal of Egmont*, 44). He took with him letters of complaint from Robert Parker, Sr., Susan Bowling, Patrick Houstoun, Patrick Tailfer and Andrew Grant, Samuel Quincy, Joseph Watson, and John West (*Col. Recs.*, 20:332–37, 494–96, 592–606). See also Gordon to the Trustees, London, 7 May 1735, *Col. Recs.*, 20:489–94.

56. Egmont described Gordon as "a conceited and unsteady Man, and favourer of the malecontents in the Colony." Yet he was entrusted with the responsibility of escorting the Indian leader Tomochichi and his party from London back to Georgia (McPherson, ed., *Journal of Egmont*, 101–2).

57. Joseph Fitzwalter to the Trustees, Savannah, 16 January 1735; William Bateman to Oglethorpe, Savannah, 3 September 1734, Egmont Papers, 14200, pt. 2, 174; pt. 1, 97. Bateman's letter was written just two weeks after his arrival in Georgia.

58. Mr. Bofin to Mr. Simond, Purysburg, 23 January 1734; Isaac Chardon to Harman Verelst, Charles Town, 17 January 1734, Egmont Papers, 14200, pt. 1, 62, 69; Eveleigh to Oglethorpe, Charles Town, 19 October 1734; Eveleigh to Verelst, South Carolina, 24 March 1735, *Col. Recs.*, 20:641; 21:118.

59. Christie to the Trustees, Savannah, 28 May 1735; Chardon to the Trustees, Charles Town, 28 September 1734; Dobree to the Trustees, Savannah, 17 October 1734, *Col. Recs.*, 20:330, 22, 28–29.

CHAPTER TWO

1. There is no biography of Tailfer. The present account draws heavily from Clarence L. Ver Steeg's introduction to *A True and Historical Narrative of the Colony of Georgia. By Pat. Tailfer and Others. With Comments by the Earl of Egmont* (Athens, 1960). Tailfer received a five-hundred-acre land grant in 1733. Soon after his arrival he moved into Savannah, where he set up practice as a surgeon and physician. See Patrick Tailfer, Patrick Houstoun, and Andrew Grant to the Trustees, Savannah, 21 January 1735; Patrick Tailfer to the Trustees, Savannah, 19 March 1735, *Col. Recs.*, 20:494–96, 448–49.

2. Tailfer and others to the Trustees, n.p., n.d., recd. 27 August 1735, Egmont Papers, 14201, 108–12.

3. Thomas Jones to Jo. Lyde, Savannah, 18 September 1740, ibid., 14205, 64–67. Jones alleged that among the Lowland Scots only Tailfer had enough capital to purchase slaves.

4. Larry E. Ivers, *British Drums on the Southern Frontier, 1733–1749* (Chapel Hill, 1974). Most servants were indentured for four or five years.

5. William Byrd to the Earl of Egmont, 12 July 1736, in Elizabeth Donnan, ed., *Documents Illustrative of the History of the Slave Trade to America*, 4 vols. (Washington, D.C., 1930–33), 4:131–32.

6. Causton to the Trustees, Savannah, 20 November 1735, 26 November 1736; Henry Bishop to Thomas Bishop, Ebenezer, 26 August 1735, *Col. Recs.*, 21:56, 272–73, 66.

7. Martyn to Oglethorpe, London, 26 September 1733, ibid., 29:35; Roberts, ed., *Diary of Egmont*, 2:41; Martyn to Oglethorpe, London, 21 March 1734; Verelst to Causton, London, 14 January 1736, *Col. Recs.*, 29:35, 331; McPherson, ed., *Journal of Egmont*, 230.

8. E. Merton Coulter, ed., *The Journal of William Stephens, 1741–1745*, 2 vols. (Athens, 1958–59), 1:xiv, xv; Natalie F. Bocock, "William Stephens" (M.A. thesis, University of Georgia, 1935); Thomas Stephens, *The Castle-Builders or, The History of William Stephens of the Isle of Wight esq. Lately Deceased. A Political Novel Never Before Published in any Language* (London, 1759).

9. Stephens's commission and instructions were signed on 27 July 1737; see *Col. Recs.*, 4:11, 15–17, 45–46.

10. William Stephens to the Trustees, Savannah, 19 January 1738, ibid., 22, pt. 1, 67–81.
11. William Stephens's Journal, ibid., 4:242–43, 244. The petition was kept at Robert Williams's house, where "all who came voluntarily might sign it, if they liked it, or let it alone, if they pleased."
12. Memorial to the Trustees, 9 December 1738, Egmont Papers, 14203, pt. 2, 330–35.
13. For the Salzburgers and slavery see Chapter 4 below. The quotation is from David Brion Davis, *The Problem of Slavery in Western Culture* (1966; reprint, Pelican Books, 1970), 169.
14. "The Petition of the Inhabitants of New Inverness (Darien)," 3 January 1739, *Col. Recs.*, 29:481–82. For a detailed discussion of the petition see Harvey H. Jackson, "The Darien Anti-Slavery Petition of 1739 and the Georgia Plan," *WMQ*, 3d ser. 34 (1977): 618–31.
15. Oglethorpe to the Trustees, St. Simons Island, 16, 17 January 1739, Egmont Papers, 14203, pt. 2, 185–88.
16. "The Answer of the Trustees to the Representation from the Inhabitants of Savannah the 9th of Dec. 1738," ibid., 14210, 30–32. Egmont prepared a paper that purported to show that the petitioners were the laziest men in Georgia ("Character of the Persons who Sign'd the Representation for Negroes Dec. 9 1738. A List of the Persons who Sign'd the Memorial to be allow'd Negroes," ibid., 14203, 181a–t).
17. Roberts, ed., *Diary of Egmont*, 3:54, 82.
18. Causton to the Trustees, Savannah, 1 March 1738; William Stephens to Verelst, Savannah, 3 January 1738/9, *Col. Recs.*, 22, pt. 1, 103, pt. 2, 6, 7; William Stephens's Journal, ibid., 4:40, 45, 50–51. For a detailed discussion of Thomas Stephens's career in Georgia see Betty Wood, "Thomas Stephens and the Introduction of Slavery in Georgia," *GHQ* 58 (1974):24–40.
19. William Stephens to Verelst, Savannah, 3 January 1738/9, *Col. Recs.*, 22, pt. 2, 7.
20. This account is based on William Stephens's Journal, ibid., 4:295–98, 338–41, 349; see also Roberts, ed., *Diary of Egmont*, 3:105.
21. Thomas Stephens left Savannah on 3 August 1739. See William Stephens's Journal, *Col. Recs.*, 4:382; William Stephens to Martyn, Savannah, 12 September 1741; to Verelst, Savannah, 26 July 1739, ibid., 23:105; 22, pt. 2, 191.
22. Roberts, ed., *Diary of Egmont*, 3:84. Information on events during the next few months is available largely in the records kept by

Egmont. The motives he ascribed to Stephens are open to question, but his account of Stephens's criticisms of the Georgia project tally with the points made by Stephens in his published works.

23. Egmont's Journal, *Col. Recs.*, 5:254; "Mr. Stephens the Son. His Thoughts on ye Colony of Georgia, and the Trustees Measures, 24 Nov. 1739," Egmont Papers, 14210, 95–110.

24. William Stephens assured Verelst that any "blunt & unguarded" remarks made by his son would come "from an open heart without any disguise" (Stephens to Verelst, Savannah, 26 July 1739, *Col. Recs.*, 22, pt. 2, 191).

25. Dunn, "The Trustees of Georgia and the House of Commons," 559; Taylor, *Georgia Plan*, 44–70.

26. Dunn, "The Trustees of Georgia and the House of Commons," 556.

27. Taylor, *Georgia Plan*, 44–70; Wood, "Egmont and the Georgia Colony." John Laroche, a Bristol merchant of Huguenot extraction, was the M.P. for Bodmin. See Meroney, "London Entrepot Merchants," 235.

28. "Ld. Egmont's Paper for the use of the Trustees, December 11 1739," Egmont Papers, 14210, 123–34. Egmont produced two other papers for the parliamentary Trustees: "Proofs of the Importance and Advantages of Georgia to Great Britain, if duly Encouraged" and "Answers to Queries or Objections that might arise in the Committee of Supply." See Roberts, ed., *Diary of Egmont*, 3:98–101; Egmont Papers, 14210, 138–46, 148–54.

29. Egmont noted that the document had been "Given by Mr. Tho. Stephens to the Trustees on 5 March 1739/40 but privately circulated a month before to Some Members of the House of Commons to inflame them against ye Trustees" (Egmont Papers, 14210, 62–63).

30. Thomas Stephens, "Comparison between the profit and the labour of Negroes with that of white men. Feby. 1739/40," Egmont Papers, 14210, 154–62.

31. Ralph Gray and Betty Wood, "Thomas Stephens on the Profitability of Slaveholding" (unpublished); Ralph Gray and Betty Wood, "The Transition from Indentured to Involuntary Servitude in Colonial Georgia," *Explorations in Economic History* 13 (1976):360–61, 363.

32. Roberts, ed., *Diary of Egmont*, 3:105.

33. Taylor, *Georgia Plan*, 157–67; Leo F. Stock, ed., *Proceedings and Debates of the British Parliaments Respecting North America*, 5

vols. (Washington, D.C., 1924), 5:22–29; Egmont's Journal, *Col. Recs.*, 5:299–301.

34. Stock, ed., *Proceedings*, 5:28.
35. Egmont's Journal, *Col. Recs.*, 5:378–79.
36. "Opinion of the Attorney Genl. that Negroes cant be admitted in Georgia, 30 October 1741," Egmont Papers, 14212, 38–39.
37. Verelst to William Stephens, London, 25 February 1740, *Col. Recs.*, 30:192–99. (Volumes 28, pt. 2, through 39 of *Col. Recs.* are available in manuscript at the Georgia Department of Archives and History, Atlanta.) The tract was published in London in 1743 and is reprinted in *Colls., GHS*, 2:67–85.
38. William Stephens's Journal, *Col. Recs.*, 4 (supp.):28–29, 30–31, 49–50; William Stephens to the Trustees, Savannah, 27 November 1740, ibid., 22, pt. 2, 450–52.
39. "The Remonstrance of the Inhabitants of the Town and County of Savannah, and the rest of the Inhabitants of the Province of Georgia in America. To the Honourable the Trustees for Establishing that Colony. Sign'd 22 Nov. 1740 Copy'd 2d Dec 1740 Recd 22 May 1741," Egmont Papers, 14205, 165–74.
40. Ibid., 174–82.
41. "Petition of the Malcontents in Savannah to his Majesty, or to the Parliament as their Agents in England Should advise. Sign'd 29 Decmbr. 1740. The Humble Petition of the Poor Distressed Inhabitants of the Province of Georgia in America," Egmont Papers, 14205, 241–59. It is not clear whether the petition was sent to Thomas Stephens or Robert Williams.
42. Ibid., 244, 248–50.
43. "To the Honourable Trustees, The Humble Petition of the Residents, Inmates and Others not being Landholders in & about the Town of Savannah & the Rest of the Colony of Georgia," Egmont Papers, 14205, 259–62.

CHAPTER THREE

1. Published in London in 1741 and reprinted in *Colls., GHS*, 1:153–201.
2. Ibid., 155, 157–60, 161, 165–67.
3. Ibid., 168.
4. Tailfer and others to the Trustees, n.p., n.d. recd. 27 August 1735, Egmont Papers, 14201, 108–12; Martyn, *Impartial Inquiry*, 169.
5. Martyn, *Impartial Inquiry*, 169, 171.

6. Roberts, ed., *Diary of Egmont,* 3:174–75.
7. Ibid., 178; Egmont's Journal, *Col. Recs.,* 5:427–28. Beauclerk, elected a Trustee in 1738, was the fifth son of the first duke of St. Albans. Between 1733 and 1744 he sat as the M.P. for New Windsor. Egmont described him as one of Walpole's "creatures." Heathcote was one of the original Trustees. He resigned from the Common Council in 1737 because he felt that some of the Trustees were too subservient to Walpole. He sat as the M.P. for Hindon (1727–34), Southward (1734–41), and London (1741–47).
8. Stock, ed., *Proceedings,* 5:83–87, 89–90, 92; Roberts, ed., *Diary of Egmont,* 3:179–81. Horatio Walpole referred to Carew as "a stout Jacobite" and "a crazy zealot, who believed himself possessed by the Devil." Egmont believed that Carew, who was "of fair character when in his wits," had been "prejudiced" by Thomas Stephens (Egmont's Journal, *Col. Recs.,* 5:443).
9. Stock, ed., *Proceedings,* 5:89–90; Egmont's Journal, *Col. Recs.,* 5:444–45.
10. Stock, ed., *Proceedings,* 5:104, 107–8.
11. Verelst to William Stephens, London, 27 April 1741, *Col. Recs.,* 30:321; Egmont's Journal, ibid., 5:496.
12. William Stephens's Journal, ibid., 4 (supp.):80–81, 174–75; William Stephens to Verelst, Savannah, 24 June 1741, ibid., 23:68–75.
13. Egmont's Journal, ibid., 5:525–38. It is not clear who was responsible for publishing the tract. For a discussion of this point see Spalding, "Georgia and South Carolina," 185–86.
14. Egmont's Journal, *Col. Recs.,* 5:526; Ver Steeg, ed., *True and Historical Narrative,* 4, 6, 8, 103. The Scots rested their case on the comparative profitability of slavery.
15. Egmont to Verelst, Charlton, 25 July 1741, Egmont Papers, 14212, 4.
16. Egmont's Journal, *Col. Recs.,* 5:578.
17. William Stephens's Journal, ibid., 4 (supp.):234, 235.
18. Thomas Jones to Verelst, Frederica, 26 April 1742, ibid., 23:290, 291; "Appointment for an Agent on Behalf of the People of Georgia, October 7, 1741," *Colls., GHS,* 2:153–54. The assistants were William Woodrooffe, Thomas Ormston, Peter Morell, John Lyndall, and William Ewen. Jones mistakenly believed that Andrew Duche, and not Peter Morell, had been elected.
19. Jones to Verelst, 26 April 1742, 293, 294; William Stephens's

Journal, *Col. Recs.,* 4 (supp.):274. It does not appear to have been suggested that financial aid might be forthcoming from English sympathizers.

20. See Betty Wood, "A Note on the Georgia Malcontents," *GHQ* 63 (1979): 264–78.
21. Ready, "Economic History of Colonial Georgia," 44; Robert V. Wells, *The Population of the British Colonies in America before 1776* (Princeton, 1975); Harold E. Davis, *The Fledgling Province: Social and Cultural Life in Colonial Georgia* (Chapel Hill, 1976), 31. Contemporary estimates of the size of Savannah's population were as follows: 275 (1738), 109 freeholders (1739), 100 people (1740), not 40 English families (1740), 292 whites (1741); and not above 100 (1741) (Ready, "Economic History of Colonial Georgia," 46). Between 1733 and 1742, 869 foreign Protestants went as charity settlers to Georgia, (Coulter and Saye, eds., *List of Early Settlers*).
22. William Stephens's Journal, *Col. Recs.,* 4 (supp.): 274; "Appointment for an Agent," 153–55.
23. Dunn, "The Trustees of Georgia and the House of Commons," 562–63.
24. Egmont's Journal, *Col. Recs,* 5:583–86.
25. Ibid., 607–8; Roberts, ed., *Diary of Egmont,* 3:261; Stock, ed., *Proceedings,* 5:132–33.
26. *An Account shewing what Money has been received by the Trustees for the use of the Colony of Georgia. And How they discharge themselves thereof with Observations thereon* was published on the same day, and it is likely that Thomas Stephens was also responsible for this work.
27. Thomas Stephens, *The Hard Case of the Distressed People of Georgia* (London, 1742), 1–4; emphasis in original.
28. Egmont's Journal, *Col. Recs.,* 5:607, 615–16; "The Petition of Thomas Stephens for and in behalf of the People of Georgia in America," Egmont Papers, 14212, 94–95.
29. Egmont's Journal, *Col. Recs.,* 5:635–40.
30. Ibid., 642. The parliamentary Trustees "perceived so great a Spirit" to save Stephens "that they thought it best not to move the reading it."
31. Ibid., 643, 644.
32. Martyn to Oglethorpe, London, 10 August 1742, Egmont Papers, 14213, 36–40.
33. Egmont's Journal, *Col. Recs.,* 5:648–49.

34. Stock, ed., *Proceedings*, 5:163–64, 167–68; Egmont's Journal, *Col. Recs.*, 5:677–78.
35. Reprinted in *Colls.*, *GHS*, 2:87–161; see esp. pp. 89, 93, 99, 100.
36. In 1759 he wrote *The Castle-Builders.* Ostensibly a biography of his father, this tract sought to vindicate the author's behavior as agent for the people of Georgia.
37. William Stephens to Verelst, Savannah, 27 October 1742, 14 December 1742, 27 January 1743, *Col. Recs.*, 5:685; 23:449, 473–74; Coulter, ed., *William Stephens's Journal*, 1:98–99. Thomas Stephens subsequently remarked that at the time of his reprimand he was "scarce able to purchase a supper" (Stephens, *Castle-Builders*, 108).
38. *Col. Recs.*, 13:501, 502, 504; 7:202. That Stephens waited until 1761 to present his petition suggests that he might then have been in a financial crisis and that his earlier activities on behalf of the malcontents provided a likely solution to an immediate problem.

CHAPTER FOUR

1. For the sympathy generated by the Salzburgers' plight see *A Serious Call to the City of London, and thro them to the Whole Nation, to the Relief of the Persecuted Protestants of Salzburg. With a Postscript giving some Account of their Sufferings, and the Numbers that were forc'd out of their Country* (London, 1732). An old but still the standard work on the Salzburgers in P. A. Strobel, *The Salzburgers and Their Descendants* (Baltimore, 1855). For more recent studies see the WPA project, *Beginnings of the Salzburger Settlement Ebenezer in Georgia*, 5 vols. (Savannah, 1937–51), and Milton Rubicam, "Historical Background of the Salzburger Emigration to Georgia," *GHQ* 25 (1951):99–115.
2. McPherson, ed., *Journal of Egmont*, 4. Urlsperger's notes and letters provide an invaluable commentary on all aspects of the Salzburger settlement. See George Fenwick Jones, ed., *Detailed Reports on the Salzburger Emigrants Who Settled in America . . . Edited by Samuel Urlsperger*, 5 vols. (Athens, 1968–). The Society for Promoting Christian Knowledge paid the Salzburgers' fare between Augsburg and Rotterdam.
3. McPherson, ed., *Journal of Egmont*, 11, 22; *Col. Recs.*, 1:129, 141. There was some danger that the entire scheme might be thwarted by the "Popish Part" of the Augsburg authorities, who were unwilling to allow the Salzburgers to leave. The problem was

resolved through the good offices of the English minister in Vienna (ibid., 138–40).

4. Historians have paid surprisingly little attention to Bolzius. He was born in 1703 and educated at the Latin Orphan House at Halle. From there he proceeded to the University of Halle. Bolzius was ordained at Wernigerode on 11 November 1733. He died in Georgia on 19 November 1765. See Lother L. Tresp, *Pastor Bolzius Reports "Life in Georgia among the Salzburgers"* (Philadelphia, 1963); George Fenwick Jones, ed., "Johann Martin Bolzius Reports on Georgia," *GHQ* 47 (1963): 216–19; Jones, ed., *Detailed Reports;* Klaus G. Loewald, Beverly Starika, and Paul S. Taylor, trans. and eds., "Johann Martin Bolzius Answers a Questionnaire on Carolina and Georgia," *WMQ*, 3d ser., 14 (1957): 218–261; 15 (1958): 228–52.

5. *An Extract of the Journals of Mr. Commissary Von Reck. Who Conducted the First Transportation of Saltzburghers to Georgia* (London, 1734), 9.

6. Ibid., 9–10; Jones, ed., *Detailed Reports*, 1:57.

7. Strobel, *The Salzburgers*, 61.

8. J. M. Hofer, "The Georgia Salzburgers," *GHQ* 27 (1943):102.

9. This account is based on Jones, ed., *Detailed Reports*, 1:56–106. The slaves were loaned by a Mr. Jenys of South Carolina (Thomas Causton to the Trustees, Savannah, 16 January 1735, Egmont Papers, 14200, pt. 2, 176–77).

10. Jones, ed., *Detailed Reports*, 1:76, 117.

11. Causton to the Trustees, Savannah, 2 April 1735, Egmont Papers, 14200, pt. 2, 295.

12. Hofer, "The Georgia Salzburgers," 102; von Reck to Oglethorpe, Savannah, 7 March 1736; Oglethorpe to von Reck, 16 March 1736; Oglethorpe to Vat, 16 March 1736, *Col. Recs.*, 21:129; *Colls., GHS*, 3:25–26, 22.

13. Oglethorpe to the Trustees, on board the *Simonds* in Tybee Road, 13 February 1735/36, *Colls., GHS*, 3:13.

14. Von Reck to James Vernon, Ebenezer, 24 June 1736; Bolzius to Martyn, Ebenezer, 8 October 1736, *Col. Recs.*, 21:172–73, 238.

15. Bolzius to the Trustees, Ebenezer, 28 July 1737, ibid., 493; Hester W. Newton, "The Agricultural Activities of the Salzburgers in Georgia," *GHQ* 18 (1934): 255; Nehemiah Curnock, ed., *The Journal of the Rev. John Wesley, A.M.* 8 vols. (London, 1909–16), 1:375. William Davis, ed., *George Whitefield's Journals, 1737–1741* (Gainesville, Fla., 1969), 456, 153. Whitefield visited

Ebenezer again in 1738 and on that occasion expressed his surprise at the Salzburgers' "order and industry." He reported that they "have the best crops of any in the colony."

16. Egmont's Journal, *Col. Recs.*, 5:674. Bolzius told the Trustees that Ebenezer's population totaled 256 and included 77 men, 70 women, 60 girls, 42 boys, and 7 "maidservants."

17. Bolzius to Verelst, Ebenezer, 3 June 1746, 29 November 1750; Bolzius to Martyn, Ebenezer, 4 September, 22 November 1750, *Col. Recs.*, 25:60–63; 26:45–49, 71, 74; Newton, "Agricultural Activities," 338–40.

18. Loewald, Starika, and Taylor, eds., "Bolzius Answers a Questionnaire" (1957):226.

19. The Salzburgers at Ebenezer to James Oglethorpe, 13 March 1739, *Colls., GHS,* 1:189–90.

20. *Col. Recs.*, 3:428–31; Bolzius to George Whitefield, Ebenezer, 24 December 1745; to Verelst, Ebenezer, 14 March 1739, ibid., 24:434–44; Egmont Papers, 14203, 200.

21. *Col. Recs.*, 24:436–38, 441–42; the Salzburgers at Ebenezer to James Oglethorpe, 13 March 1739, 190; Bolzius to Verelst, 14 March 1739, Egmont Papers, 14203, 200; Jones, ed., *Detailed Reports,* 1:57.

22. Bolzius to Whitefield, 24 December 1745, 435–36.

23. Ibid., 442–43; Bolzius to von Munch, Ebenezer, 6 May 1747, *Col. Recs.*, 25:168.

24. Bolzius to Whitefield, 24 December 1745, 437.

25. Causton to the Trustees, Oxted, 1 December 1741; Isaac Gibbs to the Trustees, Abercorn, 3 October 1738, *Col. Recs.*, 23:159; 22, pt. 1, 272–73.

26. Bolzius to Verelst, Ebenezer, 22 February 1745, 3 June 1746, ibid., 24:359, 361; 25:62.

27. Bolzius to Whitefield, 24 December 1745, 439.

28. Bolzius to Verelst, Ebenezer, 30 June 1743, *Col. Recs.*, 24:53–54.

29. *Colls., GHS,* 2:121, 123. Three of the depositions were sworn on 20 October 1741. Spielbiegler swore his affidavit in South Carolina on 16 December 1741. It was probably no coincidence that Thomas Stephens was in Charles Town at the time.

30. Bolzius and Gronau to Verelst, Ebenezer, 18 December 1742, *Col. Recs.*, 23:456, 457.

31. Bolzius to Martyn, Ebenezer, 29 August 1747; Bolzius to Verelst, Ebenezer, 29 August 1747, ibid., 25:200, 206, 209.

32. Bolzius to Martyn, 29 August 1747, 204.

33. Bolzius to John Dobell, Ebenezer, 20 May 1748, ibid., 25:283–85.
34. Ibid., 285; Bolzius to Martyn, Ebenezer, 27 October 1749, 29 August 1747; to Vernon, Ebenezer, 17 October 1749, ibid., 25:438, 425; 205.

CHAPTER FIVE

1. Martyn to William Stephens, London, 26 July 1742; Stephens to Martyn, Savannah, 1 December 1742, *Col. Recs.*, 30:456; 31:45.
2. Ibid., 445–46.
3. Ibid., 446–47.
4. John Dobell to the Trustees, Savannah, 18 July 1743, 11 June 1746, ibid., 24:62–64, 25:72.
5. "The Constables of Savannah Appointed to Seize Blacks or Negroes," *Col. Recs.*, 32:416–18. The Trustees required "all Persons to be aiding and assisting to the said Constables." In March 1741, Henry Manley and William Germain received £1.6.0 and £5.4.0, respectively, for reporting that Thomas Upton employed a slave at Frederica. The slave was sold at public auction for £13. Manley, who had signed the 1738 petition for slaves, and Germain received their payments from the proceeds of the sale. William Moore and Thomas Hird, the two constables involved in the case, were awarded £1.10.0 and £1, respectively, as compensation for "certain charges and loss of time in holding and Trying the said Negro." The balance was set aside "to be applyed to such Charitable uses as shall from time to time Appear . . . necessary" (Town Court, Frederica, 30 March 1741, "Copy of the Proceedings Relating to a Negro Slave Condemned in the Town Court of Frederica Pursuant to the Law Against Negroes"; Thomas Jones to Oglethorpe, Savannah, 18 March 1741, Egmont Papers, 14205, 275–76, 274).
6. The Trustees to William Stephens, London, 27 April 1741, *Col. Recs.*, 30:324.
7. Egmont Papers, 14205, 178; Ver Steeg, ed., *True and Historical Narrative*, 153.
8. William Stephens's Journal, *Col. Recs.*, 4 (supp.):272; William Stephens to the Trustees, Savannah, 31 December 1741, ibid., 23:185–86.
9. Henry Parker, the first bailiff of Savannah, was dismissed in 1739 for "drunkenness debasing the character of a Magistrate" and for

"countenancing the insolent application . . . for introducing Negroes & changing the Tenure of lands." Thomas Christie was removed from office in 1740 (Coulter and Saye, eds., *List of Early Settlers*, 30, 9–10).

10. Margaret C. Davis, "Fort Frederica and the Battle of Bloody Marsh," *GHQ* 27 (1943):111–74. Ettinger recognized the significance of Bloody Marsh when he termed it "the decisive battle, as decisive for Spain as two decades later the Plains of Abraham proved for France, or Yorktown two decades later yet for Britain" (*Oglethorpe*, 243).

11. See below, chapter 6.

12. Dobell to the Trustees, Savannah, 4 July 1746; Bolzius to Dobell, 20 May 1748; Bolzius to Martyn, Ebenezer, 29 August 1747, *Col. Recs.*, 25:74, 284, 206.

13. Alexander Heron to the Trustees, Frederica, 11 May 1748, ibid., 294–95.

14. Dobell to the Trustees, Charles Town, 27 April 1748, ibid., 280–82.

15. Martyn to Bolzius, London, 16 May 1746; "To the President and Assistants of the Province of Georgia in America. An Instruction from the Trustees . . . to be Signified to the Inhabitants of Georgia. That the Introduction and Use of Negroes will never be permitted by the Trustees into that Colony," 17 March 1748, ibid., 31:124; 1:506–7; 33:361–62.

16. The President, Assistants and Councilmen to Martyn, 10 January 1749, ibid., 25:347–48. The letter was signed by William Stephens, Henry Parker, William Spencer, Samuel Mercer, Patrick Graham, George Cadogan, Noble Jones, James Habersham, John Barnard, David Cutler Braddock, Charles Watson, Johann Martin Bolzius, William Horton, and Patrick Sutherland.

17. Ibid., 348–49.

18. *Col. Recs.*, 1:530–34, 550–51.

19. Martyn to the President and Assistants, London, 7 July 1749, ibid., 31:309–14.

20. The President and Assistants to the Trustees, 26 October 1749, ibid., 25:430–37. The letter was signed by William Stephens, Henry Parker, William Spencer, Samuel Mercer, Johann Martin Bolzius, Bartholomew Zouberbuhler, J. L. Meyer, Noble Jones, Charles West, Newdigate Stephens, Peter Morel, Patrick Houstoun, Richard Hazard, Griffith Williams, Patrick Graham, James Habersham, Charles Watson, John Milledge, J. Farmur, John

McKintosh, Middleton Evans, Peter Baillou, John Harn, John Barnard, Francis Harris, Henry Yonge, and Thomas Delegal, Jr.

21. To Their Excellencies the Lords Justices in Council the Memorial of the Trustees, 8 October 1750, ibid., 33:467–68.

22. "An ACT for repealing an Act Intituled (An Act for rendering the Colony of Georgia more defencible by prohibiting the Importation and Use of Black Slaves or Negroes into the same) & for permitting the Importation and Use of them in the Colony under proper Restrictions and Regulations, and for other Purposes therein mentioned"; Martyn to the President and Assistants, London, 15 August 1750, ibid., 1:56–62; 21:442–44.

23. This section of the code was probably a response to the yellow fever epidemics experienced by South Carolina in 1745 and 1748. See ibid., 1:58; John Duffy, *Epidemics in Colonial America* (Baton Rouge, 1953), 138–63.

24. *Col. Recs.*, 1:60.

25. Ibid., 58. The South Carolina slave code of 1740 prescribed a maximum fine of £100 sterling for any white person found guilty of maiming or murdering a slave (Eugene R. Sirmans, "The Legal Status of the Slave in South Carolina, 1670–1740," *Journal of Southern History* 28 (1962): 462–73).

26. *Col. Recs.*, 1:59–60.

27. Gray and Wood, "Transition from Indentured to Involuntary Servitude," 365.

CHAPTER SIX

1. Gray and Wood, "Transition from Indentured to Involuntary Servitude," 363.

2. Gerald Cates has estimated that 39 percent of the "5,604 colonists sent to Georgia from England between 1733 and 1752 . . . had died by 1752." In his view this death rate "is not alarming considering that many family units were headed by men and women of middle age or older." He goes on to suggest that "if one excludes mortality resulting from the seasoning process, from beri beri, scurvy, and dysentery, Georgia was a remarkably healthy colony." This was certainly not the perception of most colonists. See Gerald L. Cates, " 'The Seasoning': Disease and Death among the First Colonists of Georgia," *GHQ* 65 (1980):146–58.

3. "To the Right Honourable the Lords Commissioners for Trade and Plantations. The Memorial of the Trustees for Establishing the

Colony of Georgia in America," 19 June 1752, *Col. Recs.*, 33:565–66. In July 1750 there were said to be "three Hundred and Forty Nine Working Negroes, namely two Hundred and two Men, and one Hundred and Forty Seven Women, besides children too young for Labour" in Georgia (ibid., 26:22; Governor Wright to the Board of Trade, Savannah, 15 April 1761, ibid., 28, pt. 1, 514; "Report of Governor Wright on the Condition of the Province of Georgia on 20 Sept. 1773," *Colls., GHS*, 3:167).

4. Gray, *History of Agriculture*, 1:104, 137; 2:1022; Alexander Hewatt, *An Historical Account of the Rise and Progress of the Colonies of South Carolina and Georgia*, 2 vols. (London, 1779), 2:267; G. Melvin Herndon, "Timber Products of Colonial Georgia," *GHQ* 57 (1973): 56–62; G. Melvin Herndon, "Naval Stores in Colonial Georgia," *GHQ* 52 (1968): 426–35; Kenneth Coleman, *Colonial Georgia—A History* (New York, 1976), 219–21.

5. Gray and Wood, "Transition from Indentured to Involuntary Servitude," 363.

6. Between 1755 and 1771 almost 1.25 million acres of land were granted by the Georgia authorities. Almost twice as much land (719,836 acres) was granted after 1763 than before that date (402,749 acres). Before 1754 299,903 acres were granted (Lipscomb, "Land Granting," 62, 67, 84–86; see also Percy S. Flippin, "The Royal Government in Georgia, 1752–1776, Part V: The Land System," *GHQ* 10 (1926): 2–3).

7. Lipscomb, "Land Granting," 68, 88. Between 1755 and 1769, 57,417 acres were sold in this manner.

8. David R. Chesnutt, "South Carolinian Expansion into Colonial Georgia" (Ph.D. dissertation, University of Georgia, 1973), 51; Kenneth Coleman, "The Southern Frontier: Georgia's Founding and the Expansion of South Carolina," *GHQ* 56 (1972): 163–74; Robert L. Meriwether, *The Expansion of South Carolina, 1729–1763* (Kingsport, Tenn., 1940).

9. Louis De Vorsey, Jr., ed., *De Brahm's Report of the General Survey in the Southern District of North America* (Columbia, S.C., 1971), 162; Chesnutt, "South Carolinian Expansion," 51.

10. Chesnutt, "South Carolinian Expansion," 203–4; Coleman, *Colonial Georgia*, 224; James Stacy, ed., *The Published Records of Midway Church* (n.p., 1951); James Stacy, ed., *History of Midway Congregational Church, Liberty County, Georgia* (Newnan, Ga., 1903).

11. Chesnutt, "South Carolinian Expansion," 204–6.

12. Robert S. Glenn, Jr., "Slavery in Georgia, 1733–1793" (Senior thesis, Princeton University, 1972), 63–64; Coleman, *Colonial Georgia,* 207–8.

13. Coleman, *Colonial Georgia,* 224–28; Edward R. Green, "Queensborough Township: Scotch-Irish Emigration and the Expansion of Georgia, 1763–1776," *WMQ,* 3d ser., 17 (1960): 183–89; E. Merton Coulter, "The Acadians in Georgia," *GHQ* 47 (1963): 68–75; James E. Callaway, "The Early Settlement of Georgia" (Senior thesis, Princeton University, 1935), chaps. 4, 5, and 6.

14. Based on Chesnutt, "South Carolinian Expansion," 216–30.

15. Gray and Wood, "Transition from Indentured to Involuntary Servitude."

16. Coulter and Saye, eds., *List of Early Settlers,* 26, 21, 77; Coleman, *Colonial Georgia,* 132.

17. Coleman, *Colonial Georgia,* chaps. 10 and 13.

18. Loewald, Starika, and Taylor, eds., "Bolzius Answers a Questionnaire" (1957), 261; De Vorsey, ed., *De Brahm's Report,* 162.

19. Loewald, Starika, and Taylor, eds., "Bolzius Answers a Questionnaire" (1957), 255–57.

20. Ibid., 255.

21. Glenn, "Slavery in Georgia," 69. For examples of the value of slaves see Inventory Book F (1754–71) and Inventory Book FF (1771–78), Georgia Department of Archives and History, Atlanta.

22. See, for example, Inventory Book F, 424–25, Inventory Book FF, 53–54, 70–76.

23. Harvey H. Jackson, *Lachlan McIntosh and the Politics of Revolutionary Georgia* (Athens, 1979), 8, 12.

24. William Knox to James Habersham, Whitehall, 2 January 1771, 6 November 1771, James Habersham Papers, Folder 4, Letters, 1752–70, Georgia Historical Society, Savannah; Loewald, Starika, and Taylor, eds., "Bolzius Answers a Questionnaire" (1957), 257; Ralph B. Flanders, *Plantation Slavery in Georgia* (Cos Cob, Conn., 1967), 47.

25. Gray and Wood, "Transition from Indentured to Involuntary Servitude," 361–62. As they explain, "Although the internal rate of return is higher for the 100-acre plantation, the present value of the net income stream from the 200-acre plantation is larger by more than $2\frac{1}{2}$ to 1 than that of the 100-acre plantation when discounted by the prevailing Georgia interest rate ($10\frac{1}{2}\%$), indicating that the 200-acre plantation is the superior investment" (361).

26. Glenn, "Slavery in Georgia," 65.
27. Donnan, ed., *Documents Illustrative of the Slave Trade*, 4:612–13; Chesnutt, "South Carolinian Expansion," 216–30; J. G. W. De Brahm, *History of the Province of Georgia* (Wormsloe, 1849), 21. In 1758 Joseph Ottolenghe, a missionary appointed to minister to Georgia's slaves, reported that "the Negroes of these Parts . . . are mostly African born" (quoted in Davis, *Fledgling Province*, 131).
28. Donnan, ed., *Documents Illustrative of the Slave Trade*, 4:406, 416, 419–20; Habersham to Governor Wright, Savannah, 4 December 1772, *Colls., GHS*, 6:216–17.
29. Telfair, Cowper, and Telfair to Messrs. Somerville, Noble and White, Savannah, 25 November 1774, Telfair Papers, Item 44, Letterbook, 1774–82, Georgia Historical Society, Savannah.
30. Ibid; Donan, ed., *Documents Illustrative of the Slave Trade*, 4:617.
31. Donnan, ed., *Documents Illustrative of the Slave Trade*, 4:406, 420; Habersham to Governor Wright, Savannah, 4 December 1772, 216–17.
32. Donnan, ed., *Documents Illustrative of the Slave Trade*, 4:619, 433–34, 436–37.
33. Loewald, Starika, and Taylor, eds., "Bolzius Answers a Questionnaire" (1957): 255–57.
34. Telfair, Cowper, and Telfair to Robert Macmillan, Savannah, 2 September 1773; to Thomas Wallace, 2 September 1773, Telfair Papers, Item 43, Cover 2, Letterbook, 11 August 1773–11 May 1776.
35. Telfair, Cowper, and Telfair to Messrs. Somerville, Noble and White, Savannah, 25 November 1774, Telfair Papers, Item 44, Letterbook, 1774–82; to Messrs. Samuel, Jandy & Co., Savannah, 12 October 1774; to Messrs. Chalmer, Hatchel & Co., Savannah, 9 February 1774, Telfair Papers, Item 43, Cover 2, Letterbook, 11 August 1773–11 May 1776.
36. Telfair, Cowper, and Telfair to Robert Macmillan, Savannah, 2 September 1773.
37. Loewald, Starika, and Taylor, eds., "Bolzius Answers a Questionnaire" (1957), 256.
38. Elizabeth Donnan, "The Slave Trade into South Carolina before the Revolution," *American Historical Review* 33 (1928): 816–17; Daniel C. Littlefield, *Rice and Slaves: Ethnicity and the Slave Trade in Colonial South Carolina* (Baton Rouge, 1981); Donnan, ed., *Documents Illustrative of the Slave Trade*, 4:619–25.

39. Governor Wright to the Earl of Shelburne, Savannah, 15 June
1767; Wright to the Board of Trade, 15 June 1767, *Col. Recs.*,
38:223; 38, pt. 2, 503, "An Act for laying a Duty upon Negroes
and other Slaves that have been above six Months in any of the
Islands or Colonies in America and imported for Sale in this Province," ibid., 17:358–59.
40. Donnan, ed., *Documents Illustrative of the Slave Trade*, 4:612–25.
41. The inventories concerned are taken from Inventory Books F and
FF.
42. Peter H. Wood, *Black Majority: Negroes in Colonial South Carolina from 1670 through the Stono Rebellion* (New York, 1974),
153, 160.
43. Habersham to Knox, 24 July 1772, *Colls., GHS*, 6:193–94;
Wood, *Black Majority*, 163–65.
44. Wood, *Black Majority*, 153, 163–64; Hugh E. Egerton, ed., *The
Royal Commission on the Losses and Services of American Loyal-
ists 1783 to 1785. Being the Notes of Mr. Daniel Parker Cole,
M.P. One of the Commissioners during that Period* (Oxford,
1915), Book 1, 14–19.
45. Callaway, "Early Settlement," chap. 4, 16–17, chap. 6, 1–14.
46. Governor John Reynolds to the Board of Trade, 5 June 1756;
Lieutenant Governor Henry Ellis to William Pitt, 1 August 1757;
Governor Ellis to the Board of Trade, 28 January 1759, *Col.
Recs.*, 27:239; 28, pt. 1, 58, 256; applications for land grants,
1755–59, ibid., 7:102ff. The average holding of those who applied for lands between these dates was fractionally under ten
slaves.
47. Lipscomb, "Land Granting," 75–76. Bonner has suggested that by
1773 Georgia's sixty leading slaveowners held over half the colony's slaves (*History of Georgia Agriculture*, 8).
48. Gray and Wood, "Transition from Indentured to Involuntary Servitude," 363.
49. For an excellent discussion of plantation management in colonial
South Carolina see Philip Morgan, "The Development of Slave
Culture in Eighteenth-Century Plantation America" (Ph.D. dissertation, University of London, 1977). See also John D. Duncan,
"Servitude and Slavery in Colonial South Carolina, 1670–1776"
(Ph.D. dissertation, Emory University, 1971).
50. For the names of those who sat in the Commons House of Assembly during the royal period see Donna M. Rabac, "Economy and
Society in Early Georgia: A Functional Analysis of the Colony's

Origin and Evolution" (Ph.D. dissertation, University of Michigan, 1978), 205–6, 239–42. For a list of the South Carolinian land claimants between 1747 and 1765 see Chesnutt, "South Carolinian Expansion," 216–30.

CHAPTER SEVEN

1. Jones, ed., *Detailed Reports*, 1:56–106; Loewald, Starika, and Taylor, eds., "Bolzius Answers a Questionnaire" (1957), 233–34; (1958), 240; *Extract from the Journals of Von Reck*, 9–10.
2. The President, Assistants and Councilmen to the Trustees, Savannah, 10 January 1749, *Col. Recs.*, 25:347–48.
3. Bolzius to Dobell, Ebenezer, 20 May 1748, ibid., 15:282–86.
4. "AN ACT For the better Ordering and Governing Negroes and other Slaves in this Province," March 1755, ibid., 18:102–44.
5. Thomas Cooper and David J. McCord, eds., *The Statutes at Large of South Carolina*, 10 vols. (Columbia, S.C., 1836–41), 7:397–417; William W. Wiecek, "The Statutory Law of Slavery and Race in the Thirteen Mainland Colonies of British America," *WMQ*, 3d ser., 34 (1977): 265–66; A. Leon Higginbotham, Jr., *In the Matter of Color: Race and the American Legal Process, the Colonial Period* (New York, 1978), 151–266. In 1768 the Georgians stated categorically that the code "was framed on the plan of that of So. Carolina" ("Collections of the Georgia Historical Society and Other Documents: Letters to the Georgia Colonial Agent, July 1762 to January 1771," *GHQ* 36 [1952]: 274). The letter in question was dated 19 May 1768 and signed by John Milledge, James Habersham, Noble Jones, Archibald Bulloch, Lewis Johnson, Noble Wimberly Jones, and William Ewen.
6. *Col. Recs.*, 18:6–47.
7. Coleman, *Colonial Georgia*, 228.
8. *Col. Recs.*, 18:102. Governor Reynolds's instructions required him to use his "best Endeavours to restrain any inhuman Severity, which by ill Masters or Overseers may be used towards their Christian Servants & their Slaves" (ibid., 34:48).
9. Ibid., 18:131–35.
10. Ibid., 133–36.
11. Ibid., 117.
12. Ibid., 104–6. Any slave without a ticket was liable to "be punished with Whipping on the Bare back not Exceeding Twenty Lashes."

13. Ibid., 130, 107–8.
14. Ibid., 136–37; Coleman, *Colonial Georgia*, 229. All slaveholdings had to be supervised by a white person. For holdings in excess of fifty slaves the ratio was relaxed to twenty-five to one.
15. *Col. Recs.*, 18:136, 130–31.
16. Ibid., 117–19.
17. Wood, *Black Majority*, 124–30.
18. *Col. Recs.*, 18:38.
19. Ibid., 39–40. In 1773 the assembly decreed that enlisted slaves should "not Exceed one third of the White Men in each respective Company" (ibid., 29:325).
20. Ibid., 18:40–44.
21. Ibid., 137–40. A reward of £5 sterling was offered for "every grown Man Slave" apprehended south of the Altamaha River; £3 would be paid for women and children over the age of twelve and £2 for children aged under twelve; and £1 sterling would be given for "every Scalp with Two Ears" of any adult male slave apprehended and killed in the same region. Rewards of £15, £10, and £5, respectively, would be paid for men, women, and children taken south of the St. John's River. Their owners would be held responsible for paying the rewards "excepting the Scalps which shall be paid for by the Public."
22. Ibid., 120–24.
23. "AN ACT For Regulating a Work House, for the Custody and Punishment of Negroes, April, 1763," ibid., 558–66.
24. Wiecek, "Statutory Law," 273–76.
25. Any slave found guilty of striking a white person was liable to suffer corporal punishment for the first two offenses and thereafter might "suffer Death." Any slave who "grevously" [sic] injured a white person might be executed "tho' it shall be only the first Offence." The only exceptions would be if the slave acted in defense of his owner, overseer, or owner's property.
26. *Georgia Gazette*, 7, 14 July 1763.
27. *Col. Recs.*, 18:108–9, 112–13.
28. Ibid., 110.
29. In 1771, for example, Peter Random was censured by the Grand Jury "for refusing to deliver up to Justice [a] male slave . . . said to be Guilty of Felony" (Helen T. Catterall, *Judicial Cases Concerning American Slavery and the Negro*, 5 vols. [1926; reprint, Shannon, 1968], 2:6).
30. *Col. Recs.*, 18:114–16.

31. Ibid., 126.
32. "An act for the better security of the inhabitants by obliging the male white persons to carry fire arms to places of public worship, February 1770," ibid., 19:137–40.
33. "AN ACT For establishing a Watch in the Town of Savannah, July, 1757"; "AN ACT for regulating the Watch in the town of Savannah, 1759," ibid., 18:212–17, 290–95.
34. Ibid., 18:225–35.
35. "AN ACT For the better Ordering and Governing Negroes and other Slaves in this Province and to prevent the inveigling or carrying away Slaves from their Masters or Employers, 1765," ibid., 649–88.
36. Ibid., 657.
37. Wood, *Black Majority*, 289–91; *South Carolina Gazette*, 17 January 1761.
38. *Georgia Gazette*, 7 April 1763.
39. See above, chapter 6.
40. Wood, *Black Majority*, 289.
41. *Col. Recs.*, 18:641–44.
42. Ibid., 659.
43. "AN ACT to encourage white Tradesmen to Settle in the several Towns within this Province of Georgia by preventing the employing Negroes & other Slaves being handicraft Tradesmen in the said Towns, March, 1758," ibid., 277–82.
44. For an extended discussion of the disallowances see Glenn, "Slavery in Georgia," 46–51.
45. Governor Wright to the Board of Trade, Savannah, 8 June 1768, *Col. Recs.*, 28, pt. 2, 254–55; "An act for ordering and governing slaves within this province, and for establishing a jurisdiction for the trial of offences committed by such slaves, and other persons therein mentioned, and to prevent the inveighling, and carrying away slaves from their masters, owners, or employers, 1740," ibid., 19, pt. 1, 209–49.
46. Ibid., 220.
47. *Georgia Gazette*, 5 January 1774.
48. Catterall, ed., *Judicial Cases*, 2:6.

CHAPTER EIGHT

1. "AN ACT to encourage white Tradesmen to Settle in the several Towns within this Province of Georgia by preventing the employ-

ing negroes & other Slaves being handicraft Tradesmen in the said Towns, March 1758," *Col. Recs.,* 18:277, 279–80. A number of leading planters, including Edmund Tannatt, Alexander Wylly, and Lewis Johnson, believed that the protection demanded by the white artisans reflected "the Greediness and insatiable Thirst after Gain of a few Tradesmen" (ibid., 16:269–70, cited by Davis, *Fledgling Province,* 98).

2. *Col. Recs.,* 18:677–78.
3. These are the main occupations mentioned in inventories of estates and in the *Georgia Gazette.*
4. "Account of lands Negroes & other Effects, the property of John Graham late of Georgia, stated according to the Value thereof before the Commencement of Disturbances in America," Georgia Loyalist Claims, Public Record Office, A.O. 13, Bundle 35 (microfilm).
5. See above, chapter 6.
6. *Col. Recs.,* 18:660–66, 19, pt. 1, 221–23; Hewatt, *Historical Account,* 2:97–98. The most famous, or from the Georgians' standpoint most infamous, example of the use of poison by a domestic slave was in 1774 when "a household Negress" administered poison to Pastor and Mrs. Rabenhorst (Theodore G. Tappert and John W. Doberstein, trans. and eds., *The Journals of Henry Melchior Muhlenberg,* 2 vols. [Philadelphia, 1942, 1958], 2:575, 576).
7. Davis, *Fledgling Province,* 98.
8. See the advertisements placed in the *Georgia Gazette* by William Ewen (25 August 1763) and John Eppinger (24 December 1766) and the inventories of John Eppinger (1777), John Rouviere (1767), Anthony Pagey (1765), John Smith (1770), Benjamin Goldwire (1777), and James Hamilton (1769), Inventory Book F, 147–49, 296–98, 424–25, 473–78; Inventory Book FF, 32–33, 53–54; Coleman, *Colonial Georgia,* 229–30. At least two cabinetmakers, James Love and John Spencer, owned slaves, but it is not clear whether they followed their masters' trade (Inventory Book F, 80–82, 353–56).
9. *Georgia Gazette,* 9 February 1774, 17 May 1775.
10. For the use of black women as sawyers and squarers see the contract drawn up in 1766 between James Bulloch and James Wright (Miscellaneous Bonds, Book R [1765–72], Georgia State Archives, Atlanta). For examples of the use of African-born slaves as skilled and semiskilled workers see the advertisements placed in the *Geor-*

gia Gazette by Raymond Demere, Jr. (28 June 1775), Joseph Cannon (4 October 1775), Mark Carr (22 August 1775), Thomas Lee (3 September 1766), and Nathaniel Hall (31 May 1775).

11. *Col. Recs.,* 18:117, 136, 667; 19, pt. 1, 244.

12. Loewald, Starika, and Taylor, eds., "Bolzius Answers a Questionnaire" (1957), 259.

13. Ibid., 258; Bonner, *History of Georgia Agriculture,* 19–20.

14. Bonner, *History of Georgia Agriculture,* 17–18.

15. Loewald, Starika, and Taylor, eds., "Bolzius Answers a Questionnaire" (1957), 259.

16. Ibid.

17. *Col. Recs.,* 18:136–37, 685–86; 19, pt. 1, 245–46.

18. Bartholomew R. Carroll, *Historical Collections of South Carolina,* 2 vols. (New York, 1836), 2:20.

19. Two owners, Peter Random and Samuel Douglass, were censured by the Grand Jury for failing to provide proper supervision for their slaves (Presentments of the Grand Jury [1771] in Catterall, ed., *Judicial Cases,* 2:6; Presentments of the Grand Jury [1773], *Georgia Gazette,* 5 January 1774).

20. Knox was born in Ireland in 1732. He was appointed to the council and made provost marshal of Georgia in 1756. He accompanied Governor Henry Ellis to Georgia but returned to England in 1761. By that date "62 Working hands" were employed on his Knoxborough plantation. Knoxborough had "about 200 acres cultivated with Rice besides high Lands for the purpose of raising provisions for the Negroes & Lands which produced Lumber which was a very profitable article." The annual income from this estate was said to be "above £2,000" (Knox to Habersham, Watford, 12 May 1770, James Habersham Papers, Folder 4, Letters, 1752–70; Egerton, ed., *Royal Commission,* 1–2).

21. Habersham to Knox, Savannah, 17 July 1765, James Habersham Papers, Folder 1, Letterbook, 1764–66. On the eve of the War for Independence, Habersham owned 198 slaves and operated three main plantations: Silk Hope, Dean Forest, and Beverly. See Habersham to Mrs. Mary Bagwith, Savannah, 3 February 1774, *Colls., GHS,* 6:234; Virginia L. Hudson, "James Habersham: Georgia Colonial Builder" (A.M. thesis, Duke University, 1952), W. Calvin Smith, "Georgia Gentlemen: The Habershams of Eighteenth-Century Savannah" (Ph.D. dissertation, University of North Carolina at Chapel Hill, 1971).

22. John Gibbons Papers, 1758–89, 1775–79 file, William R. Perkins Library, Duke University, Durham, N.C.

23. Agreements between William Gibbons and James Guinn, 24 February 1770; William Gibbons and Thomas Moore, 30 November 1769; William Gibbons and William May, 28 January 1769, William Gibbons, Jr., Papers, 1769–71 file, William R. Perkins Library, Duke University, Durham, N.C. In 1771 Isaac Mims was paid £2.9.6 "for overseeing for Two Months the Negroes on the Estate of John Gibbons." This might have been a short-term appointment, but alternatively Mims might have proved unsatisfactory.

24. Agreement between William Gibbons and William May, William Gibbons, Jr., Papers, ibid. Charles Watson was so pleased with the way that John Tebeau had "Discharged the Duty of an Overseer" that he gave him a slave boy named Griffith (Deed of Gift dated 11 August 1769, Miscellaneous Bonds, Book R, 466–67).

25. Loewald, Starika, and Taylor, eds., "Bolzius Answers a Questionnaire' (1957), 261; Habersham to Wright, Savannah, 15 December 1772, Colls., GHS, 6:219–20.

26. Habersham to Knox, Savannah, 15 January 1772, Colls., GHS, 6:161.

27. Henry Laurens to Lachlan McIntosh, Wrights Savannah, 10 May 1769, in Philip M. Hamer, George C. Rogers, et al., eds., The Papers of Henry Laurens, 9 vols. (Columbia, S.C., 1968–81), 6:444–47.

28. Ibid., 446; Henry Laurens to James Habersham, Charles Town, 1 October 1770, ibid., 7:376; Laurens to Habersham, Charles Town, 9 October 1770, ibid., 380.

29. Hewatt, Historical Account, 2:95–96; Henry Laurens to John Smith, Charles Town, 30 May 1765, Hamer, Rogers, et al., eds., Papers of Henry Laurens, 4:632–33.

30. Covenant between James Bulloch of Josephstown & John Stewart & John Stevens of the same place, 29 March 1765, Miscellaneous Bonds, Book O, 303–8. The slaves, who were valued at £967.10.0, included twenty-one men and boys, nineteen women and girls, and four "children." See also the contract between Lachlan McGillivray and Charles Wright, Savannah, 12 June 1760, ibid., 151–52.

31. Memorandum of my negroes work at Jones Plantation, Telfair Family Papers, Box 26, Item 432, Account Book, 1763–75, 1.

32. Habersham to Wright, 16 July 1773, Colls., GHS, 6:190–91.

33. "AN ACT To empower certain Commissioners herein appointed to regulate the hire of Porters and Labour of Slaves in the Town of Savannah, March 1774," *Col. Recs.,* 19, pt. 2, 23–26.

34. *Col. Recs.,* 18:135, 684; 19, pt. 1, 242; Presentments of the Grand Jury (December 1771), Catterall, ed., *Judicial Cases,* 2:6.

35. *Col. Recs.,* 19, pt. 2, 24–25.

36. See Chapter 10.

37. *Col. Recs.,* 18:133–34.

38. Loewald, Starika, and Taylor, eds., "Bolzius Answers a Questionnaire" (1957), 257, 261.

39. Tailfer and others to the Trustees, n.p., n.d., recd. 27 August 1735, Egmont Papers, 14201, 108–12.

40. Slaves were prohibited from raising cattle on their own behalf (*Col. Recs.,* 18:126–29).

41. Loewald, Starika, and Taylor, eds, "Bolzius Answers a Questionnaire" (1957), 235, 236, 256, 260; Habersham to Wright, Savannah, 15 December 1772, *Colls., GHS,* 6:219–20; Telfair Family Papers, Box 26, Item 432, Account Book, 1763–75.

42. See chapter 7 above.

43. Loewald, Starika, and Taylor, eds., "Bolzius Answers a Questionnaire" (1957), 259. The items supplied by owners did not change appreciably after 1750. In 1783, for example, Anthony Stokes recorded that "in the Rice Colonies . . . the Negroes in General have Rice, Indian-corn, potatoes or black-eyed pease sufficient to subsist them" (*A View of the Constitution of the British Colonies in North America and the West Indies. With a Supplementary Index* [London, 1783; reprinted London, 1968], 414).

44. Loewald, Starika, and Taylor, eds., "Bolzius Answers a Questionnaire" (1957), 259; William Knox, *Three Tracts Respecting the Conversion and Instruction of free Indians and Negroe Slaves in the Colonies. Addressed to the Venerable Society for the Propagation of the Gospel* (London, 1768), 34.

45. Loewald, Starika, and Taylor, eds., "Bolzius Answers a Questionnaire" (1957), 256, 260. As long as they had a ticket from their owners slaves who lived or were "usually employed" in Savannah could "Buy or Sell Fruit Fish and Garden Stuff" (*Col. Recs.,* 18:125–26).

46. Loewald, Starika, and Taylor, eds., "Bolzius Answers a Questionnaire" (1957), 235, 236.

47. *Georgia Gazette,* 3 August 1774, 27 September 1775, 27 February 1775, 16 September 1767, 22 September 1774.

48. Habersham to Knox, Savannah, 9 March 1764, *Colls., GHS,* 6:16–17. Habersham wanted to dress his slaves in the "very strong, cheap cloth, . . . called Foul Weather" worn by "the west Country Barge Men." He suggested that it would be worthwhile offering "a Pot of Porter extraordinary pr. suit to have them sew'd strong."

49. Loewald, Starika, and Taylor, eds., "Bolzius Answers a Questionnaire" (1957), 256; Inventory of Martin Fenton's Estate (1769), Inventory Book F, 389–90.

50. Bolzius suggested a figure of twelve shillings per slave per annum and De Brahm, thirteen shillings and three pence. Both assumed that the slave would be given shoes (Loewald, Starika, and Taylor, eds., "Bolzius Answers a Questionnaire" [1957], 236, 256; De Vorsey, ed., *De Brahm's Report,* 162).

51. De Vorsey, ed., *De Brahm's Report,* 162.

52. Joseph I. Waring, "Colonial Medicine in Georgia and South Carolina," *GHQ* 59 (supp.) (1957):142. See also Gerald L. Cates, "A Medical History of Georgia in the First Hundred Years, 1733–1833" (Ph.D. dissertation, University of Georgia, 1976).

53. Wood, *Black Majority,* 70–76; Loewald, Starika, and Taylor, eds., "Bolzius Answers a Questionnaire" (1957), 239–40; Habersham to Wright, Savannah, 29 December 1771, *Colls., GHS,* 6:159.

54. Stokes, *A View of the Constitution,* 414–15.

55. *Col. Recs.,* 12:367–68; Habersham to William Russel, Savannah, 10 October 1764, *Colls., GHS,* 6:27; "Copy of Governor Wright's Answer to the Board's Heads of Enquiry, given in Febry. 1762, with Notes & further Observations, in the Govrs. Letter of 29 Nov. 1766," *Col. Recs.,* 28, pt. 2, 427.

56. Wood, *Black Majority,* 85–91.

57. Joseph Krafka, "Notes on Medical Practice in Colonial Georgia," *GHQ* 22 (1939):351–61; Cates, "Medical History of Georgia"; Waring, "Colonial Medicine."

58. William Gibbons, Jr., Papers, 1765–68 file.

59. By the end of the War for Independence there were more than two hundred doctors in Georgia.

60. Waring, "Colonial Medicine," 142.

61. William Gibbons, Jr., Papers, 1769; Telfair Papers, 1775.

62. Habersham to Willet Taylor, Savannah, 2 April 1764; Habersham to Knox, Savannah, 18 July 1772, *Colls., GHS,* 6:22–23, 193.

63. Wood, *Black Majority,* 119–22, 289–92.

CHAPTER NINE

1. Loewald, Starika, and Taylor, eds., "Bolzius Answers a Questionnaire" (1957), 236.
2. Ibid.
3. Habersham to Willet Taylor, Savannah, 2 April 1764, *Colls.,* GHS, 6:22–23; Tappert and Doberstein, eds., *Journal of Muhlenberg,* 2:675.
4. Loewald, Starika, and Taylor, eds., "Bolzius Answers a Questionnaire" (1957), 236.
5. John Bowman to John Houstoun, 24 June 1772, Keith Read Collection; Habersham to the Countess of Huntingdon, Savannah, 19 April 1775, *Colls., GHS,* 6:242–43.
6. *Georgia Gazette,* 6 July 1774.
7. See above, chapter 6.
8. James B. Lawrence, "Religious Education of the Negro in the Colony of Georgia," *GHQ* 14 (1930):41–42; see also Reba C. Strickland, *Religion and the State in Georgia in the Eighteenth Century* (New York, 1939).
9. Knox, *Three Tracts,* 16–17, 37; Lawrence, "Religious Education," 47.
10. Habersham to the Countess of Huntingdon, Savannah, 19 April 1775, 241.
11. Joseph Ottolenghe to Rev. Mr. Waring, 19 November 1758, Society for the Propagation of the Gospel Records, vol. 18, quoted by Lawrence, "Religious Education," 45–46.
12. Knox, *Three Tracts,* 38–39.
13. Ibid., 17; Ottolenghe to Rev. Mr. Waring, 19 November 1758.
14. Tappert and Doberstein, eds., *Journals of Muhlenberg,* 2:637–38.
15. Knox, *Three Tracts,* 17–18, 35.
16. Ibid., 26–27.
17. Bartholomew Zouberbuhler, for example, who served as the rector of Christ Church Parish between 1745 and his death in 1766 and who was a strong advocate of the religious instruction of slaves, left an estate valued at over £2,500, including forty-seven slaves. He made provision for the continuing instruction of his own slaves and those of like-minded planters (Inventory Book F, 253–56; Davis, *Fledgling Province,* 143–44).
18. For examples of manumission by the last will and testament of owners see the wills of John Rouviere (1767), Bryan Kelly (1766), Edward Somerville (1762), Jane Somerville (1777), John Somer-

ville (1773), and Daniel Ross (1770), Loose Wills, 1773–77, Georgia Department of Archives and History, Atlanta. For manumission by deed of gift see Miscellaneous Bonds, Book J, 2–3, 121; Book R, 450, 451, 489–90, 523–24, 527–28; Book O, 153; Book Y1, 80; and Book Y2, 372. The owners concerned were Joseph Butler, John Smith, Josiah Tatnell, James Habersham, Jr., Richard Hazzard, John Harn, Daniel Ross, Samuel Savery, Moses and Daniel Nunez, and Charles Morgan. Altogether they manumitted fifteen slaves. Blacks who received their freedom were not obliged to leave Georgia.

19. Georgia's ministers of religion complained about the small number of slaves who were allowed to attend divine worship or receive instruction. The irregularity of their attendance was also a matter for comment. In 1758, for example, Ottolenghe complained that "Some Times I have had fifty & more at once, & perhaps in a month or two after is not half that Number, and at others not Ten, and so on, more or less alternately; again some will attend for 6 months & then disappear for 6 Months or a year, & some two, before I see them again" (quoted in Lawrence, "Religious Education," 47).

20. For an account of Liele's ministry and the initial development of the black Baptist church see [George Liele and Andrew Bryan], "Letters Showing the Rise and Progress of the Early Negro Churches of Georgia and the West Indies," *Journal of Negro History* 1 (1916): 69–92, and James M. Simms, *The First Colored Baptist Church in North America Constituted at Savannah 20 January 1788* (Philadelphia, 1888).

21. Hewatt, *Historical Account*, 2:103.

22. Loewald, Starika, and Taylor, eds., "Bolzius Answers a Questionnaire" (1957), 259–61.

23. Knox, *Three Tracts*, 39; Charles C. Jones, Jr., *Negro Myths from the Georgia Coast* (Columbia, S.C., 1925); Wood, *Black Majority*, 172.

24. Presentments of the Grand Jury (December, 1771), Catterall, ed., *Judicial Cases*, 2:6; "The PRESENTMENTS of the Grand Jurors for the Province of Georgia . . . 14 June 1768," *Georgia Gazette*, 6 July 1768; "Presentments of the Grand Jurors, meeting 10 December 1766," ibid., 24 December 1766; "Presentments of the Grand Jury of Georgia, 14 December 1773," ibid., 5 January 1774; Letter to the Editor of the *Georgia Gazette* signed "R.L.," ibid., 1 September 1763.

25. "The PRESENTMENTS of the Grand Jurors for the Province of Georgia, 14 June 1774," *Georgia Gazette*, 22 June 1774; "The PRESENTMENTS of the Grand Jurors for the Province of Georgia . . . 9 June 1767," ibid., 22 July 1767.

CHAPTER TEN

1. Wood, *Black Majority*, 239.
2. This figure does not include slaves apprehended in Georgia and advertised in the *Gazette* or children taken away by adults.
3. There are no extant copies of the *Gazette* for the months between June 1770 and November 1774. There are other, shorter gaps such as that between December 1765 and the beginning of June 1766. Some single copies of the *Gazette* are also missing.
4. In the early 1770s it cost three shillings to publish an advertisement in three consecutive issues of the *Gazette* (Davis, *Fledgling Province*, 188).
5. Ibid., 136.
6. *Georgia Gazette*, 17 June 1767, 23 May 1770. Burn reported that Yamow "has often been seen in and near Savannah" and Gibbons that Nero was "lately seen in the camp at the head of Augustin's Creek."
7. Wood, *Black Majority*, 240.
8. Ibid., 241.
9. *Georgia Gazette*, 10 May 1769.
10. Ibid., 4 April 1764, 13 July 1774, 24 May 1775. It is not clear whether the sailors were black or white.
11. Ibid., 9 November 1772, 22 November 1769.
12. Ibid., 25 July 1765, 3 September 1766.
13. The slaves were owned by Mark Carr (ibid., 22 August 1765).
14. Ibid., 23 July 1766, 22 November 1775.
15. Gerald W. Mullin, *Flight and Rebellion: Slave Resistance in Eighteenth-Century Virginia* (New York, 1972), 35–39.
16. *Georgia Gazette*, 13 May 1767, 30 December 1767, 5 July 1769, 1 October 1766, 13 April 1768.
17. Ibid., 22 August 1765, 31 January 1770, 13 December 1769, 20 July 1774.
18. Ibid., 14 July 1763.
19. Davis, *Fledgling Province*, 136; *Georgia Gazette*, 7 June 1769, 27 July 1774, 25 October 1775; Mullin, *Flight and Rebellion*, 37.
20. Mullin, *Flight and Rebellion*, 106.

21. *Georgia Gazette,* 25 January 1775.
22. See, for example, ibid., 22 June 1768, 13 July 1768. One slave claimed that "he went to the Indian nation about seven years ago" (Wood, *Black Majority,* 260). For a recent discussion of the relations between Creeks and blacks during the colonial period see Daniel F. Littlefield, Jr., *Africans and Creeks from the Colonial Period to the Civil War* (Westport, Conn., 1979), 11–25.
23. *Col. Recs.,* 14:292–93; 12:325–26; 19, pt. 1, 185; *Georgia Gazette,* 9 November 1774, 1 July 1767.
24. *Georgia Gazette,* 11 November 1767. The slave was "a cooper by trade" who belonged to Francis Arthur.
25. Ibid., 1 November 1769.
26. Ibid., 7 April 1763, 23 May 1765.
27. Ibid., 27 July 1768, 22 March 1769, 6 July 1774, 27 March 1775.
28. Ibid., 30 December 1767, 27 July 1768.
29. Ibid., 25 January 1769, 16 September 1769.
30. Wood, *Black Majority,* 254–57.
31. *Georgia Gazette,* 26 July 1764, 18 October 1764, 9 May 1765, 12 April 1764.
32. Ibid., 24 May 1775, 11 November 1767.
33. Ibid., 31 August 1774, 5 January 1774.

CHAPTER ELEVEN

1. Wood, *Black Majority,* 268.
2. *Georgia Gazette,* 6 October 1763, 27 June 1765. See also the notices placed in the *Gazette* by Lachlan M'Gillivrary (29 August 1765) and James Houstoun (29 October 1766).
3. "Presentments of the Grand Jurors, meeting 10 December 1766," ibid., 24 December 1766, 28 January 1767. The statement was signed by William Simpson, Noble Jones, James Deveaux, Charles Pryce, Joseph Ottolenghe, Charles Watson, Henry Yonge, John Milledge, David Montaigut, James Bulloch, Thomas Moodie, J. J. Zubly, James Whitefield, Henry Preston, John Maclean, James Habersham, Francis Harris, James Edward Powell, Grey Elliott, Lewis Johnson, and James Read (ibid., 6 July 1768).
4. Presentments of the Grand Jury, 9 June 1767, 14 December 1773, 14 June 1774, ibid., 22 July 1767, 5 January 1774, 22 June 1774.
5. Ibid., 6 July 1768.
6. Ibid., 7 December 1774.

7. Information on slaves condemned during these years may be found in Catterall, *Judicial Cases,* 2:6; *Georgia Gazette,* 7 December 1774; *Col. Recs.,* 19, pt. 1, 48–49, 121, 161–98, 481; Davis, *Fledgling Province,* 129. Although masters received financial compensation for their executed slaves they sometimes interceded on behalf of slave defendants. In 1771, for example, John Glen requested that one of his slaves who had been condemned to death for "breaking into a shop and stealing sundry goods . . . might be Transported and not executed." His plea was rejected (Catterall, *Judicial Cases,* 2:6).

8. *Georgia Gazette,* 13 July 1768.

9. In 1770, for example, William Gibbons paid Alexander Patterson six shillings "for whiping a Negro in the work [house] named Will." Two years earlier Gibbons had paid three shillings for the "correcting" of two slave runaways (William Gibbons, Jr., Papers, 1765–68, 1769–71 files).

10. See chapter 4 above.

11. Letter to the *Georgia Gazette* signed "R.L.," 1 September 1763.

12. Ibid., 28 July 1763, 4 August 1765.

13. Eugene D. Genovese, *Roll, Jordan, Roll: The World the Slaves Made* (London, 1975), 616–17.

14. *Georgia Gazette,* 6 June 1765.

15. Jackson, *Lachlan McIntosh,* 21–23.

16. Davis, *Fledgling Province,* 147.

17. Allen D. Candler, ed., *The Revolutionary Records of the State of Georgia,* 3 vols. (Atlanta, 1908), 1:41–42.

18. For a detailed discussion of the antislavery resolution of 1775 see Harvey H. Jackson, " 'American Slavery, American Freedom' and the Revolution in the Lower South: The Case of Lachlan McIntosh," *Southern Studies* 19 (Spring 1980): 81–93. See also chapters 2, 3, and 4 of his *Lachlan McIntosh.*

19. See Kenneth Coleman, *The American Revolution in Georgia, 1763–1789* (Athens, 1958); Coleman, *Colonial Georgia,* 245–307; and William W. Abbot, *The Royal Governors of Georgia, 1754–1775* (Chapel Hill, 1959).

20. Jackson, " 'American Slavery, American Freedom,' " 87.

21. Peter Force, ed., *American Archives,* 4th ser. 6 vols. (Washington, D.C., 1837–46), 3:1385.

22. Jackson, " 'American Slavery, American Freedom,' " 87.

23. Ibid., 90–91.

24. In 1775 Governor Wright reported that Georgia's slaves were valued at £800,000 ("To the Right Honourable Lord George Germain His Majesty's Principal Secretary of State for America. The Memorial of Sir James Wright Bart. Governor of Georgia, and John Graham Esq. Lieutenant Governor of the said Province [1775]," *Col. Recs.*, 29:13.

INDEX